Powerhouse of English rugby, Lawrence Dallaglio's raw strength, determination and passion for the game run in his blood. He lives and breathes rugby.

From slight teenager to the gladiatorial player he is today, Dallaglio is one of the greats. Fiercely loyal to Wasps all his club career, his back-row dynamism and inspirational captaincy have led his team to three consecutive Premiership wins and to lift the Heineken Cup twice.

His England credentials are just as impressive: a winner in the Five Nations, the Six Nations and in the World Cup Sevens, he has represented his country in the last three Lions tours, and he was the only team member to play in every minute of every match of the outstanding 2003 World Cup-winning campaign. He has a major story to tell.

But Dallaglio's life off the field is just as compelling. In *It's in the Blood*, he reveals everything about the tabloid sting that implicated him in drug dealing and ultimately cost him the England captaincy. He talks about his and his parents' personal sacrifices to ensure he became the rugby player he was destined to be. And he also uncovers the trauma his family faced at losing Francesca – his only sister – in the *Marchioness* disaster, an event which remains the greatest sadness of his life.

From the closed, private persona to the intelligent, roguish charisma of his public face, Dallaglio finally opens up.

IT'S IN THE BLOOD
MY LIFE

LAWRENCE
Dallaglio

headline

First published in 2007
by HEADLINE PUBLISHING GROUP

First published in paperback in 2008
by HEADLINE PUBLISHING GROUP

7

Cataloguing in Publication Data is available from the British Library

ISBN 978 0 7553 1574 1

Typeset in Bliss Light by Avon DataSet Ltd,
Bidford-on-Avon, Warwickshire

Printed and bound in the UK by
CPI Mackays, Chatham ME5 8TD

Statistics compiled by Stuart Farmer

Headline's policy is to use papers that are natural, renewable and
recyclable products and made from wood grown in sustainable forests.
The logging and manufacturing processes are expected to conform
to the environmental regulations of the country of origin.

HEADLINE PUBLISHING GROUP
An Hachette Livre UK Company
338 Euston Road
London NW1 3BH

www.headline.co.uk
www.hachettelivre.co.uk

For Alice, Ella, Josie and Enzo.

Contents

Acknowledgements

I t may be tedious for the reader but it is vital I acknowledge that although my name appears on the cover, this book could not have happened without the help and support of many people, not all of whom can be listed here.

I have always been aware that without the many coaches I worked with through the years, I wouldn't have had anything like the career I had. From John Willcox at Ampleforth College to the many England coaches I have worked with, each played a part and I thank them all. If I single out Dick Best, Phil Keith-Roach, Nigel Melville, Ian McGeechan, Sir Clive Woodward, Warren Gatland and Shaun Edwards, it is only because they each made a particular impact on my life.

How can I thank all of the guys I played with and against? Rugby has always been a players' game and I've enjoyed the battles, the preparations for battle and the occasional celebrations that followed. I especially remember the Under-21s with whom I went to Australia in 1993 and those I then grew up with in the England team: Kyran Bracken, Mike Catt, Will Greenwood, Austin Healey, Richard Hill, Mark Regan and Simon Shaw. I also thank the battle-hardened warriors who introduced me to amateur rugby union, to that great game before contracts and protein shakes and ice-baths took over. They showed me you didn't have to be paid to love the game.

I was lucky to play in teams that won major trophies and that, of course, is another way of saying I was fortunate to play with some of the game's finest players. If ever I look at that World-Cup winner's medal and remember the great England team, I think of Johnno and Jonny, Jason and Jase, Hilly and Backy and all the boys. For a few years, we had something special.

If playing for England was like what we did on our summer holidays, Wasps was our nine-to-five job and I can't begin to thank all of those players who have helped to make my 17 years (and counting) at the club so much fun. We trained a lot, we won a lot, we partied a lot and we never forgot that we had to come back and do it all again the following season. As much as it can be, this book is one long thank you to all Wasps, past and present. A special thanks to Steve Hayes for his incredible efforts as Chairman of the Lawrence Dallaglio Benefit Year. Together with Mike Brooks and all the LDBY committee, they helped to raise over £1 million for various charities. A staggering effort!

All the surgeons, especially Andy Williams, who helped put me back together again. Some players more than others owe so much to all the medics, doctors, physios. For me, all those at Wasps and England including Roger Knibbs, Phil Pask and Barney Kenny. And then there's Kevin Lidlow my physio, my friend, and possibly the kindest and most modest man I have ever met.

A special mention to Andrea, Vincenzo and Flavio Riva for introducing us to Lake Como and making our wedding the most magical weekend I have ever had.

The book could not have happened without my publishers, Headline. My thanks to all the Headline team, especially David Wilson and Wendy McCance, and to my agent Richard Relton who ensured that everything was all right in the end. Thanks also to David Walsh of the Sunday Times who helped me to produce the book that I wanted, and to my assistant Claire Mason for keeping my life so organised and on track.

Of course the people who deserve the greatest thanks are my parents and family. Mum and Dad, God knows it wasn't always easy, but you were always there. And for what stability there is in my life, I thank the woman that I love, Alice. We've been lucky in many ways but most of all in having three wonderful children: Ella, Josie and Enzo.

Finally, I wish to acknowledge the memory of my sister, Francesca.

And like a rose she lived the life of a rose
The space of a morning

Foreword

I n the beginning, before money and fame and all those lovely things, why did we play competitive sport? We did it to make someone proud, generally our mum and dad. At least that's why I did it and I know that's why Lawrence Dallaglio did it. It's a feeling that produces an emotional performance and down through the years, Lawrence has given us a lot of those. I was going to say what he does on the field comes from his heart, but it's deeper than that. More like it comes from the heart of his psyche, if you know what I mean.

I've known Lawrence since my rugby league playing days. He was starting out with Wasps and I was still with Wigan. Something about the way he played the game appealed. It was his attitude. I was going to say his 'eff you' approach to the opposition, but 'belligerence' is a nicer word. After the game, no one was more willing to shake your hand, buy you a pint, and because of Lawrence, Wasps became my team in rugby union. I had played union at school. I'd actually captained England Schools at league on Friday night, captained England Schools at union on Monday night and was bollixed on Tuesday. Lawrence was my kind of union player.

Let me explain what it is about him. In every endeavour of any worth, somewhere along the way you want to give in. Lawrence could have given up when his sister Francesca was taken away, he could have stopped when he severed his cruciate ligament and you wouldn't have blamed him for walking away when he dislocated and fractured his ankle two years ago. But this old bastard won't die. Do you remember those things we used to punch as kids, how they would crumple but then bounce back up immediately? That's Lawrence.

He ruptured his cruciate ligament on the Lions tour of 2001 and towards the end of the following season he played his first full comeback match against Leicester at Loftus Road. Out of any sport – football, rugby, cricket – it was the best comeback performance I have ever seen. And like all great players, Lawrence had the ability to make other players look better than they were. If there was one time you wanted him in the team, it was when the chips were down. Like a great heavyweight in a dangerous title fight, he was at his best when it was all on the line.

We forged a close personal friendship, partly because I liked the guy and thought he was a fellow who would have been at home in our Wigan changing room, but also because we have both suffered great personal loss. Lawrence lost his sister, I lost my brother Billy-Joe and only those who have been through it can understand how tragedy affects you. There's another reason I like Lawrence Dallaglio. One day he helped a woman whose car wouldn't start in the Wasps car park. At the time he didn't know that lady was my mother. If somebody helps your mother, you're not going to forget that. And if somebody is rude to you her, you're never going to forget that either.

Shaun Edwards, OBE.

Prologue

I t is 20 October 2007. The day of the Rugby World Cup final. This evening, for England's third appearance in a World Cup final, I will start on the bench against South Africa. It is something I am not used to and definitely something I'm uncomfortable with. But hey ho, they don't allow you to write your own script in this game. You can't have the fairytale every time.

I've been thinking back over the years and I can't help smiling at how it will end. Almost twelve years ago, 18 November 1995 to be precise, I made my first appearance in an England shirt when coming off the bench against South Africa at Twickenham. Today it is all going to end in the same way, off the bench against the Springboks. Someone up there has a sense of humour and has ensured I will leave by the door through which I entered. With the final just six hours away, it is hard to describe what a rugby career in the England shirt means. Let me recall that first taste of an experience to which I would become addicted. 'How fast are you, Lawrence?' England's head coach Jack Rowell had asked me. 'Probably one of the fastest forwards,' I said, suspecting where he was coming from.

'Do you think you could play open-side?' he asked.

'Yeah, sure,' I said, willingly overlooking the fact that I had virtually no experience in a very specialised position. But I got the result I wanted – Jack named me on the bench against South Africa.

With 18 minutes left, Tim Rodber got injured and I galloped on to that pitch like a young colt having his first run in a paddock. I was 23 and all I wanted was to get my hands on the ball. It was the head-spinning speed of that first international experience that amazed me. There was no time to think, no second to draw breath, and yet I found it exhilarating. I realised my ambition in that I got my hands on the ball and more than once. The only disappointment was that it ended so quickly and walking off the pitch, I thought 'I've got to have more of this. Lots more of it.'

And that's how it panned out. I went on to play 84 times for England. We won a lot more than we lost, and if I get on the pitch this evening it will be 85 and out. Given that playing for England was what I most wanted from my rugby life, it hasn't been a bad life. We did okay, had a lot of good players who hit their peak in the years from 2000 to 2003 and after getting ourselves properly organised under Clive Woodward, we didn't mess up in Australia.

It is 4.30 p.m. and my mobile phone rings. On the screen it says, 'Private number calling.' I press the answer button. At the other end, a voice says, 'Can you speak with Lewis Hamilton?' A couple of days before, a friend of mine had rung and asked if I would take a call from Lewis on the day of the World Cup final. He wanted to wish the team good luck against the Springboks. This is a young motor racing superstar in the throes of trying to win the Formula 1 World Championship in his debut season and he wants to speak with an England rugby player. 'Of course,' I said.

We talk for a few minutes about our mental preparation for major events and I am struck by Lewis's calm. It is something we share because I'm always pretty chilled out in the lead-up to big games, although for this final, there's an inner voice wondering if being on the bench isn't the reason for my calm. I tell myself, 'No, you're always like this.'

Because so much of my career has been as a starting player, it has been hard for me to adjust to the bench. A lot of people used to say if you pick Lawrence Dallaglio, you've got to make him captain or at least have him as a central figure in the team. It was talk I used to dismiss. 'I don't need to be captain, I don't have to be a leader, I can just play,' I would say. But I now see what they meant. This is the fourth consecutive time at this World Cup I have started on the bench and it is only in the last couple of games that I have begun to get a proper grip on how to make it work. It's not as straightforward as starting. I think I had more to offer in this World Cup but you can only give what you are invited to give. My life in rugby has been about setting the tone for the team in the days before a big game, getting everyone into the right frame of mind, but you can only have this influence if you are in the first fifteen.

What this tournament has told me is that there isn't much

wrong with English rugby. Out of adversity, we have become strong. Out of the chaos, the lack of direction, the lack of leadership, we have grown as a team and I have enormous admiration for a group of players who refused to lie down. As I sit here and wonder about all that has gone on over the last three years, the thought strikes me that our achievement in getting to the World Cup final may have been because we were at such a low ebb. At times we felt like a pub team and from there we knew our only chance was if everyone, players and coaches, stayed united. This has been about a group of people who went through a lot of shit but stuck together. I am particularly pleased for guys like Martin Corry, Andy Gomarsall, Mark Regan and Simon Shaw who were on the periphery of the team in 2003 and have been central to the effort in this tournament. I may be envious but did I deserve more from this tournament than them? Definitely not.

In the end, your body or your soul gives in and you can't do it anymore. My body has been tested to the limit, broken down and built back up again. After winning the World Cup in 2003, people told me it would be a good time to quit. Get out at the top, they said. I was 31 and the lure of playing for England still overwhelmed everything else. The thought of international retirement didn't even occur to me. If I'm needed for ten minutes or 40 minutes tonight I will be ready. If I don't get on, if I never play another minute for England, I won't complain. I have had one hell of a ride. Heading off to the Stade de France, I know there are many who believe I stayed around too long but that view doesn't bother me in the slightest. What they don't understand is that when the England flame goes out for me, the rugby flame goes with it.

1

Laying the foundations

I have often wondered what it must be like to reach the summit of Everest. You have done all the preparation, got used to the thin air, learned to live with the nausea, and, finally, you are within sight of the goal. As a rugby player, I know adrenalin would take over at that point, obliterating tiredness and almost propelling you forward. I imagine how good it would feel to arrive at the top, and if the day was clear, the view would probably be the most astonishing in the whole world. What could be better than that? I will tell you what. Instead of trekking alone to the summit, you walk alongside your mate. And rather than the satisfaction of making it on your own, you have the greater joy of sharing the experience with someone. If you felt at a low ebb, the other person would be there for you – lifting your spirits, reassuring you, making you laugh, driving you on. In short, inspiring you. Then, on the final drive to the top, you catch that person's hand and when you actually arrive, you do so as one. For me, that's far better than doing it alone. And I know that what I have achieved in rugby could never have been achieved alone. Neither would it have been half as much fun without the company of those I played with and against.

Cliff Morgan, the great Welsh fly-half of yesteryear, had a commentator's voice that made you want to sit around the television when rugby was being shown. Part of the attraction was that wonderful Welsh accent, but it was also his passion for the game. He once likened playing rugby to breaking bread with your fellow man and that image has long stayed in my mind. I'm not sure why. Perhaps it implies a spiritual experience, and for me, rugby has always had that other-worldly dimension. I have broken bread with many, many men, and although we may not see each other that often, there is a bond that remains unaffected by the passage of time. On that wonderful, never-to-be-forgotten Lions tour to South Africa in 1997, our coach Ian McGeechan made the point that in future years we would see each other and there would be instant acknowledgement of something we had shared in the past – one look, he said, was all it would take. He was right.

When I agreed to write this book, it was my hope that the journey through my life would make an entertaining story – I have always loved a good story – but on a more personal level, I also hoped that by revisiting my past I would learn more about myself and maybe get to know some things for the first time. I'm not sure if this has happened but the journey has been interesting and some things are clearer than before.

Born in London, I was brought up in a modest three-bedroomed flat in Barnes, West London, by parents who lived and worked solely for the benefit of their two children – Francesca, my extraordinary sister, and me. Mum and Dad weren't well off, neither had been to university, but they were willing to work hard and every penny earned was spent on the two of us. Actually, mostly me. Francesca was such a talented dancer that she won a scholarship to Elmhurst School in Camberley, Surrey, where she boarded and spent all the free hours in the day practising ballet and other dance forms that she loved. For me, there was no scholarship to defray the expense of sending me to one of the very best, and most expensive, Catholic boarding schools in the UK – Ampleforth College in North Yorkshire. For my parents, and Mum in particular, I was fulfilling a dream, so they bore the cost of the fees and made sacrifices. Did I repay them adequately with hard work and dedication? No, probably not, and I'm not proud of that fact. But I hope, at least, that since then I've made up for that. You would need to ask them.

Why were my parents so willing to make such sacrifices and to place the quality of their lifestyle second? I don't pretend to be able to get inside the mind of another person, even my parents (although I don't mind trying to psyche out certain opponents in the name of winning a rugby match). But when I reflect on my childhood, and indeed my own character, I believe a lot of what has happened to me, and what has made me the man I am today – good or bad or a bit of both – stems from my parents. In both of them there is a backbone of passion and determination. Both have a will to succeed, to move forward and overcome the odds to be the best. They appreciate what life has to offer.

I may have developed some of those attributes a little later in life than they, or I, would have wished – certainly some of the key qualities lay dormant until after my schooldays – and we as a family might have been shaken to the very core by events beyond our control, but deep down, they have always been there. They run through my heart and soul and, if I am to do myself and my story justice, I hope they also run through the heart of this book.

On 14 March 1958, my father Vincenzo Dallaglio saw the white cliffs of Dover for the first time. At least, that's the way he likes to recall his arrival to England. He had travelled by train from his home in Turin to Paris, then on to Calais, and from there he took the ferry to Dover. Aged 23, he had accepted a job as assistant waiter at the Cumberland Hotel in Marble Arch. Vincenzo's intention was to spend two years in London and become fluent in English, adding to his fluency in Italian, French and Spanish. After London he planned to work in Germany and learn that language. He wanted one day to manage a major international hotel.

Vincenzo was born in 1934 in the Emilia Romagna province of northern Italy. His family moved to Turin when he was 10 months old, and he was still a young boy when his father, Nero, took him to the old Stadio Comunale for the first time to see Juventus play. I remember Dad telling me this the first time he took me to see Chelsea play at Stamford Bridge. He explained that while he respected my decision to follow Chelsea, he was a lifelong Juve supporter. It was all right for fathers and sons to be different – provided the respect was always there.

Vincenzo lived through the Second World War in Turin, where food was in short supply. There is a war story we tell in the family. Vincenzo's relatives were farmers in Emilia Romagna, so he and his mother would travel from Turin to their cousins in the country and return with food supplies. With no trains or buses running, they hitched lifts, and were generally picked up by lorries. Shortly before the war ended, Vincenzo and his mum were sitting on empty wine vats in the back of a lorry that was taking them back to Turin when a low-flying German plane came shooting towards them. They could see that a machine-gunner was blazing away at vehicles ahead and in an instant the lorry slowed and everyone started jumping for cover. One minute my dad was with his mother, the next moment they were separated and he was seized by panic. Not knowing if he could make the leap from the side of the moving lorry, he tried to climb off and got caught under the wheel, which ran him over, smashing bones, tissue, everything, in fact, except his spine. For three months he lay in a hospital near Parma, hanging on to life by a thread. Then he began to get better, and after six months, he was allowed home. 'It just wasn't my turn to go,' he says in a way that is typical of him.

Vincenzo Dallaglio is as Italian as you could imagine, a lover of fine food, good wine and, as I've said, Juventus, and yet he left his home country because he didn't like what was happening there at the time. He was a good student and had won a scholarship to a secondary school run by the Silesian order of priests in Turin. His father wanted him to go to university but Vincenzo spent his holidays working in hotels and grew up used to being financially independent. Besides that, he wanted to get on with his career. After starting at the Lido in Venice, he worked for a few other Italian hotels before accepting a job at the Hotel Napoleon Bonaparte in Corsica. There he perfected his French and met an Englishman who happened to be the on-call doctor for the Cumberland Hotel in Marble Arch. Through that contact, he got the job in London. He came for two years and stayed a lifetime. He felt that to succeed in Italy, he would have had to be servile and prepared to oil the wheels that ensured you progressed. Vincenzo wanted to be of service to people but he didn't do subservience. England, he has always said, didn't demand that.

With his passion for the hotel business, he did well in his new environment and became the first non-English person to be accepted as a trainee manager by Strand Hotels Limited, who owned the Cumberland and many other hotels in London. He stayed nine years at the Cumberland before moving to the Hilton on Park Lane. From there he went to the Nile Hilton in Cairo, then came back to London to various top-class hotels. He then managed an outstanding Spanish restaurant in Swallow Street called Martinez before returning to the hotel business as general manager of the London Metropole. That's the one I remember because we were moving house at the time and spent six months as a family living in the Metropole on Edgware Road. Mum or Dad would have to drive me to school in Richmond and I would turn up, having had smoked salmon and scrambled eggs for breakfast, with croissants for all my friends at playtime. In the evening I would go to the grill room for dinner and order the lemon sole or the fresh sea bass. For those six months our home was the four-bedroomed Westminster Suite at the top of the hotel. I was 12 and, as you might imagine, already developing a taste for the good things in life. It has never left me.

As a dad, Vincenzo was a disciplinarian and very traditional in the way he tried to differentiate right from wrong. If you transgressed, you had to be corrected. Punishment was a physical beating. Nowadays there is a very different approach to correction as parents try to be more in touch with their children's lives. My own feeling as a father is that physical punishment just doesn't work and I have never, and will never, smack any of our children. But I understand my dad was part of a different generation. He also had a fiery nature and, let's face it, I could be a frustrating kid. I didn't try very hard at school and ended up hanging around with the guys who saw a 'Don't Trespass' sign as an invitation to enter. Being punished was the price I paid for getting caught, but it didn't change my behaviour. In that sense, Dad's approach just didn't work for me.

Vincenzo wanted what was best for his children. Three months after starting at Ampleforth, I returned home for the Easter holidays. From telephone calls we'd had during my first term there, he knew I was getting into rugby, a sport he knew virtually nothing about. Soon after arriving home, I was in his study and noticed a book on the desk with his half-moon glasses sitting on top. It was a big book called *The RFU Guide to the Laws of Rugby Union*, or something close to that. I was chuffed that he wanted to find out more about the game that I had started playing seriously for the first time. I went to the living room where he was sitting.

'I think it's great that you've bought that book,' I said.

'Yeah, I really want to understand the game, to learn about it.'

'Well, I'm glad you bought the book for that, Dad, and didn't expect me to help you out. I've played a few games, but I can't understand any of it. From what I can see, you make up your own laws as you go along.'

Thinking of those half-moons, I remember they worried me for ages when I was a kid. 'Why only half? Can't Dad afford proper glasses? Does he have to wait until he has enough money to buy the top half?' I guess somewhere at the back of my mind I was actually aware of just how much my parents were giving up for Francesca and me. But I kept it to myself for too long.

Eileen, my mother, has always been a pretty strong character. She was born in the East End of London, the ninth of 10 children in the family of David Henry Marriott. Her mother, my grandmother, Emily, who amazingly died on the day I was born, had strong Irish roots. Mum's grandfather was a Sullivan from Mallow in County Cork and Mum says that, as a little girl, she remembers a lot of laughter and singing in the family, and a distinct Irish feel. Not surprising, I suppose. If you've grown up singing 'Danny Boy' and 'Molly Malone', you're hardly likely to feel Scottish. Mum's six sisters went to work in a textile factory but even though she too started work at 15, she wanted to do something different, and she wasn't the kind of woman who was easily put off. Her first job was in the accounts department of the local authority in Tower Hamlets. At 17 she became a dental nurse and did that for four years. Then she delivered cars for a company called Car Mart, which helped her to get a job as a chauffeur for Bowaters, the paper manufacturers in Knightsbridge.

When I say my mum wasn't easily put off, I'm probably understating the situation. She tells a story about how she left Bowaters to become an air hostess. Mum was sitting at the breakfast table one morning when she saw that British United Airways were advertising for air stewardesses, and said to her mother, 'I think I'll apply for that.' William, the eldest in the family, was listening.

'Why bother?' he exclaimed. 'You'll never get it.'

Of the 10 Marriott children, William was the only one to receive an education and apparently wasn't shy about mentioning it to his siblings. He rose to the position of Superintendent Registrar of Births, Deaths and Marriages for the local authority in Stepney, and in the East End that was close to the height of respectability. His dismissal of his sister's chances of becoming an air stewardess touched a nerve.

'Why not?' asked Mum.

'Someone with your background and lack of education? It's impossible.'

'I don't see why it should be impossible. It's only a glorified waitress in the air and I present extremely well. I'll get this job. I'm not even sure I want it but I'm going to apply for it just because you say I won't get it.'

As a driver for Lord Bowater's company, Mum was kitted out in a smart uniform with a lovely white silk blouse, and she'd had a photograph of herself taken at Royal Ascot, after chauffeuring Lord Bowater's friends there. She enclosed the photo with her application to British United Airways, and included a letter saying she was made to be an air stewardess. Always a believer in her mother's saying that 'fine feathers make fine birds', Mum turned up for the interview looking a million dollars and duly got the job.

When Mum met Vincenzo, I bet she decided early on that he was the one. They started going out together in 1961 and got married in 1968. According to Mum, like most men, he didn't want to be rushed into marriage. (I reckon he must have passed that gene on to me!) Francesca was born in December 1969, at which point Mum had to give up her job with British United Airways, where she had risen to be a senior air stewardess. Two and a half years later, in what was the Hammersmith and Chelsea Hospital (now Queen Charlotte's), on 10 August 1972 to be precise, I arrived on the scene.

Mum had used the money she'd earned with the airline to start a retail business with her sister Emily, and what began as a newspaper/tobacconist shop in the East End grew into a thriving little supermarket. But after Francesca and I came along it became very difficult for her to stay fully involved in the shop. So she passed it on to her sister Maureen and worked for a time in the gift department of the jewellers Mappin and Webb. She gave that up to be at home when we were young, but once we were going to school, she returned to work with Rediffusion, a company that rented televisions and videos. Mum thrived on this varied working life, and it's clear she's a survivor. She was always prepared to battle and do whatever it took to make some money and help provide for her family.

When I was very young, we lived in Pinkney's Green in Maidenhead, a long way from the East End of London and another reason Mum decided to step back from the shop business. I don't remember much about the place – just that it was in the country, we had a nice little house and Francesca and I had bikes and used to go horse riding. My dad worked up in London and because of the long and unsocial hours that went with the hotel business, he wasn't around as much as other kids' dads. If he was working late and starting early the next morning, he would stay in a flat in Castelnau Mansions in Barnes that he and Mum rented when they were first married. Since the rent was low, and the flat was in a great location on the Barnes side of Hammersmith Bridge, they held on to it after the move to Maidenhead. They then got the chance to buy it for £10,000 because they had been long-term tenants and as that was well below the true value, they snapped it up and we moved in. I was five. They were nice flats that rose to five or six storeys. We were on the third floor and there was a lovely view. After a little while we moved down to a similar flat on the floor below and I remember thinking how exciting that was and how it would be better to have just two flights of stairs to climb.

My greatest memory of childhood is of growing up in a loving and caring family. Francesca was a wonderfully supportive sister – the first person who believed in me – but it wasn't just my sister. It was also to do with my parents' backgrounds which made for a heady mix. From a very early age, I remember a home environment with lots of cuddles and lots of love. We were very demonstrative with each other, even in public, which is probably very un-English. I'm sure there's love in everyone's family but with us, there was always that outward expression of emotion. When Mum or Dad collected me from school, we would hug, or greet each other in the Italian way, with a kiss on each cheek. I must confess I did have the odd pang of worry about how other people might view this, but it wasn't sufficient to stop me doing something that came naturally.

Our eating habits were greatly influenced by the fact that we had a Mediterranean dad who had lived with an Indian guy when he first came to London and, as a result, had a very international outlook when it came to food. From an early age, I was aware of different dishes and styles, and even though he worked long and unsocial hours, Dad did a lot of the cooking when he was around. Friends would come round for dinner and be amazed at the care taken over the preparation and presentation, the tastiness and how much there was of it. Dad expected my sister and me to try new things and not turn up our noses without tasting something. There weren't many things I didn't like, and it gave me a love of good food that has remained.

Our most memorable holidays were when we went as a family to see my grandparents and cousins in Italy. We would drive to Dover, put the car on the ferry and then drive down through France, into Switzerland for a bit, back into France and then through the Mont Blanc tunnel and into Italy. It was an amazing journey. The magical moment for me was coming out of the tunnel on the Italian side. France is a fabulous country, I love it, but Italy was our destination; it was Dad's country.

We spent our holidays with my grandparents Nero and Guilia, Dad's brother Remo and his sisters and, of course, cousin after cousin after cousin. At first I didn't speak Italian but I began to pick a little up and before long, I could understand what was going on. Granddad (Nonno) and my granny (Nonna) ran a stall in Turin's main fruit and vegetable market and I was fascinated by the produce on display ... but not as much as I was by the currency. How could you spend a million lire on fruit in one morning? At first I helped with the unloading of the boxes and did what I was told but eventually I got to work behind the counter. By far the biggest job was convincing myself I wasn't giving everyone too much change. The Italians amazed me with their attitude to shopping; they actually talked to the sellers about the fruit and vegetables, and they were so happy when the fruit was exactly as they liked it. They could turn their visit to the market into a pleasurable experience, a thing of beauty almost, and a real exchange of views, gossip and news with the people who ran the stalls. Tesco on a rainy Saturday morning it wasn't.

Inevitably, food played a big part in those holidays. At one family wedding, I remember 18 courses being served throughout the day, in what was the most joyous celebration of family, togetherness and life. Of course, I didn't want to miss out on anything that was on offer in the food department and proceeded to shovel down as much as I could from the word go, not realising I was involved in a marathon, not a sprint. After two or three dishes I felt certain dessert must be looming, but it wasn't until after course 12 that the sweet stuff started to appear. I was struggling by that stage, I can tell you, but never one to give up, I focused and kept eating. I'm pretty sure I managed at least the tiniest of tastes of that final cake, or whatever it was, before retiring hurt at six in the evening. I could hardly move out of my seat.

The wedding was a joyous event, but the truth is that everything about family eating in Italy was an occasion and a celebration. Although polenta was our staple food on those holidays, Francesca and I would also make fresh pasta at the table with my mum and my nonna, which we would then pass to my nonno who would roll it out, making sure he got the right texture. Then we'd make spaghetti and spoon in the delicious meat sauce that was usually to be found in a bowl somewhere in the kitchen. It was a lovely way for the family to prepare the evening meal and to feel that everyone belonged. Francesca and I loved it and I hope I've instilled some of that feeling of warmth and family in my kids around meal times. It is important, I think.

As little ones, both Francesca and I went to the local Catholic school, St Osmund's, which was a good state school in Barnes. But three years into my time there, Mum moved me to King's House school in Richmond, which was a private, boys-only, fee-paying school. I was eight years of age and for the first few mornings my Italian nonno Nero, who was here on holiday, took me on the bus. After that, I went on my own. I wasn't the kind of kid who wanted anyone holding his hand. The number 33 got me from Barnes to King's House. These were the old-style buses that you could jump off and on so easily, and you knew every conductor and they knew you. I remember not having the right money at different times and the conductor telling me it was OK, he would see me the following day. If he didn't have the right change, he would promise to come back with it in a few minutes and he invariably did. There was a lot more trust in those days.

Mum's decision to send me to King's House came about because of Francesca's gift for dancing. For as long as I can remember, Francesca loved to dance and long before she ever had lessons, she moved naturally to the sound of music. A Polish lady called K. K. Lam who lived in our old flat, above us, and was a good friend of Mum's, saw Francesca dance and was mesmerised by her. 'We've got to get that little girl taught. I've got a friend who works for the Royal Ballet,' she said to Mum. Francesca herself couldn't wait to have lessons. Mum was unsure because she knew how hard ballet dancers have to work and she reckoned that with Francesca's personality and physical beauty, there had to be easier ways of getting on in life. But Francesca's enthusiasm decided it and off she went. After four lessons, the teacher said they were auditioning at the Junior Associates of the Royal Ballet School and Francesca should give it a shot.

One day after school, Mum collected Francesca and me from St Osmund's and took us to the Royal Ballet School on Talgarth Road. I was six or seven at the time. Parents and kids were everywhere, the mothers trying very hard to make their girls look good. I was just happy to have a bit of space and to run around. Mum has a better memory of the afternoon. She remembers all the other girls wearing pink stockings and having their hair pulled up and tied in ribbons. Francesca just had a black leotard and black ballet pumps. A woman from the Royal Ballet asked if Francesca's hair was not going to be pulled up and Mum asked if it was necessary. 'Well, yes,' the lady said, 'we have to see the line.' Borrowing two hair-grips, one for either side, up went the hair in 10 seconds flat. Francesca waited 10th in a line of 12 and as Mum said goodbye to her, she remembers thinking, 'My God, girl, you still look the part.'

Parents weren't allowed to watch the auditions, so Mum read a newspaper as I ran around. When Francesca returned and Mum asked her how it went, she said there were four ladies in the room who asked her to go deep into her pliées. Well, Francesca might as well have been speaking Chinese.

'Pliées?' said Mum. 'What are they?'

'Mummy,' said Francesca, 'you must get deep into your pliées or else you can't dance.'

'Oh I see,' said Mum, still not having a clue.

It took time for the auditions to be completed, over 4,000 girls were assessed, and three weeks later, a letter arrived saying she had been accepted. Everyone was thrilled. It was so unexpected. We knew how little training Francesca had had and from that moment, it was obvious she had a special talent. Mum and Francesca talked it over and eventually decided that instead of taking up the Royal Ballet place she would go to a ballet school in Teddington where Susanna Raymond became her teacher. Francesca wanted to be able to concentrate on dancing and frantically set about getting the training and qualifications that would give her a chance of winning a scholarship to a school that specialised in dance. She moved through to senior grade in one year. Mum would whiz her off to dance class at five o'clock, Dad would prepare dinner and have it ready when they arrived home at eight.

Each year the borough of Richmond-upon-Thames awarded three scholarships for Classical Dance and Musical Theatre Arts. Francesca was 10 and determined, and when she won one of them, it meant she could board at Elmhurst Ballet School in Camberley, Surrey. That was going to be her future and Mum felt a little guilty about my progress at St Osmund's. God bless her, Mum always wanted the very best for us. She used to tell people we were her two jewels. 'Francesca,' she'd say, 'is the diamond that sparkles like the star she will one day be. Lawrence is the emerald, from the Irish side of my family, the green eyes, the love of life and laughter.' If loving life and laughter meant wanting to have a good time, then Mum's description is accurate. I didn't do particularly well at St Osmund's because for me school was just another place to have fun. I liked all the playing we did at breaks, I loved every sport but saw most of the classes as spoiling the party.

However, when Francesca moved on to boarding school, Mum decided I deserved the chance of a change as well, so off I went to King's House. In equal measure, I was terrified about the move, because I was leaving all my friends behind, but I fancied getting a new uniform and the longer bus journey was going to be exciting.

One of the things about my journeys on the number 33 was that there were lots of different kids on it, travelling to state schools, and as an eight-year-old in corduroy shorts, grey shirt, blue jumper and grey socks, I certainly wasn't going to chance sitting upstairs. I whiled away the time looking out of the window, day-dreaming no doubt. One morning early in my time at the school, I missed my stop and panicked, thinking I would miss the whole day at school. So instead of waiting, I launched myself out of the moving bus, using my school satchel as a makeshift surfboard. I was badly cut up, but alive and really relieved to have got off the bus. Had I stayed where I was, I could have got off at the next stop, about 200 yards down the road, and I would still have got to school about 40 minutes before the first lesson. But you don't think like that when you're eight years old. At least,

I didn't.

They encouraged us to get to school at eight o'clock even though the first lesson did not begin until 8.45. I think they believed that boys needed to let off some steam, otherwise the first two lessons would be a nightmare. As far as I was concerned, the perfect way to start the day was with half an hour of my favourite sport – football. In my five enjoyable years at King's House, I did well in most sports, but football was always my number one. Apart from the pure pleasure, sport also allowed me to mix with older boys, which I seemed to want to do anyway. My mother is right when she talks about my love of life, and when I was young, I always wanted to do things sooner than other kids of my age. At the start of my second year at King's House I was watching guys from the classes above me having a kick-about. Most of them were three or four years older than I was. After a while, their ball got punctured. They looked at me, saw a football under my arm, and said, 'Hey, can we borrow your ball?'

'Sure,' I said, 'as long as I get to play.'

'No, no chance. You can't play, you're nine.'

'Well, then, you can't have the ball.'

'OK, come on, just don't get in the way.'

I'd played a lot of football with friends at home in Barnes and without wishing to be cocky, I could hold my own against these older boys. Getting the ball, I went past two or three of them and put it in the back of the net.

'Where's that come from, you cheeky little sod?' one of them said.

I played with those lads every day after that, whether it was my ball or someone else's, and became friends with some of them.

Hanging around with an older crowd began at an early age and continued right into my rugby career. One of the many things I loved about Francesca was that she would let me come out with her and her friends, even though I was two years younger. A group of us in Barnes had this thing called a 'bike club' where we would all meet up on our bikes – big surprise – and head off somewhere. I was allowed along solely because I was Francesca's younger brother. Actually, I say we'd 'head off somewhere' but the reality was that the bike ride was more pretend than real. In truth, we just met up to have a laugh, chase each other around and, if you were lucky, get involved in a little bit of snogging action. Very occasionally we would head out on the bikes.

It's odd reflecting now on those pre-teenage days. Are patterns set way back that in time shape your life ahead? A passion for sport, independence, older friends, a certain recklessness, a love of larking around, food, family, laughter. My parents' attitudes gave me my core values, I believe, but after that? Did the environment I grew up in shape me? Or did I shape it to suit myself? God knows. But whatever the longer-term impact, they were happy days. And I'm so glad much of them were spent close to my sister, because that particular happiness was ultimately to be taken away.

2

Another suitcase in another theatre

Sometimes, when I'm with friends and we're passing the Prince Edward Theatre in Soho's Old Compton Street, I mention the time I used to perform there. 'You, in the theatre? No chance. Mate, you're a rugby player,' one of the lads invariably says. I am a rugby player now but there was a time when I wasn't and I was paid for singing and performing on stage. Sounds a bit crazy but it's true. The Prince Edward Theatre holds special memories because that's where I had my longest run and earned most money for being part of a small choir that performed in *Evita*. It was all down to an extraordinary guy at King's House. Michael Stuckey was choirmaster and music teacher and hugely talented. His love for music was infectious.

I was 9 or 10 when I came under his influence at school and I got on with him from the beginning. He had a certain style: he drove an Alfa Romeo car and was obviously a bit of a playboy. He was just a really good guy. As well as that, he saw something in me that he liked and he encouraged me to join the school choir, if only to see how I got on. There were two reasons for being in the King's House Choir – firstly, it was very good and, secondly, Michael. In the three years that I spent singing with them, it actually became cool to be a member. That, again, was down to Michael. He also taught me the piano and he believed I had a lot of musical potential, but he never forced it on me. He came to our house to talk to Mum and Dad. He told them, 'I'd really love Lawrence to learn the piano.' Mum said that with the school fees at King's House, she would be hard pressed to pay for lessons. He said the money wasn't important, and he would do it because he wanted me to have the chance. So we arranged a trade-off – Michael would come to the house to give me piano lessons and Dad would cook a fantastic meal. Michael would stay to have dinner with my parents over a bottle of good wine.

As well as his personality and attitude to life, I was also struck by the fact that if Michael liked you, he liked you whether you were right or wrong – our family had great conversations and debates when he was around. I wasn't the best singer in the world and I often thought Michael wanted me in the choir more because I helped the other kids to interact in a way that made being in the choir a fun experience. I could sing fine but didn't want to be a soloist and didn't want to stand out from the others. My approach was to identify someone who consistently sang in tune and stand alongside him. If the person next to you is hitting the wrong notes, it's very hard to stay in tune. What I really loved about the choir was the opportunities it opened up, the places we got to see and the things we got to do. Michael's reputation meant that King's House Choir was highly rated.

In the England rugby team over the last few years, Joe Worsley has had the mickey taken out of him because he likes to play the piano and is good at it. Well, I don't take the mickey out of Joe for that – maybe for other things but not that – because I envy him and other people who can play properly. Michael used to tell me I had enormous talent for music, especially the piano. I've these big hands and I can play reasonably well. Our two daughters, Ella and Josie, have also taken up piano and when I'm showing them where the keys are, their frustration is the same as mine was 25 years ago. They want to get it straight away, and it annoys them when they can't.

To play really well takes hard work, and frankly I wasn't prepared to put in the time. For me it just didn't compare with the fun I had playing football or hanging out with my friends, and I tended to go with what I enjoyed. Even though I didn't really dedicate myself to the piano, Michael continued to work with me because I think he enjoyed my parents' company. When the time came for me to go to Ampleforth, Michael could see it was going to be the end of my music. 'I knew you were going to come to this crossroads,' he said to me, 'where it would be music in one direction and sport in another. And you are going to choose sport.' We stayed in touch and then, one day while I was at Ampleforth, my mum rang to say that Michael had died following a tragic accident. He had choked on his own vomit. I was deeply affected by his death – it made me intensely sad because I thought it was just such a waste of a young and great person. He was 33, and that was too young to die, especially for someone who was so talented and had so much to give.

Michael arranged trips for the choir, and we got to do things that you wouldn't dream of. I mean, we sang at Andrew Lloyd Webber's marriage to Sarah Brightman at his house in 1984. We went to Abbey Road Studios and sang the backing track for Tina Turner's song 'We Don't Need Another Hero'. We told our mates who weren't in the choir that we were recording with Tina Turner but the truth is she recorded on a different day from us. Being in the studio where The Beatles had worked was enough for me, and of course we went to the famous zebra crossing. There was a lot of waiting around at the studio – that's the way the recording industry works – but it was a fantastic experience. I loved it. A few years ago someone realised we should have been paid for our work on the song, so we all received a royalty payment.

To me, these experiences were what life was about, not a biology class with some teacher trying to interest you in photosynthesis. Another day we had to record an ad for Colgate toothpaste, and one Christmas we were asked to do a carol service at St Paul's Cathedral. I remember singing the St Matthew Passion at St Paul's, and you can be as blasé as you like about buildings, but St Paul's Cathedral is incredible. It absolutely blew me away, but it was still just another job for us members of King's House Choir. You've got to give a performance, whatever and wherever you're singing. I know this sounds corny and I'm not sure if I should mention it, but we also backed Barry Manilow live at the Royal Festival Hall – in front of a packed house, it has to be said. It's amusing to think back because we actually stood behind him in traditional choral gowns. We got about £5 per performance so the money made it worth it. But *Evita* was the experience that stands out.

For almost three years, from when I was 10 to 13, the King's House Choir was one of a small number of choirs that provided six singers for *Evita*. Throughout the summer, Christmas and Easter holidays we would be rotated and it worked out that I would have two or three performances each week. We were picked up in Richmond by a chaperone who drove us to the West End, sometimes with boys and girls from different schools, and after we arrived at the theatre's stage door, we were taken to the changing rooms. It was a tight little theatre. We had to go down a set of narrow stairs and were invariably met with an explosion of activity. We ended up having to climb through a trapdoor to get to where we needed to be, and everyone we passed was wearing an amazing costume.

We were required for three different parts of the show. Our first contribution was a Latin song, then we had to do a little bit of acting in boy scouts' uniforms and the third part was where we came on with lighted candles and sang a Spanish song. Although we were kids, as soon as we got out on that stage, we had to look as though we knew what we were doing. In those days, the mid-80s, *Evita* was *the* show in the West End and it was always packed out. I don't remember worrying about the audience, even though you could see how many people were there. I just loved being on stage. The whole experience – being driven up to Soho, which was a fascinating place and very different from what it is today, being backstage and seeing how a musical was made to work on the night, watching everyone racing around and changing costumes in seconds but still having a laugh – I loved it.

During my years in the show, I saw both Elaine Paige and the late Stephanie Lawrence play Eva Perón, and somewhere I've got the autographs of people who were part of the show. Nowadays if I'm in a hotel lift or bar and 'Don't Cry For Me Argentina' or 'Another Suitcase in Another Hall' is playing, I find myself singing it and remembering the fun we had. They were good songs from a musical that has stood the test of time.

Our fee started off at £5 for each performance and rose to £7.50 by the time I'd finished. That really added up for a young pup of around 12 years old. At the end of the summer holidays, it could be up towards £200 and that was a lot of money back then. Even though my parents could have done with it, they let me hold on to the money because I had earned it. Unfortunately, I'm not very good with cash. My attitude is that it is for spending, not saving, and the rainy day is something I can never see coming. That philosophy has stayed with me all through my life. In the early days, especially, I was prepared to have one big night as opposed to lots of little ones. When the money disappeared, that was fine. I would get on without it, although it is easier to do that when you're young and without responsibilities.

One year we went on tour to America, which was great fun. We sang in New York City and also in Buffalo, in upstate New York. I was 12 at the time and we were fostered out in the places where we were singing, two or three of us staying together with a local family. One of the more vivid memories is arriving at one of the homes and the mum saying, 'You must be hungry.' She started putting on breakfast for us – pancakes served with maple syrup.

Absolutely delicious. But then that was followed up with lovely steaks and then ice cream. And this was breakfast! Needless to say, I accepted everything offered and ate every morsel. I was a tall and skinny lad who looked like he needed fattening up, but it didn't matter what I ate, I stayed skinny.

Our hosts were typical middle-class American families – nice, big houses, carport, basketball hoop, big back garden with loads of space – and all so eager to please. *What else can we do for you? Anything else you would like to eat?* I also remember they were genuinely warm and loving towards us. The second family I stayed with had a couple of attractive daughters and that was great because we had a lot of fun together.

The thing I most remember is the fuss they made about 'the King's House Choir, from Richmond, Surrey, England'. One of the places was opening a big new centre of some sort and they saw it as an honour to have us sing at the event. We were a good choir, of course, and that was down to Michael Stuckey. All the incredible experiences we had as kids in that choir came about because he knew how to teach music, and he was so well connected.

Away from school, I enjoyed a very different life. From the age of about eight, Spencer Franks, who also lived in Barnes, became a very good friend and his dad, Derek, was a sports lover. Although I played rugby and cricket in junior school, football was what I was most interested in, but through Derek Franks, I got to play more rugby and cricket outside of school. My parents worked long hours and when they weren't working, they were often taxi-ing

Francesca to and from dance classes. With Spencer's dad providing the lifts for me, I played cricket at Thames Ditton and began to play rugby for Staines. That was my introduction to the culture of club rugby and it was a lovely, traditional place. Staines put out a lot of teams, they had a great atmosphere in the clubhouse and they represented all that was good about the game at this level. There was a smell in the bar that I think of as typical of a rugby club bar. At the time, that meant Coca-Cola and prawn cocktail crisps for me, but the older guys had their sing-songs and played their drinking games, and you could sense the camaraderie and the fun that everyone was having.

Spencer was a couple of years older than I was and a member of the team that went to mini-rugby tournaments. I had only just started but would still go to the tournaments to watch. At one competition in Guildford, Staines got to the final. Their opponents were a player short and I got to play for them. All I remember is getting thumped and Staines winning the match easily. But I soon got in the Staines team and we did well on the mini-rugby circuit. To be honest, one of the main attractions was the excitement of going somewhere without my parents. Derek Franks was a lovely man and by taking me to the Thames Ditton cricket club and the rugby in Staines, I had the opportunity to learn sports I would later play at King's House.

The more rugby I played, the more I liked the game. At cricket, I scored a lot of runs and was presented with a couple of balls for hitting a 50 and a 100 but I've since thought about that and decided the bowlers mustn't have been too hot if I was making those scores. I really wasn't very good. I did well at sport at King's House and, because it was a small school, I was picked for the football team when I was two, or even three, years younger than the rest of the lads and ended up scoring goals in most games.

Rugby, at that point, was an offshoot of my football and, naturally, I played fly-half. The part of the game I most looked forward to was kicking the conversions. My first time playing at Twickenham was for King's House in one of those games where our playing area was half the width of the full-sized pitch.

Barnes Eagles was the football team I played for from the age of eight right up to the Under-14s. That was an interesting experience because it took me out of the cosy prep-school environment and put me into a team where most of the players were from the local council estates. It gave me two very different lives. King's House was a good school, with excellent facilities, good teachers and the smaller classes you get at private schools. Most of the pupils came from sheltered middle-class and upper-middle-class backgrounds. Mum wanted me in that environment and I got on well at the school, made friends and had the usual sleepovers at mates' houses. Back home, though, I hung out with my Barnes friends and it was a different story. Barnes isn't exactly the roughest of areas and our flat was in a neighbourhood that was on the fringes of being lovely, but you only had to go around the corner to the local council estate to find a bit of edge, and that had its pros and cons. It was good because it showed me another side to life and made me grateful for everything that my family was giving me, but it also introduced me to kids who knew how to get into trouble, and for someone as easily led as I was, that was bound to cause difficulties.

My Barnes mates didn't have it easy. There might be seven in a family, living in a house that was really meant for four or five. My mum always talked about there being two sides of life and she moved heaven and earth to get me into what she saw was the right side, but I couldn't help being tempted by the other. The lives of some of my friends weren't as scrutinised by their parents as mine was. It wasn't that their mums didn't care but the kids had a licence to stay out till whatever time they liked and that seemed a pretty good arrangement to me. I wanted to do the things the older boys were doing and never wanted anyone to think I wasn't up for it. I was also curious to find out things and wanted it to happen sooner rather than later. My appreciation of what was sensible was a little distorted and, to a certain degree, that inability to say no and distinguish between what is the right thing to do and what isn't has carried on into later life.

Similar to my school team, I got into the Barnes Eagles side earlier than some of the other guys and I played on the right wing. We were a good side and won a few trophies. Because I was a bit younger, and possibly because I went to what would have been seen as a posh school, I was bullied a little, but not in any way that caused me real stress. If a ball was kicked wide and went a long way away, I was sent to fetch it, and if any of the tougher guys needed to let off a bit of steam, I was the one who was beaten up. But I kept going back so I must have been enjoying it – the football, I mean, not the beatings.

The boys on the team and other friends I had from the council estate were into all sorts of different mischief, mostly the things that kids do – shoplifting, drinking a little, smoking, vandalising. I wasn't a ringleader but I'd go along with whatever the other guys were doing. I was happy to be involved, whether it was going off to do a bit of nicking from shops, or to knock on people's doors and run away, or throw stuff off buildings, or spend the evening spray-painting. We would drift off somewhere and come upon a reservoir that had lots of signs saying 'Keep Out', and that meant we had to climb over the wall or sneak under the fence. We were at an age and had an attitude that made everything forbidden seem attractive. Hanging out with these guys meant I talked in a different way from the average prep-school kid and it gave me an edge.

It also led to brashness and cockiness, which is not something I'm proud of and it didn't help me much, although when I went to Ampleforth, I had a certain confidence that enabled me to deal with a new and very different environment. In a curious way, I don't think I ever committed to either world. Part of my life was spent at King's House with my friends there, another part of it was spent with the guys from Barnes, and yet I don't feel I ever truly belonged in either place. It was an exciting time, I had a lot of fun but the fact is that I don't see any of the guys from those days any more. It makes me think that I floated from one group to the other without putting any roots down in either camp. Without great difficulty, I was able to disappear from the gang who knocked around together at home while many of the others were in it for the long haul. At King's House it was the same – friends when I wanted to be, able to head off somewhere else when I didn't. It was lovely in a way, being all things to all people, friends with everyone, but still independent.

My parents, especially Mum, were conscious of the trouble that was likely to come from staying out late at night, and while they were prepared to let me out, they specified a time by which I had to be back. The general rule was that I had to be home before dark.

Of course, I tried to push my luck and stay out, but Mum would get in the car and drive around the neighbourhood until she found me. When she did, she would embarrass the hell out of me in front of all my mates. She would drag me to the car and give all the lads a mouthful as well. All the way home, I would get continuous grief and once we got there, Dad would have his say, too. I can see it from their point of view more now – they were working incredibly hard to send me to a very expensive private school in Richmond, they were also paying for Francesca's boarding fees at Elmhurst, even if the scholarship covered her tuition fees, and it seemed to them I was wasting the opportunities being offered to me.

Towards the end of my time at King's House, Mum went to see the principal, David Derle, to talk to him about secondary schools that might be suitable for me. He mentioned a few but said these schools needed an overall 65 per cent in all subjects – I was on 55 per cent. The reason for that was a straightforward neglect of homework. I must have been hugely frustrating because every report said the same thing: 'Lawrence would do really well if only he was prepared to work hard.' There were times when things would go well and the teachers would be pleased with my work, and the school was very proud of what I did on the sports field. But there were other times when I was a pain in the neck. In the classroom I could be disruptive, at the centre of a little group who made life difficult for the teacher. I knew the trouble the Barnes guys were getting into at their school so my problems seemed pretty minor, but at a school like mine they were considered to be very serious. Mum received a number of phone calls from the principal and most of them would begin, 'I am sorry to have to tell you, Mrs Dallaglio . . .'

My situation at home wasn't helped by the fact that Francesca was the opposite. She had a huge workload with her dancing and her studies and managed to get excellent grades in both. Most of her dance classmates struggled to find time for the academic side but not Francesca. I used to think it was easier for her – living away from London in a boarding school meant she didn't have to deal with alternatives to study, such as being tempted out to see your mates. It should also be said I wasn't incredibly bright and after starting out being an average student in King's House, I slipped a bit from there. That was totally to do with the fact that I would only do as much study as I needed to do to get by. For all the time I was there, I never really grasped the idea that the harder I worked, the easier it would become. Instead, my only desire was to enjoy school as much as possible, and I didn't see how working really hard allowed you to do that. Of course, you get older and wonder what the hell you were thinking, but my sole aim was to do enough to make sure I wasn't disgraced in the classroom and that no one could call me thick or stupid. While Mum's approach was to talk to me constantly and try to persuade me to work harder, Dad would physically punish me when I stayed out later than I should or did something wrong. That led to a traditional smacking and, to Mum's concern, it was often too severe. My reaction was to accept it as a fair punishment because I knew when I had done wrong. Also, unknown to my parents, I had already been there.

When I was younger, from when I was about six, they would sometimes leave me with another family to be looked after. If I did any little thing wrong, the father of the family would punish me by beating me up. The thing that made it different was that he used to take pleasure in hurting me. I never told my parents because I knew they would be devastated to find out they had left me with someone who was physically abusing me. He was a strong man and maybe he didn't realise he was hurting me, but I would be screaming for him to stop and he'd just carry on. It definitely had an effect on me in that it made me tolerate being hit, to a point where I accepted it as normal. I'm not sure how else it has affected me but I imagine it has.

Throughout the days of disappointing school reports, occasional phone calls from the headmaster and Mum pulling her hair out because of her belief that I was wasting a great opportunity, Francesca was fantastic. She would tell me how hard Mum and Dad were working to send me to my school and that I really needed to work much more and appreciate what they were doing. Then, after I had left the room, she would put her arm around Mum and reassure her everything was going to turn out fine. 'Don't despair about Lawrence,' she would say, 'he'll come good in the end, I promise you he will. He's the kind of person who'll be a millionaire before he's thirty. He's got so much going for him. It's just a question of growing up.'

3

Little Lord Fauntleroy goes north

My mother, as you may have picked up, is a strong character. When she gets an idea in her head, especially something she thinks is right, she will generally see it through. Coming from a strong East End and Irish Catholic background, she had pangs of guilt about taking me out of St Osmund's, a state Catholic school, and sending me to a Church of England school, King's House. Her faith is important to her. If at all possible, she wanted me to go to a Catholic secondary school and from a brief look at the possibilities, the name Ampleforth College kept cropping up. Over lunch with her friend Sonia Kennedy, who knew about these things, the question of my future was discussed.

'Have you decided where to send Lawrence?' asked Sonia.

'I'm not sure yet, but one thing's for certain – I won't be giving up work. Vincenzo's got promoted so things aren't too bad but even still, I thought we might look at Ampleforth.'

'Oh, it's a superb school, Eileen. Although it's far up in North Yorkshire – it's the premier Catholic public school in England. It would be wonderful to send him there.'

You could say my fate was decided there and then. There was still a year to go before I finished at King's House but Mum wrote to Ampleforth to register my name. A letter from the school arrived shortly afterwards, saying there were three lists of potential candidates from which the following year's intake would be chosen. The letter went on to point out the school nearly always filled its enrolment from those on the first list, occasionally they took some applicants from the second but they rarely needed to go to the third list. 'Unfortunately, Lawrence would be on the third list,' stated the letter. Mum replied, 'As it is by divine providence that I wrote to you in the first place, please register Lawrence's name anyway. If Almighty God wants him to go to Ampleforth, it really won't matter what list he's on.'

I was invited up for an interview during that year, so we drove up to see the school and meet the principal, Father Dominic Milroy. At the time we had a small MG car, which wasn't brilliant if you were a gangly teenager squashed up in the back seat on a 400-mile round trip. Before our interview with the principal, a monk met us to take us on a tour of the school's facilities.

'Where is your car parked?' he asked. This wasn't a school you toured on foot.

'Well, I'm afraid we won't all be able to fit in our car,' Mum said.

I can still see the shock, the complete horror, on the monk's face at the prospect of having to walk around the grounds.

Mum and Dad were in awe of what they saw — wonderful buildings everywhere, an old library with individual cubicles, a fantastic swimming pool. I just noticed all the rugby pitches. Even though I knew that rugby was Ampleforth's number-one game, nothing prepared me for the reality. We stood looking down this Yorkshire valley and it seemed to be full of rugby pitches, for as far as the eye could see. Even though I had played the game at King's House and at Staines rugby club, I was still a Londoner and more into football. I started to count the pitches and got to 27, and they were only the ones I could see. King's House had one. Immediately, for no reason other than all those pitches, I saw rugby differently. 'God, this game is quite serious up here,' I thought.

The important part of that first experience of Ampleforth was meeting Fr Dominic. He was a professor of languages and had a love for Italian, which may have been why he noticed our surname in the first place. Once we got talking, he got on well with Dad and there was a little bit of Italian spoken. Then Fr Dominic turned to me.

'And Lawrence,' he said, 'do you know what's special about the name Lawrence?'

Perhaps it was my mother's belief in divine providence, but I just said, 'He's the patron saint of the Benedictine Order.'

My parents sat there thinking, 'Where did that come from?' I was asking myself the same question because, no word of a lie, it just came out and to this day I don't know why. Father Dominic was impressed and later asked when I was born.

'Tenth of August,' I said.

'And do you know what's special about that day?'

'Yes, it's Saint Lawrence's day.'

Again, I had no idea how I knew that but obviously sometime in the past, I'd been told. It was enough to persuade Fr Dominic that I would be a good addition to Ampleforth and I was offered a place.

We couldn't quite believe the huge clothing list that arrived before term started. It went on for pages. Some of the stuff was optional but my mother went out to buy every single item mentioned. She didn't want me to feel in any way inferior to my classmates at Ampleforth and she spent pretty much all the cash she had at the time. For some reason I started at Ampleforth in January 1986, halfway through the school year, and having spent a lot on the uniform list, Mum didn't have enough money to drive me up to North Yorkshire. So there I was, dressed up like Little Lord Fauntleroy and sent off to my new school on my own on the train, from King's Cross to York. A school mini-bus took me the rest of the way.

Setting off on my own didn't bother me because I'd been going to school on the bus by myself since I was eight years old. 'Don't worry, it's not a problem,' I told my mother, when in fact it was a bit worrying for a 13-year-old who hadn't spent much time in the north of England. There were other Ampleforth kids on the train, sixth formers sitting at a table drinking cans of beer, but I found a quiet seat and kept my head down because I was so obviously a new boy.

Three bags plus golf clubs was a lot to carry and I just about managed it, but you wouldn't have wanted a long walk. Well, that

January evening it was snowing, in London and in Yorkshire, and as I discovered, there's London snow and then there's real snow. It was eight o'clock in the evening when the shuttle bus dropped us in the main square at Ampleforth. Five or six inches of snow lay on the ground and it was still coming down heavily.

In my innocence, I thought the bus would take us to our different houses. Not a chance. You got dropped in the square and had to find your own way to your house, in my case St Thomas's. I had come armed with directions but it was hard to make out anything in the driving snow. Everyone else quickly scuttled off and I was left struggling with my map getting wetter by the minute. Eventually I found where St Thomas's was marked on the map and, of course, it was the farthest away from where I stood, located on the top of the hill. You may have heard me at different times in my career say that I didn't do any weight training until I was in my early 20s. It's a lie. I had that one evening of serious weight training in Ampleforth – three bags, one set of golf clubs, and a significant trek through the snow on my first evening at the school. Eventually I got there, put all the bags down, knocked on the door and Fr Richard Field, the housemaster, noticed me. He was saying goodbye to parents who had come with their kids.

'And who are you?' he asked.

'Lawrence Dallaglio,' I replied. 'I think I'm in St Thomas's. I hope I'm in the right place.'

'Oh, you are, you are. Where are your parents?'

'My mother,' I said, 'wasn't feeling very well and I decided to travel up on the train on my own.'

He looked at me curiously, and gave the impression that I was the only pupil to have turned up alone for his first evening at

Ampleforth College, which I may have been. It made for an interesting relationship because I felt from that moment that Fr Richard looked on me completely differently from everyone else.

Not knowing anyone at the school, I tried to get the hang of what a newcomer needed to do to survive. That meant taking a few minor beatings from boys two or three years older than you and accepting that if they asked you to do something, it made sense to just do it. I learned very quickly that if you did what you were told, provided it wasn't inhumane, that was best. I ended up spending almost four years at Ampleforth and enjoyed being there.

For the first two years I got on well and a number of the teachers were writing good reports, saying positive things about me. I was responsible enough to become a house monitor, even head of house, but there was still that other side to my character that wanted to enjoy life and not worry about the dangers or the implications. The balance between acting responsibly and irresponsibly was fragile throughout my school life and has remained so through my rugby career. I believe the wayward side of my character has held me back and anyone who saw how I conducted myself at Ampleforth would not have been too surprised that I got, and then lost, the England captaincy. That sums up a lot about my character back then.

Ampleforth was just an amazing place and had so many good points. It allowed me to become independent because I was in an environment where the support and love of my parents was not immediately available. Boarding school taught me how to deal with things I didn't like but couldn't change. To make the system work, there had to be a lot of routine, and there were plenty of things we had to do. You had to attend mass on Sundays, you had to do prayers in the morning, prayers in the evening, and follow a routine that gave each day structure.

The Ampleforth way of life certainly prepared me well for my life in professional sport; I learned to take orders, to survive in a male-dominated environment and to accept the rough with the smooth. I had a lot of fun there and, perhaps more importantly, it was the place where I learned the game of rugby. But I also saw the less attractive side of the boarding-school system. I went there at the age of 13 and became friendly with boys who had been at Ampleforth since they were eight. Apart from school holidays and occasional weekends, they would have no physical contact with their parents for 12 years. I think there's something fundamentally wrong in that. In one sense, boarding schools are like a very expensive prison.

A lot of boys were there because their parents had, like mine, made unbelievable sacrifices to come up with the fees, but plenty of others came from wealthy families. That fact didn't go unnoticed by my parents. As I've said, for most of my upbringing in Barnes, I was mixing with people who were a million miles from Ampleforth. They were stuck on the other side of the fence and I had always been drawn towards them. The kids whom I hung out with on the council estate might not have got into serious trouble but there were always minor scrapes and I was enjoying their company. At Ampleforth it was a different story. I was friendly with Lord So-and-So's son and the son of the Right Honourable So-and-So. There were boys whose fathers, grandfathers and great-grandfathers had been to Ampleforth. I often wonder whether Mum and Dad's decision to send me there was partly a conscious choice to introduce me to a different peer group.

I was a carefree teenager and so really enjoyed myself. Homework was OK, provided, just like at King's House, it didn't stop me having a good time. If I enjoyed a class, I excelled at it, but to be honest, there wasn't that much I liked. I did manage to avoid too many bad reports in those first couple of years though – by once again just doing enough to get by. It was working out just fine but in a broader sense I'm not convinced that boarding school worked for me. I keep coming back to my view that they are an expensive prison. Boys in particular need a mentor and normally that comes from your father. If you're away at school, without even an older sibling, you're not going to get that. Having had a very strong, day-to-day relationship with my parents up to the age of 13, I then disappeared from their sight at a crucial time. Those teenage school years shape you and, even though my parents always wanted to know how I was getting on and would telephone regularly, I found it easier to get away with things at school than it had been when I lived at home.

Ampleforth was quite liberal in its approach. Boys were allowed to smoke at 16 provided they had a letter from their parents. So, obviously, there was a healthy trade in forged letters. As usual, I gravitated towards people in the years above and made friends with the senior guys in the rugby team.

Among some of these older boys there was a great entrepreneurial culture in which fellows were always trying to come up with ways of making money. Most of their ideas went against school rules but that didn't necessarily put people off. I came up with one scheme to purchase Zippo cigarette lighters, which were all the rage at the time. They were advertised in a magazine from Pennsylvania, and you could order them for $4 each. You could also get whatever you wanted engraved on them. 'Fantastic,' I thought, and settled on the Ampleforth crest. There were a few of us involved, so we collected orders from all these guys around the school and bought 750 engraved lighters. Having received the consignment, I sold them for around £15 each and ended up with quite a hefty profit.

It left me with about £5,000 in cash – not exactly the best thing for a 16-year-old who liked to have a good time. In the lower sixth form, you were allowed to go to the pub for meals at certain times, so obviously we went there when we shouldn't. If someone said, 'But we can't afford to go drinking,' I was the one who would say, 'We can, money is not a problem.' Money and me didn't mix very well. Mum backed my scheme with a little capital, not realising what she was funding, and after blowing all the profits, I struggled to pay her back, even though I'd earned seven or eight times what she had lent me. Not good, I know. Another venture, with T-shirts, was not quite as successful and, again, Mum didn't get her money back. By the standards of a 16-year-old schoolboy, I had a pretty lavish lifestyle and a great talent for spending a lot of other people's money in no time.

During my time at Ampleforth, my housemaster would phone Mum when there were disciplinary problems or disappointing grades. Needless to say, there were a number of such calls. Once, my parents came up from London after a series of interesting exchanges with Fr Richard, and Dad took me for a walk around the grounds. For a while we chatted about everything except what he really wanted to talk about. Then I asked, 'Has Fr Richard spoken to you and aren't you going to tell me off?' Dad's normal style was to get to the point when there was a problem and let me know in pretty forceful terms what he expected of me. So I kind of wanted to get it over with. But this time he went through everything Fr Richard had told him and stayed totally calm, which was unusual. Listing the complaints one by one, he said that on each occasion I had been faced with a choice and if I had made a different decision, there wouldn't have been any subsequent problem. What he said made sense and he asked me to try to be more responsible in the choices I made. He explained that the consequences of my actions were down to me. You couldn't argue against the logic and I said I would try to follow his advice in the future. But, in reality, I wasn't ready or mature enough to start doing all the right things at that point in my life. That just wasn't me.

No school in England could have prepared me better for my future career than Ampleforth. You could even argue that I wouldn't have had that career had it not been for the school and its rugby masters. I said earlier that teenage boys need mentors and, far away from their dads at boarding school, they often don't have one. That's true, but fortunately for me, John Willcox was the games master at Ampleforth and he became my rugby mentor. John played 16 times for England at full-back, was an Oxford blue for four consecutive years, and as a rugby coach, he was way ahead of his time. His record as coach to the Ampleforth team was outstanding and that was down to his understanding of how to prepare a team. We were by far the fittest school rugby team in England at that time.

Many of the boys at Ampleforth didn't particularly care for rugby but what you couldn't do was ignore it. Walking from your house to the school, or anywhere around the grounds, you were surrounded by the game. I didn't immediately take to it. My experience of playing at King's House and at Staines meant I was always going to play at Ampleforth, but for the first two years I was considered a back, and played outside centre and wing. At 13 and 14, I was tall but skinny and I just didn't have the physique to play in the forwards. I was also pretty quick, but when you played in the backs for a schools team in the north of England, you didn't often get the chance to show how fast you were. In a general sense, the skills levels among teenagers then were not fantastic, and we were also playing a lot of our matches in sub-zero temperatures and Arctic winds. At the time, I would have preferred football because I wanted to be centrally involved in every game I played.

Things started happening for me when I began to develop physically. It wasn't that I suddenly got bulky, but I did get taller, broader and put on enough weight to be looked upon as a potential back-row forward. Bizarrely, it was my economics teacher, Mr McAleenan, and my geography teacher, Mr Booth, who suggested I have a go in the forwards. Frank Booth had been a good player himself and his son, Richard, was then an excellent scrum-half for Ampleforth who would go on to play for England Schools. Frank wanted me to play No. 8 and as soon as I made the switch, rugby became a lot more fun and my last two years at school turned into one long and fantastic rugby experience. As well as playing No. 8 in the 15-a-side game, I got involved in Sevens rugby. Ampleforth had a great tradition in that format, and they attached a lot of importance to it.

John Willcox was the key to everything that was achieved. For the period coinciding with my being there, and a year or two before and after, Ampleforth enjoyed glorious years. The first team remained unbeaten for six or seven years and always seemed to have an amazing set of players. It wasn't necessarily the individuals but the preparation that was amazing. We played rugby through the first term of the school year, concentrated on Sevens in the second term and then on cricket for the final term. During Michaelmas term, we would turn up for line-out practice during the first break at school, about 10.30 in the morning. We didn't have a formal school uniform but had to wear a shirt, jacket and tie – jeans and trainers were not allowed – and so when the first and second teams showed up for that morning session, we would just take off our jackets and ties, open our top shirt button, change our shoes and get on with it. Not quite what professional teams do today but this was 20 years ago. Not surprisingly, we hardly ever lost a line-out.

Our principal training session took place in the afternoon and would last two hours. Relative to our physique at the time, the fitness sessions were brutal and as tough as anything I've done with England, but John was both a tough disciplinarian and a perfectionist in his attention to detail. He didn't take nonsense from anyone and wanted everything done correctly. I don't think I could have had a better training environment. And the key, as it is with every coach, was that John got the best out of his players. Ampleforth was a pretty challenging place to train, purely in the physical sense. As well as the north of England winters, the rugby pitches were so far distant from St Thomas's that they had a different postcode. We'd go down to the rugby pitches six or seven times a day and that's a lot of extra walking and running each week, which had a big impact on our fitness.

Apart from the thoroughness of our preparation, what was great about rugby at Ampleforth was its inclusiveness. A lot of boys in the school played. We were a little like the old amateur rugby clubs, we had teams that went from the first down to the seventh. As long as you could walk, there was a team for you.

The logistics of getting the Ampleforth rugby circus on the road must have been a real headache for the teachers. For away games we would sometimes take seven or eight senior teams, five Under-16 teams, five Under-15 teams and so on. It felt like the whole school sometimes. Our regular circuit involved some wonderful fixtures against our northern neighbours, Sedbergh, Stonyhurst, Leeds Grammar, Newcastle Royal Grammar, Pocklington, Wakefield and Mount St Mary's near Sheffield. It was tough rugby and a good place to spend your formative years. To make sure we didn't get above ourselves, John Willcox would organise games for us against the Under-19 teams at Harrogate and West Hartlepool rugby clubs and, because we were playing against guys who were a year out of school, that was really hard, but it made us a better team.

We played on the northern circuit, and not many opportunities arose for us to test ourselves against teams from the south. The Rosslyn Park Sevens was one exception and Ampleforth tended to do well there. In 1989, when in lower sixth, I was picked for the school's Sevens squad for the tournament. Two competitions took place over four days – the Festival for teams that played rugby during just one term, and the Open for all schools who cared to enter. As we played the 15-a-side game in one term only, we were eligible for, and entered, both tournaments. Plenty of good sides took part. Millfield were always very strong and there were great teams from Wales. But more important for me was the fact of going down to London and playing in a tournament that was just down the road from where I lived.

We stayed in a dormitory at Crystal Palace, which was once a hotbed for athletics, and did our final preparation there. On the Saturday night, two days before the start of the Sevens, we all went to see Nigel Benn fight at the Royal Albert Hall. He was starting out on what would be a successful career, but I can't remember the name of his opponent that evening. Mind you, he probably can't remember much about the fight either because Benn caught him with an uppercut about 30 seconds into the bout. I still have a mental picture of this guy's legs leaving the canvas and then him falling violently on his back. We didn't have ringside seats but even though we were a little bit away, you could still feel it. I had done some sparring at a gym in Putney when I was a kid but this was bone-chilling. Benn ruined this guy – it wasn't for nothing he was called the Dark Destroyer.

For a few of the Ampleforth team, it was their first time in London. On the Monday morning, we travelled by mini-bus to Rosslyn Park. Standing on the pitch there was a bizarre experience for me as memories came flooding back. All those journeys to prep school on the number 33 bus had taken me past the ground twice a day for five years. At first I sat downstairs but in later years I would sit on the upper deck from where you looked down on the pitch. I never imagined I would be back playing there.

At home matches in Ampleforth, it seemed like the whole school turned out to support the team but the crowd at Rosslyn

Park was different because they were there to watch everyone. The four days couldn't have gone better for us. We played 16 matches and won all of them, taking the cup for both the Festival and Open tournaments. It wasn't without a few scares, though. I remember we had a very close match against Neath College and battled long and hard against King's Worcester in the final of the Open tournament, which was the more difficult to win.

Dad rifled through the newspaper reports the next day and I remember Brendan Gallagher's article in the Daily Telegraph. He's now a senior reporter at the paper and he wrote some nice things about Ampleforth and picked out a few of the players. I remember Dad getting annoyed because none of the reporters spelled my name correctly. I have since become a patron of the Rosslyn Park Sevens and occasionally give out prizes at the end of the tournament. A few years ago, I presented an award to Paul Sackey, who was playing for John Fisher School when they won it. Paul, who now plays alongside me at Wasps and for England, often reminds me of the fact and, of course, he does so in front of all the lads at Wasps and makes me sound like his grandfather.

During the summer holidays of 1989, I wasn't sure I wanted to go back and complete what would have been my final year at school. This was surprising because the 1989–90 school year would have been my time to make the school's first XV. In my lower sixth form year, I played mostly for the seconds and a few times for the firsts but in making the Sevens squad for the Rosslyn Park tournaments, I'd shown that I was improving and it was pretty certain I'd be in the first XV the following season. There was also a chance that I would be captain and yet I was very much in two minds about returning. Even though it was obvious I could play rugby, the school wasn't thrilled by the prospect either. There had been problems and I had been suspended for a couple of weeks around Easter that year.

The issue revolved round one of those unauthorised pub trips I mentioned earlier. On this occasion I was with a couple of other guys and the girlfriend I was with at the time. Traditionally, animosity exists between young guys from the local community and the sixth formers from Ampleforth. We were all thought to come from privileged backgrounds, which in many cases was true. They didn't hide their resentment and we didn't appreciate their attitude – it's not as though people can choose the families into which they're born.

I have to say, my girlfriend was totally blameless for what happened. She was as nice as could be, but the presence of a girl can often be the spark that starts the fire. Something happened in the pub, I can't remember exactly what, but I do know I ended up defending her and it all got a bit out of hand. At the end of a brawl that resulted in the hospitalisation of a few people, I managed to walk out of there under my own steam. But, of course, an investigation followed and I got my suspension. I was 17 at the time and have to accept some responsibility for my part in what happened. In my defence I felt I was standing up for someone, that was my motivation. The suspension irritated me because I didn't believe the school dealt with the problem very well. Certain schools it seems, and I include the Ampleforth that I knew in this, have a straightforward policy when dealing with tricky situations – pass them on to someone else. In my case it was turfing me out so the problem was shipped back to my parents. But the point is my parents paid vast amounts of money to send me there and, in doing that, handed over responsibility for my development to the school. Then as soon as there was a difficulty, the school handed the 'issue' straight back to my parents. It just didn't seem right.

Why I ended up so often in and out of trouble, I'm not sure. I guess part of me didn't want to be caged, didn't want to be locked away in a school, didn't want to be restrained and told, 'This is what you can do, this is what you can't do.' Obviously, there has to be a timetable, a set of rules, and a bit of structure in everyone's life, but it wasn't something that sat very comfortably with me, 200 miles from home. I found it easier to break the rules than to keep them. Yet it is also true that I had a fantastic time at Ampleforth. I had a lot of fun and learned the game of rugby in a way that was technically correct and would stay with me. When I look back I wish I'd worked a damn sight harder at my books. I was one of those irritating children who had the ability but not the application. Every report from Ampleforth said if I applied myself, I could be very good. For my parents, that was far more frustrating than receiving a report that indicated the pupil was not the brightest, but tried very hard.

But for all the fun times at Ampleforth and the prospect of a great rugby year to come, I went home for my summer holidays not at all sure I wanted to go back – not even sure that the school wanted me back. Then something happened and the decision was made for me.

4

Francesca

Breakfast at Ampleforth was typical of what you'd expect at boarding school. In your first year you sat at the table farthest from the action – the food – and you served everyone else before yourself. You started with the older guys and worked your way down. This natural hierarchy taught you to respect your elders and if there was any food left, good luck to you. So you had to learn some cunning plans because it was a dog-eat-the-other-dog's-food environment. After your first year, things improved a little until, eventually, you were one of those served first. My cunning plan was fairly basic – get my mum to send food parcels that contained chocolate. It was essential, I told her, because I was a growing boy. But the authorities were cunning, too. They handed out the day's post at breakfast, which was one way of a) ensuring everyone got up for their first meal of the day, and b) everyone else knew who had received a food parcel . . .

The handing out of the post was important to me because Francesca used to write often. She was naturally gifted like that and wrote wonderfully long letters, sometimes four or five pages, and I looked forward to them. She was in Camberley, while I was 250 miles away in North Yorkshire and we could go months without seeing each other. My parents couldn't afford to come up and see me very often, so Francesca's letters took on added significance.

When I got a letter, I would disappear to my room immediately to read it. My sister would tell me all the news from home, because even though she was at boarding school, too, she and Mum talked a lot and kept in touch by letter as well. She would ask me to write to Mum and say that if I couldn't find the time to write, I should phone. I would always mean to but just didn't always get round to it. As well as trying to get me to do the right thing by my parents, Francesca wanted to know how I was doing. She also reminded me how much it was costing our parents to have us both in boarding schools and we should really make the best of the opportunities we were getting. She was incredibly sensible. 'It's the way girls are,' I'd say to myself. 'They mature quicker.' All of my memories of Francesca are fond memories. She went away to boarding school when I was eight and five years later I went away to school, so we were only together at home during holiday periods. I've often wondered whether that's why we got on so well. Perhaps we didn't see enough of each other to have the kind of rows common to brother/sister relationships. It amazes me to hear of brothers who don't speak with their sisters. Even my mum, who came from a family of 10 and had six sisters, was always falling in and out with her siblings; but bigger families tend to have their own politics I suppose. Francesca and I never had a situation where we wouldn't speak to each other. Our relationship wasn't like that.

One of the many differences between us was that Francesca was born to dance whereas I don't believe I was born to play rugby. As I've said, I didn't play the game seriously until I was 16 and up to that point, it was just one of a number of sports I enjoyed. Then at 16, I grew taller, got stronger, and the game became easier for me. Suddenly, it became my number-one sport. Two or three years after that, I began to dedicate myself to the game. But pretty much from day one, dancing was all Francesca wanted to do. Her acceptance into the Royal Ballet School after four lessons showed how gifted she was. And she knew from that first experience aged eight that she wanted to be a dancer. She knew what she wanted and went all out to get it.

To be a dancer, you have to be highly disciplined and incredibly hardworking. Francesca understood that and accepted the demands, and yet she did it in a very nice way. Dancing was fiercely competitive and it was not unusual for one girl to bitch about another but, as far as I could see, Francesca stayed above all that. My earliest memory of watching her dance was of Mum, Dad and me travelling down to Camberley to see the end-of-term show put on by the girls. It was an eye-opener for me on two counts. First, it was a chance for me to see just what an incredible dancer my sister was, and, for a young boy growing up fast, it was also interesting to be among so many good-looking young ladies. Francesca was getting honours in all of her dance exams but to see how she commanded the stage was something else. When I watched the show, my eyes were fixed on her. 'She's my sister,' I'd think to myself. I was very proud of her.

Francesca managed to get good results in her O-levels and later her A-levels and every teacher, especially the dance teachers, talked about how much they enjoyed working with her. That wasn't a surprise. Her generosity and kindness endeared her to people and she was incredibly beautiful. She was a stunning looking young woman who had time for everyone. From my parents' point of view, she was a joy and very different from her younger brother. The reports from Elmhurst were always good but even though I went to very good schools, Mum lived in fear of the phone call from my form tutor relating the latest indiscretion.

Dancing is not everyone's cup of tea but for those who appreciate it, there is something wonderful in watching someone who can do it brilliantly. It's like hearing the piano played beautifully. When Francesca was dancing, you could picture her at Covent Garden. She had danced at the Royal Albert Hall, the Royal Festival Hall, in front of Princess Diana, and she had been on a tour to Yugoslavia. She had danced for her country. From a very early age, it seemed as though her life had been mapped out.

I was proud of Francesca because she was my sister, not necessarily because I was in love with what she was doing. People who were not family were amazed she could dance the way she did. I saw her on stage many, many times at Elmhurst, in ballets such as *Sleeping Beauty*, *Swan Lake* and *The Nutcracker*. But for me, it was more about Francesca than the ballet itself. From the moment she decided to focus on dancing, it was complete dedication. By the time she got to her last two years at Elmhurst, she was on a full scholarship and working unbelievably hard. At that point she was dancing 10 hours a day, four days a week, and five and a half hours on two other days, and she was also preparing for A-levels. Along the way, and especially during the early years, the criticism from dance teachers can be very harsh, the kind of stuff you hear in professional rugby team rooms when everyone is being honest. Dancers have to deal with this criticism from the age of eight or nine. It's not quite Chinese gymnasts but it's not far off – there is a brutality common to both. To survive, you need to have a huge amount of self-belief but also the maturity to realise it is criticism of you as a dancer, not you as a person. Francesca understood that and enjoyed very good relationships with her teachers. In terms of commitment, dancing to Francesca was what professional rugby would eventually be to me. In our house, she was the star and I felt if I ever achieved in rugby half of what she achieved in dancing, I would be doing well.

When she left Elmhurst in early August 1989, she had her ARAD (Associate of the Royal Academy of Dancing) qualification, and she had also passed the Royal Academy student teacher exams, and the Society of Spanish Dancing exam, all with honours or distinctions. She was ready to go out into the working world and was accomplished in so many dance forms, but her greatest love was Spanish dancing. Maybe it appealed to her Latin side but she really enjoyed the excitement of it. She applied for different jobs, and accepted an offer from the Austrian national ballet, with whom she was due to begin in September. It was a good starting point because the position would allow her to continue dancing but also included opportunities to teach and to model a little. The last bit would have come easy to Francesca because of her stunning good looks.

The way I saw it, this was going to be her time. She loved what she did and had spent years learning how to do it to an incredibly high level. That summer of '89, the years of adhering to a tough regime were behind her – the warm-ups that began at 6 a.m., the last class that didn't finish until 8 p.m. She had invested everything she had in this, worked her fingers to the bone to get to the point where she could enjoy the fruits. And then it was all taken away.

I don't have a clear memory of Saturday evening, 19 August 1989. Perhaps that's because I have been trying for a long time to run away from all that happened. It was coming towards the end of the summer holidays, I'd done holiday jobs and still wasn't sure if I was going back to Ampleforth for my final year. Francesca was finished with school and looking forward to starting in Austria the following month. Mum had invited her sister Emily to dinner and also her friend and my godmother, Gloria Featherston. Francesca and her boyfriend, John James, were there. John was a friend of mine from Ampleforth. I was dating his sister, Rachel, and Francesca got to know John through me. Francesca, John and I had all been invited to a river disco being held that night on board a boat, the *Marchioness*, which had been hired by a friend of John's.

When I first heard about it, I'd been keen to go. John's friend, Antonio de Vasconcellos, was known to throw great parties and I wouldn't normally have had access to that kind of thing. I have never been one to shy away from a night out but that afternoon I had a bit of a headache and didn't feel great. Over dinner, I said, 'I don't think I'm going to go.' Even to this day, I wonder why I cried off. Mum also remembers me talking about a headache but I normally didn't get headaches and for a party animal, this was the kind of occasion you didn't want to miss. I mean, I can't ever remember turning down any other party invitation in my life. Not going that night has played on my mind for a long time, still plays on my mind, but I have to accept, somehow, that it was God's will, one of those things that happens.

Mum wasn't very keen about Francesca going, mostly because it was an all-night affair, starting at one o'clock. She tried to talk her out of it but Francesca could be stubborn and reminded Mum that she was now 19 and independent. They talked about what time Francesca had to be home by, and it was agreed she would get off the boat at Tower Bridge and come home with John from there. Mum grew up in the East End when the Krays and the Richardsons were on the go and she was always aware of the unpleasant things that could happen. So she asked John to make sure he looked out for Francesca and that whenever a drink was poured for her, it was his responsibility to see no Mickey Finns were slipped into them. And Mum would have said 'Mickey Finns' because when it came to her children, she was never afraid to say what was on her mind.

Francesca tried to get me to go. 'Come on, you'll change your mind. There's going to be some lovely models there.' She said she would call me around 11, to see if I'd changed my mind. After dinner, I went to my room and lay down on the bed. Mum came and asked me if money was the problem and I said no, I genuinely didn't feel great and didn't want to go. As Francesca and John left the house, she came back to give Mum a kiss and they said goodbye in the way they often did. 'Bye, you bitch,' Francesca said. 'Get out of here, go on, you bitch,' replied Mum. Francesca did call me as she planned but I had decided and that was it.

Some time between three and four o'clock in the morning Commander James, John's father, rang our house. Mum picked up the phone. He said there had been a collision on the River Thames involving the *Marchioness* and that John was in St Thomas's Hospital and Francesca was missing. Mum says she went into a type of psychological shock from which she did not recover for 15 years, when all the inquests, hearings, appeals and legal battles ended. She also says that hearing the words 'Francesca is missing' drained her of any will to live.

Mum was still hysterical when she woke me at around seven o'clock. She told me the boat that my sister was on had been involved in a terrible accident and had sunk. She was saying lots of other things too but I was struggling to take it all in. The one thing I heard above everything else was, 'And we still haven't heard from your sister.'

'What time did the boat sink?' I asked.

'About one forty-five,' Mum said. It was now five hours later. I didn't need to hear any more details because I knew immediately that Francesca was dead.

I didn't say so to Mum, how could I? But my sister had more common sense than anyone I ever knew, and I also knew that the first thing this sensible, caring and responsible person would have done was to call her parents the second she got out of the water. So I just decided at that moment she was gone. It didn't occur to me she might have banged her head and been taken from the water in a concussed state. I am now 35 years of age and I know that, in similar circumstances, my reaction would be very different. I was then a kid, just turned 17, who loved his sister and whose natural instinct was to believe the worst. I got dressed very quickly and went downstairs. The house was already filling up with my mum's family. We could hear the helicopters flying overhead, people were watching the news and slowly piecing together what had happened the night before. Mum called in to the police station in Barnes on her way to eight o'clock mass and gave them photographs of Francesca. She also told them the name of our dentist so they could get her dental records. More people kept coming to the house, drinking tea and coffee and waiting for news of my sister. But there was none. The next day, another long wait for news and still nothing. Bodies were being found all the time but no news of Francesca. Four days would pass before her body was recovered.

When I now see news on the television of someone who is missing and there are genuine fears for that person, it brings it all back to me – the waiting in the house, with so many family members and friends, and the feeling of being totally powerless. My parents tried to protect me from most of the details but I was aware that after two days, most of those who died had been found. Francesca's body was eventually found under Battersea Bridge, which is about four miles from where the *Marchioness* went down near Southwark Bridge. Then a few days later, it just all became too much for me. I couldn't stay in the midst of all the grief and people offering sympathy and all my family being devastated, so I left home and went to stay with a friend of mine from Ampleforth, Nicky Strauss, whose family lived in Yorkshire. Even though our house in Barnes had been full of people who were all concerned about me, I felt alone and wanted to be among my friends. A day or two later, Nicky and I and a number of other Ampleforth friends went to York races, which will seem odd to people, given what had just happened. How could I be out enjoying myself at such a time?

I felt comfortable being around friends. It wasn't as though I was trying to pretend it hadn't happened but I did want to get away from what was going on at home. I found it too hard to see my parents broken-hearted. I don't know what a 17-year-old can do in that situation. Mum had her sisters and brothers around her, Dad's family were also there, and I just didn't feel I could do anything. Being among my friends was easier, although I felt they were a bit uneasy with me being around them – 'You know this guy's sister has just died and he's here with us, is that right?' Everyone was as nice as could be but I could still sense that.

They didn't see all the times I cried, because when there are people around, your manly instincts take over and you try to put on a brave face. I don't know whether that's a good thing for you psychologically, suppressing a lot of emotions and not being able to grieve openly. Francesca's death drove our family in three different directions. Dad was in one place, trying to be very stoic and behaving as he thought the head of the family should behave. Mum is very emotional and she was overcome with grief and clearly traumatised by the whole thing. My dad's efforts in trying to hold things together must have caused emotional damage because he didn't express the huge sense of loss he was feeling inside. Three years later, he suffered a mild heart attack and the specialist who treated him believed it was connected to what he had been through after Francesca's death.

Grief is a very private thing. Dad went one way, Mum went her way and I was sent in yet another. We were just blown apart. I believe it was the best part of 10 years before we began to come to terms with what happened and, in a sense, we're still coming to terms with it. Life is never the same after the tragedy of losing someone that close. It changes your relationship with the world, and the nature of your relationship with your family. I don't think it's ever the same again. That's not to say it goes from good to bad, it just changes. I saw the pain my mother was suffering and continued to suffer over the following years. I saw the pain it caused my father. My reaction was to try to accept what had happened but not necessarily deal with it. When you are 17 you don't have the ammunition to cope with something like that. You don't understand life as you will later on. You see it at the time and you just want to move away from it and move on as quickly as you can. But for the following two years, I lived on another planet.

I was devastated by the loss of Francesca but had conflicting emotions. Her death made me angry. To die at the age of 19 was just far too young, especially for someone who had worked so hard all through her life and was about to reap the rewards. Her career as a dancer was about to take off when her life ended and she was taken away from us. It made me wonder about the fairness of life, and to ask what was the point of working so hard and then ending up with nothing to show for it, certainly not in this life anyway. I also felt a responsibility to be there for my parents more than I had in the past. Francesca was going to be successful, they were going to be proud of her and now, I thought, I would have to do something to help them cope. But I wasn't ready or able to face up to that because, without my sister, I was lost and angry and intensely sad and the only way I could deal with those emotions was to suppress them. I had lost someone who totally believed in me, who had always intervened on my behalf with Mum and Dad. 'Don't worry, Lawrence will turn out fine.'

Unsure whether I wanted to go back to Ampleforth in the first place, my sister's death made up my mind. The trouble I had been in at school before the summer holidays and the trauma of losing Francesca meant it was in everybody's interests that I didn't go back. I didn't feel I could cope with a boarding school at that point in my life. Despite trying to get away from the grief, I couldn't stop my mind from wandering. What if I had gone to the party, maybe I would have been able to save her life. And then another part of me says, 'You weren't there and therefore you couldn't do anything.' I miss her hugely, but I'm fortunate that my parents are still alive and I still have a strong relationship with them. But the tragedy wreaked havoc in our lives – one night we were all sat there having dinner together, the next and from then onwards there was an empty place at the table. One minute we were having the most wonderful conversation, 'Oh Mother, don't worry, I'll be fine,' the next minute she was gone. Grief affects people differently, but I don't think there's ever a positive effect, certainly not in the short term.

That September I started at a tutorial college in Oxford and the plan was to complete my second year in the sixth form, do my A-levels and go off to university after that. It was more my parents' hopes than anything. I didn't have a plan and was living from day to day. Oxford seemed a good idea because it meant I wouldn't be living at home and wouldn't be wrapped up in the lives of my parents, who were in bits over Francesca. How could I be of any help to them, when I wasn't interested in helping myself? I went for some counselling but got myself out of that as quickly as I could. The appeal of the tutorial college in Oxford was that no one would know my background and as I made friends there, I would tell them briefly about Francesca, they would sympathise and that was it. They hadn't known her and hadn't known me before she died. They didn't know my history and that's how I wanted it. Many of the people at Oxford went on to become good friends and remain so today.

The tutorial college was called d'Overbroeck's and, for pretty hefty fees, it offered intense teaching and back-up to those who wanted to study. It was a completely different set-up from Ampleforth, operating with an almost university approach. You had to make your own way to lessons, which were located in different parts of Oxford, and if you didn't show, no one came looking for you. I was one of those who didn't want to study. Less than a month had passed since my sister's death and I was all over the shop. I couldn't or didn't want to sit down and work, anything and everything distracted me, and I just wanted to be out with my friends all of the time. I rented a room from a lovely lady in south Oxford, Jenny Coulbourne, and she seemed to understand and looked out for me. When she felt I was partying too much, or needed to be reined in, she would call my mother who would come up and have a chat. All the time a voice in the back of my head was whispering, 'What's the point of everything if one minute you have a great future and the next minute you have nothing?'

I pushed my parents into allowing me to go to Oxford and have that space. Once I got there, all I wanted was to find new friends and constantly surround myself with them. I would still go home on some weekends and during the holidays but it would be very emotional. We would hug and kiss and that closeness was never lost but we had to learn again to be comfortable in each other's company. You were always thinking of when there were four, and now there were only three. I preferred to be out of that situation. Then I would go back to Oxford and try to obliterate everything by having a good time. I was lucky to meet a lovely group of people there, people who, like me, hadn't excelled at their previous schools and didn't really excel there either.

When I look back on this time in my life, I wonder how much of my behaviour was attributable to Francesca's death and to what extent I was just a chancer who loved school for everything other than the work? Ultimately, it was a combination of the two and, almost, my sister dying gave me an out. 'Well, I'm not ready to do anything,' I could tell myself. I didn't want to accept responsibility. Today I still feel some remorse about my attitude and behaviour because my parents were still working very hard to give me the opportunity to be there. But then I reflect on the subsequent events in my life and realise I shouldn't continue to beat myself up over how I was in the two years after Francesca died.

During my time in Oxford, rugby became very much a secondary influence in my life. After I decided not to go back to Ampleforth, I spoke to John Willcox, who was very keen that I keep up my rugby. Ironically, the year at d'Overbroeck's coincided with the time I should have made the England Schools team. John said it would be better for me to play for Middlesex rather than Yorkshire, because there was a bit of an anti-Ampleforth feeling in the north of England. It may have been that John ruffled a few feathers, it may also have come from the perception that Ampleforth was the posh public school, but whatever the reason, we agreed I would have a better chance of trying out for Middlesex. The only problem was, I turned up for training a couple of weeks late and then appeared at Ealing late for my first session. Not surprisingly, the coach, Len Cole, was not impressed. He made me run around the pitch about 12 times but we eventually sorted out the difficulties and I made the team.

After Middlesex, I went to the trials for the London/South-East divisional team and made that selection as well. Not helping me, however, was the fact that I was no longer from a rugby school; I was living in Oxford and going to a tutorial college there. What this meant was that at the trials I was on my own and if the guys picking the trial teams had too many back-row forwards and not enough second rows, I was the one shoved into the second row – which is exactly what happened when it came to the England Schools try-out. That took place at Trent College in Nottingham and the guy they had in mind for No. 8 was Eben Rollitt, whose dad, Dave, was a fantastic player for England in his day. Eben was a bit more established than I was at the time. He played No. 8 for Middlesex and his dad was a vociferous presence on the sideline. Ironically, Eben went on to join Wasps so we played together and I got to know his dad.

In that England Schools trial, I scored a try but played just OK. Second row was not my position. After the trial, they picked a 30-man England squad, which was later reduced to 23. I made the

23. We then played Rosslyn Park. They selected a probable first XV who played as England, the remaining eight joining up with seven from Rosslyn Park to form the opposition. I was one of the ones who played for Rosslyn Park. Afterwards the squad was cut from 23 to a final 22 and I was the 23rd man. Not making the team devastated me and I resented what I saw as the unfairness of the England Schools selection system. What seemed to matter was the school you attended, who your parents knew, what club you were at, who your school's coach was, who he knew and whether your father had played to a high level. For me, it all added up to nepotism.

Dick Tilley was coach of that England Schools team and I did speak with him after I was cut from the squad.

'I don't think you're fit enough,' he said. 'I think you've got a lot of ability but if I'm honest, I don't think you're in good enough condition.'

He didn't know how I had been living for the last eight months and his assessment was absolutely right. That didn't mean I agreed with the decision to omit me. I was thinking, 'Well, it wouldn't actually take that much to improve my fitness,' but I said nothing because I was in a state of shock from what had been a kick in the teeth.

A little later, when I was moping around feeling sorry for myself, Dick came back to me and tried to offer encouragement.

'Look,' he said, 'I'm sure if you carry on, they [the England Schools selectors] will find a place for you somewhere.'

Dick's a smashing bloke and he wasn't trying to offend me but when he talked about the selectors 'finding a place for you somewhere', it really irked me. I didn't need that sort of patronising bullshit and what annoyed me even more was that I knew I was better than the lads who were in the team. I felt I should have been selected but that it had suited them to find something wrong with me because other guys were better connected. That's how I saw it, anyway.

I left Rosslyn Park bitterly disappointed and hurting. To make sure the other guys didn't see me, I walked past the first bus stop and went to the next one. I cried and was still upset when Kyran Bracken, spotting me waiting for a bus, stopped the car in which he was travelling. He was with his parents, I think. We had played against each other in the north of England, Ampleforth against Stonyhurst, and even at that point in his career, he was recognised as a star of the future. There was no debate about who would play scrum-half for that England Schools team.

'Are you all right?' he asked. 'Can I give you a lift anywhere?'

'I'm fine,' I lied.

'For what it's worth,' he said, 'I thought you played very well. I'm surprised you're not in the team.'

'One of those things,' I said.

What I like about travelling on a bus, which I had done all through my years at King's House, is that you can be surrounded by people and yet be on your own. And that was what I needed coming away from Rosslyn Park, for this was the first major setback of my rugby career. As with most disappointments in my life, my first reaction is to show my hurt, because I am an emotional person who can't really hide things like that. At that moment, I think the whole world is wrong and everyone is against me. Then the anger and disappointment subside and once I've begun to lick my wounds, I start assessing the situation. That's what it was like then. When I thought about it, it was clear I had done well to get as close as I had to that England Schools team. I'd had virtually no rugby since leaving Ampleforth nine months before, no real preparation for all those trials and average fitness. Back in Oxford, it went on in my head for some time and I decided that never again would anyone leave me out of a team because I wasn't fit enough. 'When the next opportunity comes, I will be as fit as I can possibly be and I will prove these fuckers wrong.'

D'Overbroeck's never really worked out. I had done so little work and attended so few classes, there was no point in sitting my A-levels. You could say it was a waste of time and money but at that particular time in my life, I wasn't able to cope. At the beginning of the following school year, instead of repeating the year, I began to work for an old mate of mine, Laurie Hicks, who used to run the youth club in Barnes. He had set up, and was managing director of, a ski-tours business and it was one of those classic situations I seem to get myself into. Because I knew Laurie, I half had the job before being interviewed. 'One thing,' Laurie said at the end of the interview, 'you will need a car. Have you got your driving licence?' My driving test was the following week and I just said, 'Yeah, no problem, I've got the licence.' It put me under a little pressure not to mess up the test and, thank God, I didn't. I started work for Laurie's company three days later.

I really enjoyed that job. We were selling ski holidays, which meant I got to go to Austria for a few weeks where I learned to ski. How it worked was that a school would go to Adventure Express and we would organise their trip from beginning to end.

Laurie wanted me to work in all the different areas of the company's business and I enjoyed learning. Then, after about four months, the company suddenly went into liquidation, unable to exist alongside the really big players in the market, such as Thompson and Quest. It was a shame. It was now February, getting into March, 1991 and it was beginning to dawn on me that without A-levels, I was going to struggle.

During my time in Oxford, I'd met a private tutor, Chris Sivewright, who worked at the Oxford School of Learning. Chris looked a little like a hippy and was very relaxed, so we got on well from the moment we met. After Adventure Express went to the wall, I spoke with Chris and discussed the possibility of doing a couple of A-levels. Chris had a reputation for helping people get through exams and he was also a lovely guy who put on classes in business studies and economics for unemployed people on Wednesday evenings.

'Don't worry,' he said. 'We'll pass you, we'll get you through these exams. You come to the Wednesday evening classes because they won't cost you anything. But I've got to charge you something for the one-on-one stuff we do.'

By this point, I had begun to realise my parents did not have an inexhaustible supply of money and said so to Chris.

'Look, I can't afford to pay you a lot, my mum's signed enough cheques for the last five or six years and she's not keen on signing more.'

Chris wasn't too bothered about what he was going to get out of it.

'Oh, don't fret about that. We'll not worry about the money side of it yet. Pay me what you can afford.'

Mum and Dad did dig into their pockets again but it certainly wasn't what Chris was worth. I did three classes a week with him for three months, and went to the classes for the unemployed on Wednesday evenings. It was all worth it as I ended up getting Cs in both Business Studies and Economics – not bad for three months' work.

When I had first suggested going back to Oxford to do my A-levels, Mum screamed, 'What? Well, you're not going to live up there again. You'll get on the train every morning, go up there and come back every evening.'

It was bizarre going back to Oxford, sitting in all the places where I'd had such fun the year before, but now everyone was gone and there was no one to play with. My life was moving on in other ways, too. The storm inside my head was beginning to calm and I started asking myself what Francesca would say about that first year in Oxford. 'You know how much it's costing Mum and Dad, they don't go on fantastic holidays, they don't stay in fancy hotels, they don't do that because their money is going on your fees.' The more I thought about it, the way Francesca had lived her life, the way she believed in me, the more I realised things had to change. I spoke with Mum and Dad. 'I know I've given you a lot of problems over the last eighteen months and I know Francesca would not want me to carry on like this. She would be ashamed of the way things have been in my life.' I was ready to go forward, get my A-levels, return to serious rugby and see what happened.

It helped that the experience of not making the England Schools team stayed with me. When you know you had a lot more ability than the guys who got picked, that hurts, and as time passed, I realised it was mostly my fault. 'Come on, Lawrence, you didn't give yourself any chance at all. If you'd been half-fit, you'd have walked it. OK, OK, but what are you going to do it about it now?' On the back of how close I'd come to being selected for England Schools, I was picked for a North of England Schools XV against Middlesex Colts at Wasps. We played on the back pitch in a howling gale on a horrible December night, which felt like home for us guys who had learned our rugby on the northern schools circuit. I must have done OK in the match because I was contacted by Wasps soon after and asked if I would be interested in coming to their club and having a go. I'd also seen an ad in the *Daily Telegraph* inviting prospective rugby players to join Wasps and I liked that – you could turn up pretty anonymously and just say you had seen the ad.

From the moment I stepped inside its modest ground at Sudbury, I liked Wasps. After Ampleforth with its 27 pitches and magnificent facilities, it felt like I had walked into a working-man's club where everything was pretty basic. Yet Wasps was one of the best teams in England – how did they manage that? What I especially liked was the eclectic group of people drawn to the club. They came from all kinds of backgrounds. You got guys who had been to Oxford University, City bankers, builders, electricians, jewellers, students who were still at college, guys who had been through the state education system, others who had been to private schools. It didn't matter at Wasps. It was how you played the game and what kind of bloke you were that mattered, and it was a million miles from the elitist rugby environment I'd been used to.

Another thing I liked about the club was that it gave me space.

No one there really knew my background, no one there had been to Ampleforth, they were aware of what had happened to Francesca but they weren't connected to the tragedy of her loss in any way. They judged me on what they saw, no preconceptions. We trained on Tuesday and Thursday evenings, played a game every Saturday and most Sundays, because Wasps had a good Colts – Under-19 – side and there were a lot of fixtures. Doubling up every weekend was never a problem because we were young and able to bounce out of bed on Sunday morning. Our Colts team remained unbeaten that season and we had a lot of fun. You played a good hard game on Saturday afternoon, you had a few beers afterwards and, whether you played home or away, you all went back to the rugby club where you would have a few more beers. Then you would go out for a curry. A lot of the guys who played in that team stayed together and spent many happy years at Wasps.

Team-mates would stay at our house and next morning Mum would cook everyone a fry-up and then we'd be off to play our second game of the weekend. Occasionally, we would have to bail someone out of a police cell if they had been unlucky enough to end up in some harmless altercation with members of the establishment. Playing for Wasps gave me the platform to challenge for a place on England's Colts team.

It was the same route as the year before – Middlesex trials, Middlesex team, London/South-East divisional team – only this time I made the England team and was one of the fittest players there. It was also my first experience playing with and against guys who would be team-mates and friends for years. Simon Shaw played for London, as did Tony Diprose, Richard Hill played for the South-West, Austin Healey played for the Midlands, Will Greenwood for the North, and when you mention those names, we should have had a reasonable England team. In fact, we were terrible, losing four games out of five. We even needed the floodlights at Harlequins to malfunction halfway through the match against Argentina for our one victory – we were winning at the time and so were awarded the game.

The first game, and our first defeat, was against Italy at Grange Road in Cambridge. In the second, Kenny Logan scored the winning try for Scotland in a game played at Stirling, a result I might have forgotten if Kenny, God bless him, hadn't reminded me about it every week for years at Wasps. We then played Wales at Fylde in Lancashire and lost 37–7 – so much for home advantage. That match is remembered for the fact that their No. 8, an 18-year-old mountain called Scott Quinnell, scored four tries. Though that doesn't look great for me, most of the time Scott picked up off the back of a scrum and swatted away our No. 6 before putting the ball down. Scott had a beard at 18 and physically, he was on a different planet from the rest of us.

Everyone, of course, was talking about him and the papers were full of it the next day. You can't ignore a young man who has scored four tries against England and who is the son of Derek Quinnell, the famous Welsh international of the seventies. Yet really good players like that had never fazed me. I came off that pitch believing I could be every bit as good a player as Scott. It was just that with our different physiques, I would need a little more time to develop. John Willcox, my old rugby coach from Ampleforth, turned up at the game and even if the result was a let-down, it was still great to see him. Wanting to show my appreciation for all he had done for me at Ampleforth, I gave him the England jersey I wore that day.

'Today,' he said, 'wasn't the best, but I guarantee you will one day take your revenge on Mr Quinnell.'

We would indeed have many battles in the future, and I would get to win a few of them.

5 | A woman's heart

When my mother wanted to tell me off for something I had done, she would say, 'Lawrence, when you do that, you offend me.' I would say, 'Mum, you do know how to get to me.' She was very resourceful in that way. Ultimately, she and Dad were also incredibly supportive parents. It was like that when I was 15 and now, at the age of 35, it's still the same. Wherever I play, they are pretty certain to be in the crowd, cheering me on. After getting my two A-levels in Oxford, I decided to do a course in Urban Estate Management at Kingston Poly, now Kingston University, in south-west London. My choice of course was determined by rugby. Things were going really well at Wasps and a good friend at the club, Lawrence Scrase, was doing the same course at Kingston. Urban Estate Management was surveying by another name and Wasps were sponsored by DTZ, a surveying company, and a number of Wasps players worked in surveying. But it was also time for me to leave the family nest and that's where Mum's resourcefulness again proved useful.

She was of the view that I should move out into the world and learn to be independent. Neither she nor I was keen on paying London's exorbitant rents, but I wasn't in a position to take on a mortgage. 'Why don't we look at some houseboats?' she said. 'The rent won't be much.' We started to look for something appropriate but there was nothing, except one for sale in Twickenham with an asking price of £8,000. It needed a bit of work but we liked it. I borrowed £13,000 to buy the boat and fund the necessary repairs and refurbishment. I wouldn't have had a hope on my own but Mum guaranteed the loan and Lawrence Scrase decided to move in with me so his rent virtually paid the mortgage. The houseboat was called *Bardot* because the woman selling it, who was a lovely, lovely lady whom we all liked, was a fan of the actress. Lawrence and I worked on smartening up the boat and Mum got us a carpenter, Roger, who came over from Ireland for six months to live and work with us on the houseboat. It was a bit of a squeeze but he transformed *Bardot* into a work of art.

And so my address for three years was: *Bardot*, Swan Island Harbour, Strawberry Vale, Twickenham. Different tenants came and went. Lawrence Scrase stayed for a while and moved on. My good friend Spencer Franks stayed for about two years and we had so much fun. It was a lovely way of life, being part of a community of about 30 boats, in the heart of Twickenham and yet not really part of mainstream London life. To get home, you crossed a bridge, walked through a boatyard and onto a pontoon. What fascinated me were the people who chose to live like this. They were a really mixed group. Everyone had something different about them, otherwise they wouldn't have chosen to live on a boat, and the community spirit was not what you normally found in London. Everyone looked out for everyone else's boat and when you had a problem, people were always willing to come and help you sort it out. For me, just starting out at university, it was a fantastic place to live. Since our boat was the last one on the pontoon, it could be difficult on a summer's evening to reach home. As you walked down towards the boat, people would be on their roof terraces having a beer and they would often invite you to join them. Of course, it would have been rude not to accept such kind offers.

To people who knew my background, it seemed a strange choice to live on the river that had claimed my sister's life. Some thought it was a deliberate decision to be closer to Francesca, others imagined living on the Thames would be a constant and painful reminder of what had happened. The truth was neither of these. When Mum and I bought the Thames houseboat, it was not because of Francesca, at least not consciously. But once I began to live on the river, I found it both comfortable and comforting. Francesca's body had been found about four or five miles up river and, as time passed, I felt a sense of being close to her, in a beautiful way. Being on the river was never a painful memory. Perhaps a lot of things were happening subconsciously because I grew to love being woken by the sound of water washing against the boat, and I also loved the sense of being away from it all.

Mind you, it got a little bit cold down there in winter but that was far outweighed by the magic of summer evenings, sitting on the terrace with a beer and being among some quirky and fascinating people. When anyone said to me, 'Ah, you live in Twickenham, that's because of the rugby I suppose,' I would reply, 'Well, not quite.'

As soon as I took rugby seriously, rugby took me seriously. The day after my first-ever match in an England shirt, the Colts game against Italy, I received a phone call from the Italian team manager. He got to the point.

'Your name is Dallaglio, sì? Why are you playing for England?'

'Well, I was born in England,' I said.

Two other phone calls followed, one from an official at the Rovigo club, another from Milan. I was flattered and curious enough to pursue it. The offer from Milan appeared the most attractive because they were also offering a place at Bocconi University in Milan, which has Oxbridge-like status in Italy for some disciplines, but this was four years before the game turned professional, so there wasn't any money on the table – not in so many words, anyway. What they would do was get me a place at the university, have all my fees and accommodation taken care of and pay me a living allowance of £2,000 per month. With everything else taken care of, that was a pretty decent amount of money. The idea was to play club rugby with Milan and go on to play for Italy.

Mum and Dad travelled with me to Milan to see exactly what

they were talking about. We were put up at the Jolly Hotel, owned by Silvio Berlusconi. It was an eye-opener to speak with the Italians because, in the politest way, they made it clear they didn't expect me to make this move purely for the love of my Italian side. Of course, there would be an incentive. Amateur rugby? Do me a favour. But to be fair to them, they were also adamant that education had to be a part of the deal. If I accepted their offer, my commitment had to be both to the university and to the rugby. Mum and Dad liked this part of it and I was impressed. Dad, especially, would have liked me to accept their offer. They showed us where I would stay, an amazing sports complex called Milano Due, built by Berlusconi because he owned the football team (A.C. Milan), the basketball team, the volleyball team, the ice-hockey team and the rugby team. With the exception of the footballers, all the athletes were accommodated here and I was awestruck by the set-up. David Campese, a legend in the game, was living there with his Italian girlfriend.

I went to dinner with Campese and another Aussie legend, Mark Ella. Campese was playing for Milan, Ella was the team coach and I was an 18-year-old kid from England of whom no one had ever heard. I watched Milan play L'Aquila in an Italian first-division game in front of 500 people. This was 1991 and the standard was poor. Campese was playing full-back and I imagine he was earning a lot of money, enough so he could put up with it. He didn't do much in the game but every now and then he would show his skill and class. It was a good situation for him because he was earning a decent living and could then return to Australia and play proper rugby through their season.

Still, for me it was an amazing offer and a fascinating

opportunity. Back home I thought about it very seriously and had a long chat with Mum and Dad. I felt it was one of those decisions that, once made, would be final – that is, there would be no turning back. I would go to university in Milan, play for Milan and Italy, learn to speak Italian and end up going into business in Italy. I just wasn't prepared to go down that route.

I felt I had dual nationality from my Italian dad and English mum, but I was born in Shepherd's Bush, I felt English, and I had already worn the England shirt in a Colts international. Maybe I was a little scared at the prospect of leaving home and trying to settle in another country, I'm not sure. What is certain is that if I had accepted, I would have been giving up on my ambition to play for England. So while no one could say Kingston Poly was anything like Bocconi University and there was no chance of Wasps offering me any kind of 'package', I said no to the Italians. I still love the country, the food, the lifestyle, and feel lucky that part of me is Italian. But the greater part of me is English. Simple as that.

Sometime after the offer from Italy, I agreed to meet England internationals Peter Winterbottom and Brian Moore and Australian Kent Bray for a drink in Richmond. This wasn't to be just a social pint. They had come to convince me of the virtues of their club, Harlequins. They put up a lot of arguments as to why it would be right for me to join 'Quins – how I could be the next No. 7 for England, how I could learn from Winterbottom, how I would benefit from playing alongside outstanding forwards such as Jason Leonard, Moore, Paul Ackford and Mickey Skinner. Geographically, it would have made a lot of sense for me to play for 'Quins because I lived just down the road and I wouldn't have had to take the bloody Piccadilly Line to Sudbury Town every other day. That part of it definitely made sense. Supporters believed, and it was written in some newspapers, that I couldn't join 'Quins because of their rivalry with Wasps but I didn't see it like that. They're a fine club and there are good reasons why excellent players went there, not least being the fact that players from the club seemed to find an immediate avenue to the England team. Kent Bray and Peter Winterbottom were both very passionate about their club, probably more than any Harlequins players I've met.

I couldn't leave Wasps, though. I joined the club in the 1990–91 season, a few months after Wasps had won the Courage League. Rob Andrew captained that team and it was still pretty intact when I started to make a name for myself there. In those days, you had nine league games per season, four Cup games if you got to the final, divisional games if you were good enough, and internationals if you were among the élite. There were no substitutions, very few injuries and the senior players pretty much ran the show. If you were 21 years of age, you were considered too young and were expected to be patient. In fairness, given the way the game was then played, you *were* too young. At the time Harlequins approached me, I might have played a few 'friendlies' for Wasps' first XV but I hadn't played a competitive match. I should rephrase that because if England were playing Wales in Cardiff and you got selected for the Wasps' first team against Neath at The Gnoll on Friday night, I'm not sure it would be right to call that experience friendly.

If I'd moved to Harlequins, I would have done so without achieving any of my ambitions at Wasps. It was the same situation as with the Italian offer – accepting it meant giving up my England dreams and I wasn't prepared to do that. There was much that I wanted to do at Wasps and I hadn't even begun. Although I wasn't a first teamer, a year later I made the England Under-21s. As well as adding some excitement to a rugby life mostly spent with the Wasps second team, playing for England's representative teams was helping to get me noticed and I did my first proper interview with a newspaper when Chris Jones, rugby correspondent at the *Evening Standard*, was writing a piece on me. I've got to know Chris over the years and we often laugh about that first article. I was living on the houseboat in Twickenham and, during our chat, I told him about the lucrative offer I'd had from Italy but explained that I'd decided to stay with Wasps. It was a fun article and a photographer from the paper even came and took a picture of me sitting on deck to go with the piece. But best of all was the headline: '*Bardot*, Not The Money', a reference to my choosing to stay on the houseboat rather than accept the millions of lire on offer.

In the years after Francesca's death, I gradually accepted the fact that my parents would be depending on me more than ever before. Their lives would be better if I could do something positive and pretty soon it was obvious that rugby offered me an opportunity to make something of myself. All my efforts went into that. I couldn't deal with the grief of losing my sister, and so, like my dad, I suppressed my feelings. In the beginning I wanted to be with people who didn't know Francesca and barely knew what had happened to her. Time passes, other people forget and denial becomes easier. Then I learned to speak about her in a superficial way. For years I was unable to express my emotions. Through this time, my mother and many others fought an incredibly brave battle to have the circumstances of the tragedy properly explained and to have those responsible for the loss of 51 young lives held accountable. I was incapable of being involved in any of the great work done by the families of the victims – but I have huge admiration for Mum, Margaret Lockwood-Croft, Tony Perks, Barbara Davis, Billy Gorman and all the others who gave up much of their lives to the cause. What they did was truly heroic.

In Mum's telling of the story, the starting point was 23 April 1990, eight months after the *Marchioness* disaster. It was the day of the first inquest at the Coroner's Court and Mum had gone there believing she and the family members of the other victims would hear the reasons why their loved ones had died on the Thames. What they found in the court was a small army of legal people representing every party except the members of the public whose sons and daughters had been lost in this tragedy. Then she heard the coroner, Paul Knapman, conduct the first inquest. 'Name?' And the name was read out. 'Person that last saw him?' Name was given. 'Location?' 'On the bow of the *Marchioness*.' 'Cause of death?' 'Drowning.' And then it was on to inquest number two.

Mum decided there and then that she didn't want Knapman to proceed with the inquest into Francesca's death. She needed to know how, where and why Francesca had died and she didn't care how long it took, she wanted answers to those questions. Six other families did likewise and the inquest was adjourned. Mum was put under a lot of pressure to allow the inquest to go ahead but she refused. My mother had been an air stewardess and had been trained in survival at sea. Because of that, she could not understand why her daughter was almost 10 minutes in the river after the *Marchioness* went down and not rescued. She had been taught that if you survive the impact and escape from the wreckage into the sea, you had a good chance of being saved. The way she saw it, this boat had sunk in the middle of London on a clear moonlit summer's night and yet more people died in the water than on the boat.

On the road to getting justice for the victims, there were some pretty bad turns. Douglas Henderson, the skipper of the 1,475-tonne dredger the *Bowbelle* that ploughed into the Marchioness, was twice prosecuted for failing to keep a proper lookout and failing to provide his crew with walkie-talkies. Twice the jury could not agree on a verdict. My mother and the Marchioness Action Group were also appalled by the behaviour of the coroner, Dr Knapman, and by the failure of Ready Mixed Concrete, owners of the *Bowbelle*, and Tidal Cruises, owners of the *Marchioness*, to ensure proper safety standards on their vessels. Knapman said the Marchioness Action Group were a small minority of people who were seeking publicity from this tragedy, and he described Margaret Lockwood-Croft as 'unhinged'; he also called others, including my mother, 'mentally unwell'. After the initial, aborted, inquest, he refused to re-open it. The families of the victims sought a judicial review of that decision and lost. It was expensive and many families could not afford to continue. My mother and Margaret Lockwood-Croft applied for legal aid and were twice refused. Mum's solicitor, Sallie Booth, warned her of the danger of proceeding without it.

'You could lose your home,' she said.

'A house?' my mother replied. 'What are houses when you're in search of peace and contentment.'

At the third time of asking, they were granted legal aid and that allowed them to challenge Knapman's refusal to resume the inquest at the Court of Appeal.

Then the tide began to turn for those seeking justice. The Court of Appeal case, taken on by Mum, Margaret Lockwood-Croft and six others, found that Knapman had acted with 'an appearance of bias' against the victims' families and should be removed as coroner. A new coroner, Dr John Burton, decreed that the inquest should be resumed. It took six years from the night of the disaster to get a result from the inquest. Throughout that time, Mum and about 20 friends from the Marchioness Action Group protested at the Annual General Meeting of Ready Mixed Concrete. The idea of my mother as a placard-bearing protestor would have been funny if the issue had not been so serious. She bought one share in the company so that she could attend the AGM, and spoke passionately, saying that, as the company's vessel, the *Bowbelle*, had caused the disaster, it should be funding the families' fight for justice. The chairman replied that the matter was in the hands of their insurers. That didn't discourage Mum, and she returned to that AGM every year and made the same case.

The inquest took place at Hammersmith Town Hall, a stone's throw from our family home in Barnes, and lasted five weeks. Michael Mansfield, the Queen's Counsel representing families of the victims, said to Mum that he felt the best they could expect was an open verdict. 'No,' said my mother, 'that's not the best we can expect. You and I both know that Francesca and the other fifty victims in this tragedy were unlawfully killed and we are here to convince the jury of that fact.' Mum had gone through legal books, studied merchant shipping laws dating back to 1894 and understood what a prudent shipmaster should have done on a voyage on the river. She spoke for 43 minutes in the witness stand, concentrating as much as she could on the many mistakes and sloppy standards that had led to the collision. She spoke too about the terrible grief she and others had suffered through the years, some of the unavoidable emotional fall-out caused by the tragedy, and also about the unnecessary trauma caused by the behaviour of the coroner's office.

She talked about the tradition in her family of bringing the deceased home, in the Irish way, and having a wake in the house. She had done this with her mum and dad in the East End, and every member of the family had been able to kiss their parents goodbye. Mum was denied this right, and Francesca's body is the only one in her family that's never come home. That's one of her deepest regrets. She knows now that should never have happened; years later she saw photographs of Francesca's body and she was very recognisable.

Our family wasn't the only one – a number of others were denied access to the bodies of their sons and daughters. Three years after the tragedy, the families learned that over half of the victims had their hands severed by Dr Knapman and his assistant, Dr Dolman. It was justified on the basis of speeding up the identification process but it was totally unnecessary and was a horrific discovery; Mum's panic attacks started after this came out and Dad had his minor heart attack.

When the jury came to state its verdict at the inquest, the

presiding coroner reminded the chairperson of the jury that the verdict should not conflict with the result of any other criminal proceedings. Most considered this a direct reference to the inability of two juries to convict the captain of the *Bowbelle*, Douglas Henderson, of failing in his duty to keep an adequate lookout. The young woman to whom Dr Burton directed his advice did not react in any way.

He then said, 'Have you reached your verdict?'

'Yes, we have.'

'Very well, then. What is your verdict?'

'We are unanimous that all forty-four were unlawfully killed.' (It was 44 not 51 because the other seven victims had already been dealt with in the original, aborted inquest.)

The tears flowed down my mother's face, as they did for many of the family members present. After six years, it was a release of pent-up emotion. They had known negligence was the cause of that collision and the loss of so many lives but for so long no one was prepared to listen. What the verdict meant was that some person or persons were responsible for the deaths of 51 people on the Thames in the early hours of 20 August 1989. It is a travesty of justice that no one has been held to account for the unlawful killing of so many young people. But that verdict did lead to the Deputy Prime Minister, John Prescott, announcing in 2000 a public inquiry into the sinking of the *Marchioness* and a separate one into the identification procedures used by the coroner and his assistant. One of the recommendations was that this barbaric procedure of removing victims' hands for identification would never happen again. Lord Justice Clarke chaired the inquiry and his main report blamed poor lookouts on the *Bowbelle* and the

Marchioness for the collision and criticised the owners and managers of both vessels. He said it was a tragedy that 'should never have happened'. He was highly critical of the skipper of the *Bowbelle* who had drunk at least six pints during the day before his vessel left its berth at around 1.25 a.m.

How much of this would have come about if the Marchioness Action Group had not campaigned? Probably very little. On the evening of the 'unlawfully killed' verdict, my mother walked into the pub in Barnes to be greeted with the words, 'There's one helluva woman.' Mum knew the guy who'd said it. He had reared five children on his own after his wife died. 'She and her friends took 'em all on, the coroner, the lawyers, the judges, played 'em at their own game and got the verdict that was right. What a wonderful woman, and now I'm going to buy her a drink.' Mum had a half of Guinness and as she downed it, all the expense and emotional turmoil involved in fighting a powerful establishment seemed worth it. Other times she thinks about the fact that no one was convicted of wrongdoing in a tragedy that was caused by negligence, but to keep her sanity she focuses on what she and the other campaigners achieved.

Getting Dr Knapman stood down in the Court of Appeal made legal history and opened the door for others who disagree with a coroner's decision to have it judicially reviewed. She is also pleased that Lord Justice Clarke's inquiry, when its findings were published in 2002, made wholesale recommendations for the improvement of safety standards on our rivers. Now there are new lifeboat stations on the Thames, and the Royal National Lifeboat Institute (RNLI) have high-speed boats that can be used to get to the scene of an accident very quickly. The old, huge dredgers have been removed and safety standards on pleasure boats are more carefully monitored. Mum complains that some of Clarke's recommendations are still to be implemented and she is going to stay on the case until they are. For 15 years after my sister died, my mother was consumed by the struggle and only in the last three years has she begun to get her life back.

My mother says the young cope with tragedy in different ways and that I chose the right way, which was to pick up the torch Francesca had lit. I don't know if there was much choice in my reaction to the loss of my sister. For over a year I was lost and didn't know why, but I tried to forget about it. When that phase passed, part of me wanted to be there for my parents, to give them something to counter what they were going through. I wasn't alone in caring for them because once Mum and Dad started coming to my Wasps games, which was pretty much from day one, they were welcomed with open arms into one of London's great rugby families. It seemed everyone at the club understood their situation and if Mum needed to talk about something that was happening in the case that week, as she often did, there were always people at the club who cared enough to listen. But mostly it was a refuge from the madness, somewhere they could come to watch rugby, talk rugby and meet their friends.

6

'Dallaglio? Sounds like a wine bar.'

Coming towards the end of the 1992–93 season, I was almost 21 years of age and a little restless. After almost three seasons at Wasps I had yet to start a league game. At the time I was playing for England Under-21s, I had played for England Colts and everyone was telling me I should move – to this club, to that club, to any club that would give me first-team opportunities. England's Under-21 coaches said I needed to start playing first-team rugby, as most of my Under-21 team-mates were doing. But they weren't playing at Wasps, where the competition was fierce. My two back-row colleagues in the England Under-21 team, Richard Hill and Tony Diprose, were playing in the Saracens first team but they had just been relegated and that gave the club the opportunity to blood younger players. Still, it was frustrating for me and I needed to stand back and take stock. For starters, the end goal was to establish myself in the Wasps team and because there were a lot of good players at the club, that wasn't going to happen overnight. I also appreciated that when I made the first team at Wasps, I would be a more rounded player than some of my contemporaries at other clubs. Secondly, Wasps were my club and if I left before becoming a regular first-team player, that would be to admit failure. Finally, I was having a bloody good time.

Remember, these were the amateur days. We trained Tuesday and Thursday evenings. The highlight of the Tuesday session was a Firsts versus Seconds match that was full on and a reminder to me that the Wasps No. 8 at the time, Dean Ryan, wasn't prepared to give up his place easily to some young kid who happened to be playing for England Under-21s. It was also clear Dean saw some potential in me but he believed I was a bit loose and needed to develop the tight aspects of my game. To do that, he got me to play No. 6. On the pitch, Dean was a great guy and a complete psychopath, the like of whom you don't really see nowadays. His team-mates loved him for it but, in those days, you didn't want to play against the Wasps pack. They were all horrible – Matt Greenwood, Jeff Probyn, Paul 'The Judge' Rendall, Alan Simmons, Francis Emerua, Buster White and Dave Pegler as well as Dean. Nowadays, hardness is measured in how hard you hit the other guy in the tackle – in those days it was whether your punch knocked him out. I don't say this to glorify the old days but that's the way it was. And Wasps, like Leicester and Bath, were very good at this game.

As a 21-year-old, my body shape wasn't ideal for the way the game was then played. I was 22 before I saw the inside of a gym but now young players are using weights from the age of 14. Having said that, I'm glad to have been around when I was, to have been part of the amateur generation. I would have said, 'The gym? I'm sorry, not interested. I play rugby for fun, sitting in a gym for three hours is *not* fun.' I thought I was big enough, I thought I had a decent frame, but when I look at the photographs now, I wince to see that tall, skinny, lanky kid, and think, 'Play with that body now and you'd snap in half.' At that time, rugby clubs might have found room somewhere in the clubhouse to install one of those multi-gyms that you got out of an Argos catalogue.

Earlier in that season at a training session, Dick Best was introduced to us with the words, 'He's England coach and will be taking the training this evening.' We knew who he was and that he had been coach at Harlequins before the England job. Dick was a players' coach, a very funny, dry bastard who happened to be very good at what he did and was known for making training fun. Occasionally, to get his point across, he would ridicule one player in front of the other 30 in such a way that they wouldn't be able to stop themselves laughing. I suppose he was a bit of a bully and you either took to him or you didn't. Well, I liked him from the start, partly because I found him very entertaining but also because I'd been hardened over the years and was never too bothered by stuff like that. Once you rose above it, you saw just how hilarious it was.

So this evening, I dropped a pass – just one of those mistakes that happen but it was Dick's opportunity. The whistle sounded. Everyone stopped.

'You,' he said. 'Yeah, you. What's your name?'

'Law . . . Law . . . Lawrence Dallaglio, sir,' I said, as nervous as I'd ever felt in my life.

'What, what did you say?'

'Dallaglio, sir. Dallaglio.'

'Dallaglio?' he said. 'What sort of a fucked-up name is that? Sounds like a wine bar. Well, mister Dallaglio, why don't you fuck off back to the wine bar and stop ruining my training session.'

After Dick's scary but memorable visit, good things followed. Somehow I had impressed Dick and, through his influence, I was picked for the Public School Wanderers select team to compete in the Lord's Taverner's Sevens at Harlequins' ground. That was a prestigious tournament and we actually drew with the England Sevens team. Following that, I was picked to play for England in the Dubai Sevens and, because of an injury to Nick Beal, ended up playing at centre.

We did well in Dubai, reaching the semi-finals, and I revelled in the atmosphere, playing at night before big crowds in televised matches. Sevens was a game I loved, having learned it under John Willcox at Ampleforth. Take half the number of people off the pitch so everyone else has to cover twice as much ground and there is a premium on your ability in one-to-one situations. It's very rare you get that in the 15-a-side game, but in Sevens you're going to get the chance to use a bit of skill, or a bit of speed, to beat the other guy. And I did enough in Dubai to get picked for England's team at the inaugural World Sevens held at Murrayfield. It was one of the very best weeks of my rugby career.

Although we were mostly a team of young and up-and-coming players, I thought it was an inspired selection. They made Andrew

Harriman captain and picked Matt Dawson, Damien Hopley, Adedayo Adebayo, Chris Sheasby and Nick Beal together with Sevens specialists Dave Scully and Justyn Cassell. I think Tim Rodber was the only one in the squad who had played for the senior England side.

To make Harriman captain was a stroke of genius. Within the game, he was a real character – we're talking legendary. His background lay in wealthy Nigeria and when he spoke, the first thing you thought was, 'aristocrat'. The stories about him were so fantastic. I couldn't do them all justice but let me tell one. Harlequins were playing away and the team bus was due to leave the car park of their ground at a certain time. In rugby, you're frowned upon if you arrive late for anything but on this day, they couldn't leave on time because Andy hadn't shown up. Standing up on the bus, Dick Best was fuming, 'Where the fuck's Harriman?' and everyone else was thinking Andy was going to get it when he showed.

Then a brown Bentley rolls sedately into the car park, does a big circle and slows to a stop alongside the team bus. Dressed in a smart uniform and peaked cap, the driver gets out, opens the boot and takes out a kit bag. He then walks round to the back door on the left, opens it and out steps Andy. As he gets on to the bus, the chauffeur hands him the kit bag, and says, 'There you are, Mr Harriman, have a good day.' Dick is looking at all of this in complete shock. He cannot believe it. Before he can say anything, Andy is in there. 'So sorry I'm late, Dick. The Ferrari wasn't behaving itself. Had to borrow Dad's Bentley.'

And Dick, the master of put-downs, just shook his head and sat down. The rest of the Harlequins boys were pissing themselves laughing because that was Andy. No one was ever more suited to playing for 'Quins, and even though I'm Wasps through and through, I've a lot of admiration for the kind of characters who played for Harlequins. They're just different and rugby needs different clubs.

The Sevens turned out to be a fantastic week. We travelled up to Edinburgh on the Monday, which, it so happened, was Damien Hopley's birthday. We were both at Wasps, so I knew Damien and felt very comfortable with him. Since it was our first night together as a squad and some us were virtual strangers to each other, Damien said, 'Come on, let's all have a night out together to break the ice.' Not one to pass up a few beers, that sounded a good idea to me, and we well and truly smashed the ice that Monday night. It turned into a sensational party and we didn't get to our beds at the luxurious George Hotel until five o'clock in the morning.

The tournament was not due to start until the end of the week and because they would be cramming so many matches into a weekend, games were scheduled to begin at 8.30 in the morning. That was fine, but our coaches, Les Cusworth and Pete Rossborough, wanting to get us into the swing of early morning games, had organised one against the Hawick Sevens team for eight-thirty on the Tuesday morning. If you'd wandered into the ground that morning, you would have thought Hawick were England and we were the Hawick Milkmen Sevens team. It's hard to play your best rugby on two hours' sleep but our coaches knew nothing about that. I noticed Pete Rossborough pull Andy Harriman to one side.

'Who's this Dallaglio? I mean he's a fucking kid. Can't catch the ball, let alone make a run. We have a serious selection problem here.' I was feeling particularly shabby but Andy smoothed things out.

'Don't worry, boy's had a bit of a late night. Everything will be all right.'

Pete wasn't convinced. 'Fucking hell, I'm not so sure.'

The coaches didn't know me from Adam. But needless to say, we sharpened our act as the week went on. We didn't touch another drop of alcohol, trained like demons, and it soon became clear that we were actually a decent team. Harriman was an outstanding Sevens player, as were Adebayo and Sheasby. Rodber and I, if we got the chance, had the pace to go the length of the pitch. We beat Hong Kong, Canada and Samoa in our group and then New Zealand, Australia and South Africa in a round robin. No one gave us a chance of getting out of that and, much to my annoyance, I was rested against New Zealand. I brooded on the sideline but the guys played outstandingly, especially Adebayo and Beal. I remember Adebayo making a fantastic try-saving tackle on Eric Rush. New Zealand were pretty shocked at the end of it – they didn't expect us to be as good as we were. I was back for the South Africa game, which we won and so guaranteed our place in the last eight. We beat Samoa in the quarter-final and had tournament favourites Fiji in the semi-final.

Not only did we beat Fiji but we beat them well and, for me, that was the highlight of the tournament. They had a fine side, with the brilliant Waisale Serevi as their star player, and no one had given us a prayer. It was a milestone for me to play against Serevi, whom I had always admired, and the experience became memorable when I was given the ball by Chris Sheasby and managed to sidestep Serevi in a one-on-one. After first meeting the great Fijian at that tournament, I became good friends with him. There would be many other battles in Sevens rugby, most of which his team would win, but I've always got that first victory to fall back on.

Australia in the final was always going to be a huge test. They had David Campese, Michael Lynagh, Matthew Burke and Willie Ofahengaue in their team and yet we truly believed we would win. We caught their kick-off, the ball went through the hands of every player on our team and eventually we got it to Harriman who ran at Campese, looked at him, sprinted round him and carried on to run the length of the pitch and score beside the posts – 7–0. We again caught their kick-off, passed it round a bit and Chris Sheasby put me in for a try. From their third kick-off, we again passed it about, retained possession and Tim Rodber ended up going the length of the pitch – 21–0. Apart from Lynagh three times re-starting the game, they had not touched the ball.

They got a try before half-time, came out strongly in the second half and got another two but their tries were scored in the corners and they couldn't convert them all. We won 21–17. Somehow it didn't feel as though we had won a World Cup, but that we had played well to win a good Sevens tournament. Maybe that was because we weren't a team of England internationals, and we certainly weren't given the resources that a team containing Carling, Guscott and Rory Underwood would have got. No one in the hierarchy of English rugby thought we had any chance of winning. I actually felt we were sent up there because England was obliged to enter a team. But there we were in Murrayfield, booed and jeered by the home crowd every time we took to the field, the first winners of the World Cup in Sevens. And having listened to the crowd cheer on every team we played, it pleased me no end that Scotland lost the final of the Bowl. To Japan.

What I loved about the experience was the feeling that came with winning. I just absolutely adored that. Walking off the field, I thought, 'If you could bottle this moment, it would be priceless.' It was a feeling that I wanted to experience again and again. You've never seen anything like the reaction that our victory generated from people in high places – all sorts of belated congratulations from everyone at the RFU, and from Geoff Cooke and all the England coaches. They were taken aback because England hadn't beaten Australia in previous World Cup finals, and our unlikely team had shown that it could be done. A lot of great things have happened through the course of my career but that victory in the inaugural World Cup Sevens remains a genuine highlight. It didn't do my career at Wasps any harm either, because ITV's coverage of the tournament attracted good viewing figures and people at the club were going to have to look at me a bit more closely.

I think it was partly because we were thrown together by a Union that didn't have high hopes for us that we got on famously. We actually had a great little back-up team and the coaches did an excellent job. For any collector of sports trivia, one of the most unlikely questions came out of that weekend: name the Scotsman who won a World Cup medal for England. The answer, of course, is Billy Dods. He was on the bench for us in the final because of the competition rule that allowed you to pick from a pool of 'extras' if you were badly depleted by injury. We lost Damien

Hopley in the quarter-final and needed to pick someone from the pool. Billy didn't get on the pitch but he did get a World Cup medal – for England.

A week that began with a huge party finished with a huge party. Andy Harriman was inspired. With the style he had displayed all week, he produced a very flash credit card on the evening after the final, and said, 'Right, gentlemen, this is on me. Champagne for the team.' And that was it. We drank champagne all evening.

At the end of that 1992–93 season, I went with the England Under-21s to Australia, which was another memorable trip. England had been hopeless at the Colts level two years previously but suddenly players who hadn't got into that team were playing for the Under-21s and making a big difference. We had a great group of guys. I played in the back row with Richard Hill and Tony Diprose, who both went on to have fantastic careers, and Mike Catt, Will Greenwood, Austin Healey, Simon Shaw, Mark Regan, Mark Mapletoft and Darren O'Leary were also there. Like the Sevens squad in Edinburgh, the Under-21s got on really well in Australia and we had a ball. Since I was the only member of the squad to have been part of the World Cup Sevens victory, the rest of the lads decided I should be called 'Golden Bollocks' for the entire tour. Fair enough, I thought. Before this I had never been to Australia and this trip opened my eyes to what rugby could be – an opportunity to travel to places you would otherwise never see.

It wasn't the perfect rugby tour because we lost two games, but it was pretty good. The decisive match was always going to be against Australia Under-21s, played at the Sydney Football Stadium before the senior match between New South Wales and

South Africa, which was, incidentally, the first time South Africa had played outside of their own country since the end of apartheid. For our game against the Aussies, the team management drafted in Kyran Bracken from Canada, where he had been touring with the England senior squad, and he played his part in a great win.

For me, it was a fabulous way to end the season and I was more determined than ever to break into the Wasps first team. That wasn't going to be automatic, though. Already I had made a number of appearances as a replacement but they were on the wing because Chris Oti seemed to be the only Wasp who ever got injured during a match and the powers-that-be thought that, as I was fast and could tackle, I'd be fine in that position.

My first league start came early in the 1993–94 season in a home match against Harlequins. Again, because I was seen as quick and a bit light, I was picked at No. 7 when all my rugby at that point had been at No. 6 or No. 8. But when you've waited for as long as I had, played as many second-team matches in front of one man and his dog as I had, you don't complain about where you are picked in the first team. The difference between playing first- and second-team rugby was amazing. The first team is the centre of attention, of course, and journalists were trying to find out what we thought about playing against Peter Winterbottom and Will Carling just as we were preparing to go on at Sudbury in front of a crowd of 6,000 people. It was a scrappy game, which we won 19–8, and my only distinct memory now is of getting into a post-match drinking session with Jeff Probyn, Paul Rendall and Jason Leonard. That was no good for anyone but starting a match for the Wasps first team had been one of my targets and, although everyone else expected it to happen, it was an important milestone for me.

I stayed in the team for the following week's game, again at home, against Newcastle Gosforth (as was), which we also won – things were looking up. A week later we were away at Leicester and in this collision with reality we were smashed 38–3. As is so often the case in sport, you learn a lot from the bad days. Before our trip to the Midlands, the biggest crowd I'd played in front of was at the Dubai Sevens, where 10,000 people turned up to have a bit of a party. There were 13,000 people at Welford Road, pretty much all Leicester fans, and they were there to see the Tigers maul another visiting team. In terms of my experiences in the game, this was another eye-opener. Leicester were a very good side, just about beginning to break Bath's domination of English club rugby, and while we were often up there in the top three, we weren't nearly good enough that day. On a personal level, this was proof that playing Leicester away was very different from playing Harlequins or Newcastle at home.

You expect the other team to have one tasty back-row player. Leicester had John Wells, Dean Richards and Neil Back – three of the very best at the time. I remember the game for different reasons. Obviously, their back row was outstanding. The score was humiliating and, to be truthful, we were lucky to get the three. From our team, only Rob Andrew came out of the game with any credit. Last but by no means least, this was the game in which I received my first punch that hurt in a rugby match. Early on, I was at the tail of a line-out, eyes fixed on the ball as it was thrown to our middle jumper, when Dean Richards, who obviously wasn't ball-watching, just smacked me one in the face. For a second or two, I didn't know what had happened because Deano had caught me flush with a really good punch. It felt like my nose had been broken, but it had just been seriously bruised. For that I was grateful – you can be certain it wasn't his best punch but it was good enough and it hurt. Blood was flowing out of my nose and I was a bit shell-shocked, which only added to the daze caused by the way Leicester had been totally dominating us in the game through those early minutes. Even then, I could understand Deano's thinking – 'Let's see what this young lad is all about.'

These were the good old days when there was no such thing as a blood stoppage and the sight of a visiting player with blood all over his face was a cause for cheering and applause from the Welford Road faithful. Eventually there was a break in play and our No. 8, Dean Ryan, who was used to a bit of blood himself, sometimes his own, sometimes his victim's, came over to me.

'Look,' he said, 'you've got to sort this out.' Still a bit confused, I couldn't see what he was getting at, so he explained, 'You're going to have to whack him one.' I was afraid that's what he meant. I'm thinking, 'This is fucking Dean Richards he's talking about, the guy I've been watching in the Five Nations for God knows how many years. An absolute icon, a legend in the game, and I'm just a kid, starting my third league game for Wasps. How can I be expected to whack him?' But Dean Ryan is still there, in front of me, telling me what had to be done. 'You've got to deal with this.'

It didn't seem like there was a choice, so at the next line-out I attempted to punch the great Dean Richards. Although I connected, it certainly wasn't as good a punch as the one he landed on me, but it was enough for him to acknowledge that I had retaliated, and once that had been noted, we both got on with the game.

Neil Back was the outstanding player on the pitch and it dawned on me that if I was going to play No. 7, Winterbottom in my first game and Back in my third game had shown me the standard that was required. After the game we were in the bar at Welford Road when Dean Richards came over and bought me a pint. We had a bit of a laugh and a joke and we've shared many pints and got on well ever since.

For me, the good times ended when the team was announced for the next game. Changes had to be made after such a bad defeat and it is easier to leave out a young lad who has played three games than a senior guy who has been playing for 10 years. Naturally, I totally disagreed with the decision to drop me. What's the benefit of putting a young guy in the team if you kick him out after the first setback?

The disappointments didn't end there. Having made my Wasps debut, I was selected for the London divisional team against the North, and although we won 10–9, it wasn't a good performance so I was dropped. That was important because New Zealand were touring England that autumn and scheduled to play all of the divisional teams. Phil Keith-Roach was London forwards coach at the time and he explained why I wasn't being picked for the All Blacks game. 'We just feel the other players are a bit more physical,' he said. It was true. Rory Jenkins, Chris Sheasby, Dean Ryan and Matt Greenwood were more experienced and physically stronger than I was and I had not done much to improve my strength. I still felt humiliated, as though I had again been set up for a fall. I get in the Wasps side, play three games, get dropped. I get in the London side, play one game and get chopped.

I went to the All Blacks v. London game at Twickenham and felt the people picking the London team should have been more concerned about skill, pace and flair than physicality. London lost 64–10 and, despite their best efforts, they couldn't get near enough to the All Blacks to make it a physical game. Frank Bunce was sensational that day, delivering one of the best performances I'd ever seen by a centre. As a team, we were outmanoeuvred, out-foxed, out-run, out-everythinged! Ironically, the All Blacks slipped up against England at Twickenham in the one game of the tour they needed to win.

It's funny the different way you see things with hindsight. When I was dropped by Wasps and later by London, it was like my world caved in. Having waited so long to get my chance, it was so utterly demoralising to have it all taken away so quickly. But now when I look back, I can see that I was actually making a lot of progress in a short space of time. I was a 21-year-old who had just broken into his club's first team, had got into the London set-up and had also just been named in the England squad. That meant I was going along to England training at Richmond or Harlequins and training alongside Brian Moore, Will Carling, Tim Rodber and Dean Richards. That was an outstanding environment and every time I was there, I wanted more of it.

I don't think I've ever agreed with a decision to leave me out of a team, certainly not when I first heard it, anyway. Often you will go away, think about it and, a day or two later, you can appreciate the coach's thinking. Occasionally you may even concede to yourself that he had a point – doesn't mean you agree, just that you understand his point of view. However, I don't think it's a good idea to admit that publicly. I decided it was best to leave coaches and selectors with no room for manoeuvre by making sure I was head and shoulders above any other options. It also seemed to me that if these disappointments were going to happen, it was better they came early and involved Wasps and London. The last thing I wanted was to get into the England team, play one game and then be left out. Now that would have been a disaster.

Not long after being dropped, I got back in Wasps' first team and played a pretty central part for the rest of the season. When people had been telling me I should move clubs to try to get first-team experience, one of the reasons I'd been reluctant to do so was that I imagined once I broke that barrier with Wasps, the other things would follow. Sure enough, they did. Being named in the England squad was another important step. Geoff Cooke was in charge of the team. He had formed an outstanding relationship with Will Carling and England had become the dominant European team of the early nineties. What I didn't realise was that Cooke's reign was about to end, and he was replaced by Jack Rowell, who also, luckily, wanted me in the squad. Being in the squad is one thing, though, getting into the team is another, and throughout the 1993–94 season, I felt a long way from selection.

After the 1994 Five Nations, in which Ireland beat England at Twickenham with Simon Geoghegan's try, I was at home in Barnes when the telephone rang.

'There's an Irishman on the phone for you,' my mum said. 'Noel somebody or other.' I went to the phone.

'Hello Lawrence, Noel Murphy here, chairman of the Irish selectors. Let me get to the point. How would like to wear the green jersey of Ireland?'

'That's very kind of you.'

'We've heard you like a few pints of the black stuff.'

He wasn't wrong, but it was comical really. I was in a state of shock. I mean, 'We've heard you like a few pints of the black stuff'! I've got to know Noel over the years and I've come to appreciate his manner and charm. In those days, Irish rugby was regarded as being tough, strong but never consistently good. They just didn't have the same fitness levels as England, so it was more 'kick ahead, any head'. The way Noel put it seemed part of the Irish approach at the time. From my point of view, it was brilliant to get the offer. What Noel was telling me was that he knew my mother was Irish and that her people came from County Cork. He went on to say, 'And I would hate to see you wearing a white jersey on the bench for England when you could be wearing a green jersey on the pitch for Ireland.' He lured me with his Irish charm, and played on the fact that I hadn't been going anywhere with England. My head felt sore from banging it against the wall.

Ahead of me in the pecking order were Neil Back, Dean Richards, Ben Clarke, Tim Rodber and Steve Ojomoh. They were all very good back-row forwards and I regarded myself as being in that category. Unfortunately, Jack Rowell didn't. Maybe if I had played for the club he coached, Bath, he would have rated me higher. I liked Jack. He was odd, definitely. We were told he was a business guru, a man who had done extremely well with Golden Wonder crisps and Dalgety. He obviously had a lot of intelligence and he could be very witty, but often he was the only one clever enough to understand his own wit. There was always a certain nervousness coming from Jack that unsettled me. Physically, he was incredibly tall but he had the smallest feet you've ever seen under so big a man. Clearly, he had helped to create a winning environment at Bath and a lot of people who had come into contact with Jack spoke highly of him. It was a natural progression for him to be given the England job.

Jack liked to play mind games with players, which is not necessarily a bad thing, and the Bath players, who were used to this, were able to answer him back. But if you were young and impressionable, a bit uncertain of yourself and a little quiet, you would find it difficult. Out of all those things, I was only young, but I remember Matt Dawson and Paul Grayson being bemused by some of the things Jack was asking them to do. The hard part was that Jack never asked for what he wanted directly. The request was often couched in metaphorical terms in a way that was probably more suited to the business world he had come from. Other sides of him were easier to take to. He would always have a smile on his face and was clear that he wanted to get the best out of his player. 'Might be good enough for Wasps,' he would say, 'but not good enough for England.' Or, 'Might be good enough for Leicester, but not good enough for England.'

Jack always seemed to fall back on the players he knew. If it was a tight call between you and a Bath player, you generally lost. I suppose it was understandable because he knew the Bath players and trusted them. But after training with England on a number of occasions, I didn't seem to be making any headway with Jack, and when Noel Murphy called, I was flattered by the offer.

'I can't give you an answer over the phone right now. Let me think about it for a few days,' I said. Only when I put down the phone did the seriousness of the situation hit me.

Effectively, I was being offered the opportunity to play for Ireland immediately. Not having played for England's senior side, it wasn't as if I'd be switching countries. At the time, the rules were that you could play for England Colts and Under-21s, as I had, and then switch allegiance. After putting the phone down, I spoke to Mum about it. The idea of being able to play international rugby appealed to me and it was clear from their win at Twickenham that Ireland were improving. That summer, Ireland were touring Australia, including playing two Tests. That, too, was attractive. It was all still swirling round inside my head two days later when there was another phone call to my home. This one was from Don Rutherford, technical director for the Rugby Football Union at Twickenham.

'Congratulations Lawrence, you've been selected to tour South Africa this summer,' he said.

Nothing more needed to be said. Being selected for England's tour decided everything. I was staying where I was. I called Noel Murphy but by then England's touring party had just been announced and he knew my answer.

Who knows what might have happened if I hadn't been selected for the tour to South Africa? But, as was the case with Wasps and when the offer came from Italy, I didn't want to turn my back on something that I had not yet achieved. Halfway up Mount Everest, you don't turn back because you'd rather climb another mountain.

7

Jellyfish 1–Sheep farmer 0

Your first major rugby tour for your country should be memorable. Mine certainly was and the 1994 tour to South Africa holds a very special place in my heart.

When we were in Durban early on in the trip, I shared a hotel room with Graham Dawe in an arrangement that carried on the tradition of the youngest sharing with the oldest. We were the odd couple; he was a 35-year-old farmer from Cornwall, I was a 21-year-old likely lad from London. Maybe it was my liking for being in the company of guys who have been around the block, but we got on really, really well. It was a friendship based on simplicity – I did everything I was told. But then he also looked out for me and, recognising it was my first tour, smoothed the

117

way. Dawsie spent most of his career in the shadow of Brian Moore, sitting on the bench for game after game and almost never getting on the pitch. He started just three internationals, and came off the bench twice, but he didn't complain. Everyone could see he was a fine player who would have done an excellent job for England had he been lucky enough to get more chances.

Dawsie was a great tourist. He liked to be at the centre of things – back seat of the bus – and was a tough character, totally respected by the so-called 'superstars' of the team. He and Brian Moore had a very interesting, intense and I would say complex relationship. They loved each other, they hated each other, but ultimately they admired each other. Dawsie was fascinating. You do get characters today but the difference is that their personalities are not moulded by what they do away from rugby. Dawsie had farmer's fingers – shaped like a bunch of bananas from hours spent holding a sheep's mouth open or investigating its backside – and his face had that worldly look. Dawsie wasn't the only character, though. With Dean Richards, Brian Moore, Martin Bayfield, Stuart Barnes, Adedayo Adebayo and Steve Ojomoh also touring, it was bound to be an interesting trip.

During a booze-up at a sports café in Durban one night, Dawsie sidled up to me at about 1.30 a.m.

'All right?' he asked.

'Yeah, you all right?'

'Yeah,' he said, and then, 'tomorrow morning we're going to go for a run, you and me.' At that hour of the night, it's easy to agree.

'Yeah, yeah, whatever.'

I left the bar at about 3 a.m., sailing three sheets to the wind, and the early morning run wasn't exactly uppermost in my mind.

It seemed as though I'd just put my head on the pillow when someone was trying to wake me.

'Come on,' a voice said. 'It's time.'

Now I didn't care what I'd agreed the night before, I wasn't going for any run.

'You must be joking,' I mumbled.

'Come on,' he urged, 'we're going for a run.'

I tried a, 'No, no, no, no, we're not,' but Graham has a way of letting you know he's not taking 'no' for an answer. I stumbled out of bed, put on shorts, top, pair of runners and vaguely noticed that it was a beautiful morning, which made it like every other morning in Durban. We were staying in the Elengeni Sun Hotel on the beach and the setting is sensational – not that I was seeing it clearly that morning. Suddenly we were down on the beach, running, but I seemed to be on quicksand, plodding along 10 yards behind the oldest man in England's tour party. There were lots of runners on the beach, the surf looked magnificent, the sun was warm but not too hot and I found myself thinking this would be a beautiful time to be out – if you'd had more than three hours' sleep and less than three bottles of tequila.

But, wonder of wonders, I slowly began to come round. The first thought that struck me was, 'What am I doing out here?' The beach didn't seem to be coming to an end and I was too embarrassed to ask Graham to slow down or stop. I was supposed to be the young guy, but he was one of the fittest in the squad. We ran for about three miles before we could go no farther. 'Thank fuck for that,' I thought. After getting our breath back, he said, 'Come on, we'll run back,' but he was obviously feeling it himself because he added, 'on the road.' So we started off again and it's a funny thing but when you turn a horse homeward, his nose picks up a different scent and he finds new energy. We resumed at a bit of a jog but I was now up alongside Graham, not behind, and the speed crept up. Soon the talking stopped and we were getting faster and faster. With about half a mile to go, we were still level and it became a bit of a race – he sprinted, I sprinted, eye-balls out, and we reached the hotel, side by side, covered in sweat. I felt incredibly good. Dawsie couldn't leave it at that, though. 'Come on,' he said, 'let's finish off with a swim.' If you've ever seen the early-morning surf in Durban, you'll know what I mean when I say it can be fierce. The die-hard surfers were already out there, off the pontoons, but not too many swimmers. Even though we had been told it was dangerous to swim in the sea, and Jack Rowell had been emphatic, 'I don't want anyone swimming,' Dawsie was up for it.

'Are you sure we should do this?' I asked, but with such meekness, I wished I hadn't said it at all. Thankfully, Dawsie pretended he hadn't heard and was already halfway down the beach. 'Ah fuck it,' I said to myself, 'we're only going for a swim.'

We paddled out a bit, but the surf was much fiercer even than it looked. Anyway, I'm not great in the water. I've never been the strongest of swimmers and maybe, subconsciously, Francesca's death has made me more tentative. As the waves rolled in, I tried to keep diving under them, because you don't want them hitting you each time, but as I resurfaced from one, another came along and I was diving under again only just in time.

Next thing, I couldn't see Dawsie anywhere. We were a good 80 yards out and I was thinking, 'Where the hell is he?' I looked everywhere, my heart missing beats because I was thinking the worst. 'Jesus, Dawsie, please, where have you gone?' Then it suddenly dawned on me to turn back towards the beach to see if he was there. Sure enough, I saw this figure in the shallows, on all fours, clawing his way to the beach. It took me about three minutes to swim back because of the currents and the surf. He was spewing up a lot of seawater and needed a hand to get to the beach. Once we were there, I made sure he could breathe properly and that's when I noticed he was covered with horrible marks. He'd been stung to bits by jellyfish. He looked so bad I had trouble stopping myself laughing.

Apparently, he'd been hit by a wave, swallowed a ton of water and struggled to get back in. He probably didn't even feel the jellyfish. The stings didn't look great but they were secondary to the amount of water he'd swallowed. 'The stupid bugger,' I thought. 'I should have told him not to go near that water.' But I didn't dare say that to him. He spent three days in bed, throwing up a lot of the time. Of course, Jack Rowell wanted to know what had happened.

'Lawrence, what have you done to Dawsie?' he demanded. I let Dawsie answer for himself.

'Just a dodgy tuna sandwich after training,' he said.

For those three or four days, I did my best to look after him, as any room-mate would have done, but I did want him to get back to top form as quickly as possible because I really liked him.

It was actually a pretty amazing time to be in South Africa. Nelson Mandela had just been released from prison and had become the country's first democratic president. England was the first rugby nation to visit South Africa in this new post-apartheid era and nearly everyone made himself available for the tour. Every legend of my formative years was present – Carling, Andrew, Barnes, Richards, Moore, Dawe, the Underwoods. From Wasps, Damien Hopley, Dean Ryan and Steve Bates were there, as well as Rob Andrew, so even though it was my first tour with England, it wasn't difficult to integrate. What was really exciting was the sense of being in a country still overcome with emotion following great change. Politically and economically, South Africa was in a state of delirium. What struck me was that we had come at a time when South Africa was feeling really good about itself.

Lots of people were excited about the nation's future and those in the rugby community were just so happy that normal relations were resuming with the rest of the world. It was my first visit and this tour started my love affair with South Africa, both on the pitch and off it. Very early in the tour, I realised this country was truly a superpower in the sport. Always was, always will be. It was also a very interesting time to visit because rugby was in the act of switching from amateur to professional status, and it was clear to us the change had already been made in South Africa. New Zealand had changed too, and you could say the Italians had offered me what amounted to a professional contract back in 1991. England being England, we were the last to catch up. But it was good for us to be in South Africa, to be playing against a country where the whole attitude to rugby was professional and where the players were properly supported.

The England team had other concerns. Jack Rowell had just one year to get the squad right for the 1995 World Cup back in South Africa. One of his most important decisions on that tour was whether to mix and match his teams for the early games and encourage everyone to compete for Test places, or immediately divide his squad into dirt trackers and first team. The bold thing would have been to mix and match and, as a young player trying to climb the ladder, that's what I wanted. But right from the first game, it was obvious the squad was already split in Jack's head and he selected the dirt trackers for the opening game against Orange Free State in Bloemfontein. For all of us, it was the first experience of playing at altitude and our first taste of the fervour and physicality of South African rugby. They beat us and they beat us good and proper. If there was one thing I would learn from subsequent tours, it was that no matter where you are or who you're playing against, rule number one is win your first game. Our tour got off to the wrong start.

Off the pitch, Bloemfontein was a remarkable place. Certainly in 1994, it was the kind of place that, unless you had seen it, you would not have believed existed. We had come to South Africa having heard all the news about the end of apartheid and the great change sweeping the country – but no one had told a lot of the white folks in Bloemfontein. From what we could see, there was no such thing as anti-apartheid. Stuart Barnes, our No. 10, even wrote a piece for the *Daily Telegraph* suggesting that not much seemed to have changed in that corner of the country. In the lead-up to the game, the England party had attended a civic ceremony in which both teams were paraded in public. The entire proceedings were conducted in Afrikaans, something that made it difficult for us to feel involved. The whole ceremony felt more like a Nazi rally, and Stuart had written, 'Welcome to the Fourth Reich.' The locals weren't best pleased, and if they had been able to catch him, Stuart would have been hung, drawn and quartered. So they just made us pay in the match, which they were probably going to do anyway. It was the most hostile environment I had played in and the game didn't go well for me, not that it went well for any of us.

The difficulty for those who played was that we almost agreed with Jack Rowell's view of us as dirt trackers. I had a sense that my selection was a luxury choice, a young player brought along mostly for the experience. If things were going well, I would get a lot of opportunities. When we were turned over in that first game, it was clear there wouldn't be much for me. There were seven games left and as I scanned through the list, I couldn't see myself being selected for more than another two. That was disappointing but it wasn't going to get me down. 'If I'm going to play only another two out of seven games, I might as well have the craic,' I thought to myself. These were the days of the tour allowance and on the day the weekly amount was paid, I would end up in a casino with Stuart Barnes and Damien Hopley – seriously bad company, but we had such a laugh. We founded 'The Playboy Club', which was made up of those guys who clearly weren't going to get their rewards on the pitch if you get my drift. It included a number of the Wasps lads, who seemed to have that lust for city life, and a few like-minded Bath players. We're talking Steve Bates, Dean Ryan, Barnes, Adedayo Adebayo, Hopley, Mike Catt, myself.

Early in the tour, a social committee was appointed and, as one of the younger and more willing volunteers, I was invited to take my place. Obviously, not much time was wasted before I was at the hub of the committee's activities and took it upon myself to organise a 'Goodbye to Durban' beach party on the Sunday before we left. We had been there for almost 10 days and it was a chore I took to my heart. Durban is such a beautiful place. The invitations had to be special. In South Africa, England's rose carries a lot of weight so I had the symbol embossed on the invitations, which read: 'To celebrate their stay in Durban, the England Squad cordially invites you to be their guest at a party at Umhlanga Rocks...' In the days leading up to the party, I formally handed out these invitations to various ladies, ranging from the 18–22 age group for the younger gentlemen in the squad to more mature ladies in the 45–50 age group for the senior players. The barbecue was set up, food was bought, music was chosen, fireworks were ready – we were really rocking. This was going to be a fun party.

Then, the day before, our first team lost to Natal at King's Park. Now we'd lost the first two games of our tour and things were suddenly looking bleak. We were all supposed to have a day off on the Sunday but, because of this defeat, that was cancelled. Our coaches were clearly incensed. So those players who had not been involved in the King's Park game had to train on the day of the barbecue. The first-teamers, who'd actually lost to Natal, were free to attend the party I'd helped organise. While it was going on, Dick Best was putting us through what's known as a beasting session. The frustrations he felt after two defeats were taken out on us and I can tell you he must have felt pretty damn frustrated because the session lasted almost four hours. He seemed to enjoy it, and by the time he had finished with us, we could hardly walk, let alone think about catching the end of the party. I was glad the first team enjoyed themselves, though.

Before the first Test we had the honour of meeting Nelson Mandela and it led to one of rugby's most famous stories. The protocol is straightforward; our captain walks with President

Mandela and introduces him in turn to each member of the squad. There isn't time for any kind of detailed conversation, so what you do is shake the president's hand and maybe say, 'Lovely to meet you.' He will then say something appropriate and move on to the next in line. Our scrum-half, Dewi Morris, was always known as 'the blithering idiot' among the rest of the squad, because when he got a little over-excited, he would invariably come out with a load of rubbish. As President Mandela was getting closer to him, Dewi was obviously getting nervous. He wanted to say something more than the standard, 'Pleased to meet you,' and had been thinking about it. When the president put out his hand, Dewi shook it, seemed to hold on longer than most of us and then said, 'Do you have road tax over here?' The guys around him were thinking, 'What did he just say?' By the perplexed look on President Mandela's face, he hadn't a clue whether they had or not – after all, the man had just been freed after 26 years in prison. So he turned to his bodyguard and asked, 'Well, do we?' and the bodyguard just ushered him on to the next England player. This is one of the after-dinner stories that Jason Leonard and a few of the lads tell and there's no surprise there because it is hilarious.

The irony is that Dewi is now a well-respected television analyst but he did come out with some beauties in his time, purely because he got so hyped and over-excited. Another Dewi classic happened when he was playing for England against France. There was a ruck and the ball was clearly on the English side but Dewi was struggling to retrieve it because the French were preventing it from coming back. Dewi was having a fit, because no whistle had sounded for a penalty to England, and he started to shout, 'Monsieur, le ballon est ici, le ballon, ici,' which was very impressive until you heard the next voice. 'It's quite all right Dewi, I speak English,' said Stephen Hilditch, the Irish referee.

Having lost our first two matches on tour and not really impressed anyone in our other matches, England were completely written off before the first Test at the Loftus Versveld in Pretoria. But they went out and, against all the odds, smashed the South Africans in one of the best away performances I've ever seen from an England team. Tim Rodber, whom I found particularly hard to get along with when we were players, played the game of his life. It was a pleasure to watch. Then we did what most rugby teams do after a fantastic victory – we all went out together and had a great night. We were still getting our feet back on the ground when we played our next match, against Eastern Province in Port Elizabeth, which turned into an infamous bloodbath. From our point of view, their guys played as if intent upon inflicting as much physical damage as possible on us before the decisive second Test. Jon Callard was stamped on and needed 24 stitches in his head, Tim Rodber piled in looking for revenge and got himself sent off, Dean Ryan was involved in an almighty punch-up in the first minute and was carted off to hospital with a broken hand, and I got the shit kicked out of me at the bottom of a ruck. I was fine, I wasn't complaining, but the kicking of Jon Callard was unacceptable.

The match was a mess from start to finish and the South Africans succeeded in roughing us up. We had to use players off the bench who had played in the Test match four days earlier, something that wouldn't be countenanced in this day and age. Since the only player to be sent off was one of ours, our management team felt we had to do something to defend ourselves in the media, and so John Mallett and I were photographed to show how we had been the victims. OK, we'd had a bit of shoe pie and could display plenty of scars to prove it, but my attitude was, 'So what? It happens.' However, it was pointed out that if we made people aware of how we had been kicked, that might help Tim get a lighter ban or even get off. If it didn't succeed in doing that, at least it would deflect some attention from the sending off.

Playing South Africa is one thing; playing a wounded South Africa is quite another. For the second Test in Cape Town, they changed their tactics, learning from their mistakes in the first Test. They were like savages and I mean that in a positive sense. Sure, they gave us a bit of a kicking on the pitch, but also on the scoreboard. Shortly before the game, Dean Richards pulled a calf muscle so England needed a back-row player on the bench. I could see the coaches looking around, because they felt it wasn't a game to give an uncapped 21-year-old flanker his taste of full international rugby. But there wasn't anyone else and I was named on the bench. With 15 minutes to go, Ben Clarke went down injured and I started to warm up. But Ben recovered and I didn't get on. I have often wondered if I'd started my England career in Cape Town that afternoon whether I would ever have been heard of again. There was a lot of criticism of the players after that game and you always fear that because you're the new guy, the blame for a bad defeat might be inextricably linked to you. I wasn't complaining that I didn't lose my international virginity that day.

During the tour, Stuart Barnes and I became great friends. I related to his attitude off the pitch as well as on it. He was a bit cavalier, someone who enjoyed good food, good wine and good times. As for his rugby, he wanted to win. There was no doubt about that, but he had suffered the twists and turns of the selectors' knife so many times, he had got to the point where he didn't give a shit any more. His attitude was understandable and as long as you recognised the basis for it and you, as a young player, didn't become bitter and twisted, you could really enjoy the company of someone like that. It was great being with the Wasps guys, too, and I bonded with Dean Ryan in a way that hadn't happened at our club. In this tough and hostile world of South African rugby, I guess he looked out for me and we became firm friends.

Mike Catt also became a great friend from spending time together on this tour, and I got on well with Dick Best, whom I felt had put in a good word for me with Jack Rowell and had probably been the reason I was picked for the squad. Even if we lost a number of non-Test games, we actually shared the series, one each. Put that in the context of the All Blacks never having won a series in South Africa at that point in rugby's history and that's not bad. I played in just three matches out of eight, but couldn't claim to have been hard done by. This was one tough tour and not the ideal starting point for a slightly built 21-year-old back-row forward. I made sure to work hard at training and do everything asked of me, although, on one celebrated occasion, it was a close-run thing whether I'd actually get there at all.

The trouble began after a midweek game when a group of us went out for a quiet drink. Mike Catt had been brought up in South Africa and knew someone who was having a private party in Johannesburg, to which we were all invited. As well as Mike and myself, Damien Hopley, Steve Bates and Dean Ryan made up our group. At the party, we all had a good few drinks and, sometime during the evening, I fell asleep. Of course, instead of waking me up, they left me. I woke up at eight o'clock the next morning, training was due to begin at nine, which might not have been too big a problem if it wasn't for the fact that I was in Jo'burg and training was in Pretoria, about 45 minutes away. You can imagine the horror. I was thinking, 'I've been in the England squad for all of three weeks and now I'm going to be sent home in disgrace.' I could see the plane landing at Heathrow, a few photographers there to greet me. Unfortunately, there was no car in the house where I'd slept and, in a state of complete panic, I knocked on the door of the next-door neighbour. He had a pick-up truck in the driveway.

'Look,' I said, 'I'm going to have to borrow your car, mate.'

'Well, I'm sorry, you can't.'

'No,' I said, 'I'm sorry, you don't understand, I have to borrow your car. This is a life or death situation.'

Hearing that, he sharpened up his act. 'OK,' he said, 'where do we need to go?'

'Pretoria,' I said, 'and do you mind if I drive?'

'No problem.'

We were on the motorway in no time, and got there in 30 minutes. I tore up that road. This was the era when journalists and team used to stay in the same hotel and we were all encamped at the Holiday Inn. I drove straight down to the underground car-park, thanked the guy, told him he had a friend for life, took his address and promised he would be getting a couple of England shirts. Then I thought about my situation. I was still wearing the blazer and slacks that we'd to wear for the previous day's game. What if I were to meet Jack Rowell or one of the journalists in the lift? I ruled out the possibility of the journos – far too early in the morning for them but Jack was a possibility. Fortunately, I managed to get to my floor without meeting anyone, and slunk into my room where my room-mate, Tony Underwood, was pretty startled by what he saw. A lovely, teetotal bloke, Tony just said, 'Unbelievable,' and went on down to breakfast.

I got changed double quick, grabbed a bacon sandwich and tried not to seem in any hurry as I got on the team bus. At training, the boys were chuckling non-stop. It was like they left me in Jo'burg to test me, to see if I could get back in time. Fair enough. Since that day, I don't fall asleep without setting about five alarm clocks.

With the mix of characters we had on that tour, I was like a sponge, absorbing how these guys dealt with things while they were away. But as well as wanting to learn, I wanted to have fun, which has always been my way. Anyone looking for someone to lead astray would not have had to look very far. On another memorable occasion, the squad was taking a one-day trip to Sun City. It was sort of optional but everyone was expected to go and everyone wanted to go. For most of us it was our first visit to South Africa and our first opportunity to see Sun City. But the previous evening Mike Catt, Dean Ryan, Damien Hopley, Steve Bates and I went out for a few beers. Obviously, that got out of hand and, having got back rather late, we all missed the team bus the next morning.

It was Catty who phoned me. 'Look mate, great night, but we've just missed the trip.' I thought that put us in a lot of trouble but Catty said it really was optional and once that was pointed out, I became a lot more relaxed. We met after a quick breakfast and felt a bit disappointed to have missed out on Sun City. It was about a two-hour drive from Pretoria, and by the time we'd have hired a car and got going, there wouldn't have been any point. Then Catty came up with a bright idea. He knew a pilot who lived not that far away and would be able to take us up there in his little six-seater. It was fixed up in a few minutes. We chucked in a few rand each to pay the pilot and landed an hour before the team bus. Steve Bates wouldn't remember it as that straight-forward because he was feeling pretty sick on the flight and a couple of the other boys weren't great. Luckily, I was fine. After arriving, we went to the bar and were having a quiet pint when some of the lads on the bus began phoning us. 'What idiots! Missed the bloody bus,' they said. 'Complete losers.' We never said where we were and when they arrived, their faces dropped. 'Nice trip on the bus, boys? Our flight took twenty-seven minutes.' We had a great day in Sun City and, of course, we ended up in the casino where we decided that whoever won had to pay the pilot for the return trip.

Mike Catt and I still talk about that tour because it was such an eye-opening experience. You would be going into a bar and the security guy would say, 'Gentlemen, can you leave any firearms in your possession at the door?' 'I think you'll find that none of us is carrying guns,' I said the first time. Then you'd see a fight breaking out and you'd realise it was a sensible idea to get guys to hand in their guns as they entered. For me, it was a chance to dip my toe in the water of international rugby, to meet and get to know men

I regarded as icons of the English game, and I loved every minute of it.

After the tour to South Africa, I returned to Wasps and to the job of establishing myself as a regular first-team player. Dean Ryan remained the first choice No. 8 and when I was selected I found myself slotted in at No. 6 or No. 7, depending on the particular needs for that game. Jack Rowell was picking his World Cup squad and it was obvious that four of his five back-row players had to be Dean Richards, Tim Rodber, Ben Clarke and Neil Back. Steve Ojomoh and I were the two candidates for the fifth slot, and as Steve had already been capped, that gave him an advantage. Probably just as important was the fact that he was from Bath and Jack knew him far better than he knew me. There was a trip by England A to Australia and Fiji that I could have gone on but it would have meant postponing my exams at Kingston and while I would have done that for the World Cup, it didn't make sense to do it for an England A tour. Instead, I was put on the dreaded 'non-travelling reserve' list, which meant I had to keep training and be ready to answer the call should there be any back-row injuries. I did get a phone call from the RFU's Don Rutherford halfway through my exams, saying a couple of the back-row guys had injuries and weren't able to train and there was every chance I would be called upon to go, but it never happened.

In the event, I watched the 1995 World Cup at home in London, cheering on England, feeling pure joy after the quarter-final victory over Australia and then dread as Jonah Lomu announced himself on the greatest stage and cut England to shreds in the first 25 minutes of the semi-final in Cape Town. In terms of what they expected of themselves, England's World Cup was disappointing. England's problem then was that, as they had so little contact with the southern hemisphere teams, they were always going to struggle in back-to-back matches against them. Beating Australia in the quarter-final was like winning a World Cup final for them and we were always going to be vulnerable against New Zealand the following week. The Cooke/Carling generation was very successful; they won consecutive Grand Slams and they were unquestionably the kings of Europe, but they were never kings of the world. If you look back at their fixtures, you can tell that wasn't actually part of the grand plan. Yet they were an excellent England side.

That autumn, South Africa, the new world champions, came to Twickenham and I found myself on the bench, having a conversation with Graham Dawe. 'Well, mate, you look a lot better than the last time I saw you,' I said, thinking back to the jellyfish incident.

'You know what,' he said, 'I bet you get on today. I've sat here so many times, never got on, but you'll get on today.'

Substitutions were extremely rare. Another player had to be injured for you to get on, but I didn't disagree with Graham. I felt my time had come. Every time you play South Africa, you expect blood injuries and I was there as cover for all of the back five positions. In my eyes, it had taken me for ever to get to this point and I was desperate to get my first taste of international rugby.

It turned out that both Graham and I were right. My time had come. Tim Rodber sustained his injury and I replaced him about halfway through the second half. As I've already described, my first cap was everything I thought it would be, and more – truly one of the best moments of my life, despite the fact we didn't win. It's an unreal situation, being in a losing dressing room after your first cap. All your team-mates are disappointed, but inside you're completely elated and finding it hard to keep the smile off your face. But all the guys had been through this. They'd all had their first cap and knew what I was feeling. A lot of them came and shook my hand; I especially remember Graham Dawe and Jason Leonard coming over. I have often been asked in interviews about the proudest day of my rugby life and I struggle to find anything better than winning that first cap for England, especially as it was at Twickenham. The place has always had a special meaning for me: I lived in Barnes, went to school in Richmond, played in an Under-12 tournament across the width of the pitch at Twickenham, was present as a fan when England beat France 21–19 to win a Grand Slam, I'd lived on a houseboat in the area for three years and driven past the ground thousands of times. It felt like a home from home.

It was the days when the squad stayed at the Petersham Hotel in Richmond and the after-match banquet was a grand affair that the committee men seemed to love. These banquets are difficult for the players as one team is massively happy and the other is pretty low. Anyway, ultimately there wasn't much I would remember about it as I might just, maybe, have had a few drinks to celebrate. In those days, rugby and alcohol went hand in hand; petrol and cars, bread and butter. Alcohol was the life-blood of the after-match get-together at certain levels and for some players it probably still is; you chatted and shared a pint with the man you had played against. At the time that drinking culture was beginning to change. But, my team-mates told me, there was one tradition that was sacrosanct – the new cap had to have a drink with every member of the team, the choice of poison to be decided by his team-mate. I was up for that. I fancied myself as someone who could hold his own and, over the course of an evening, I didn't imagine 14 drinks would be impossible. I should have known better. The first drink was a very large glass of red wine, the second a few shots of tequila in one glass, the third was a pint of gin and tonic, so there's no way I'm going to remember the rest.

But, I'm told, I did have a drink with every member of the team. The original plan was to carry on after dinner to a London nightclub. However, I never quite got there, ending the night in a world of pain in my hotel room. Andy Robinson, who would go on to become England coach, was one of the guys who carried me upstairs. I crashed out, feeling very little and when I woke the next morning and saw the England cap and tie in my room, I was ecstatic. Looking back now and seeing how other guys have coped with the aftermath of their first cap, I realise I was stitched up on the drinks front. But that doesn't bother me because I'd represented my country at Twickenham and it was an extraordinary experience. The following week I played for Wasps and in the team list on the match programme it said: L Dallaglio*.

*Denotes international

8

The professionals

I t was at an away game for Wasps early in the 1995–96 season that the reality hit me – the great upheaval. Professional rugby was upon us. In England the game had remained pretty staunchly amateur. No one at Wasps was being paid and as a student at Kingston Poly, I was just pleased to be allowed to send in the odd expenses claim and get a little drinking money. Through the autumn of '95, the England squad still trained at Marlow Rugby Club and there was a wonderful amateurism in the way we went about our business. Training might be cancelled, for instance, because the pitch was waterlogged or because the floodlights weren't working. Marlow was a solid and well-established rugby club, where the facilities were actually quite good and afterwards we would all go into a dining room at the back of the clubhouse to eat food that had been prepared by the mothers and wives of Marlow members. They gave up their time and seemed to enjoy catering for us and we definitely enjoyed all the soup and bread rolls, and the chocolate we had with our cups of tea and coffee.

Then one evening, at that away game for Wasps, I was resting on my hotel bed when Dean Ryan, who was sprawled on the other bed, started talking.

'What would you do,' he asked, 'if you were offered quite a lot of money to go and play for Newcastle?'

He didn't say the offer had been made to him but I assumed it had, and was shocked that everything had moved on so quickly. Overtaken by the pace of change, the Rugby Football Union had declared a moratorium for that season, asking clubs to wait to see how professionalism developed in other rugby countries. Fat chance of that happening when it was obvious the game was going professional and everyone else was already reacting to the change. From Dean's question, it was clear Newcastle were not wasting much time.

'I'd be tempted to accept,' I said, 'especially at your age.'

'I think you're probably right.'

'You would be missed if you left,' I said.

'Yeah, but it would be good for you. If I left, you'd move to No. 8. You're going to have to take this club forward.'

Early in my career at Wasps, I'd felt Dean was holding me back. It was what a young, impatient guy was going to think but once I got a little older, I realised it was the right way. Dean was a very good No. 8 with an aggressive, abrasive, almost psychotic approach to the game. He was never going to be intimidated and when you played against him, you were in for a tough time. When you played alongside him, you were very grateful to have him on your side. His belligerent streak on the pitch tended to blind people to how bright he was about how the game should be played and how tactically astute. We both wanted to play No. 8, but the fact that he was the more senior, and also the team captain, meant I had to wait my turn. It also didn't help that Dean believed I was not good enough in the tight, which meant I played much of my opening season in the first XV at No. 6. Then, out of the blue, he was on his way to Newcastle and telling me, 'You're going to have to take this club forward.' I've wondered since if he hadn't been grooming me for a leadership role at the club all along.

Dean was just the tip of the professional iceberg. Soon afterwards, our international fly-half, Rob Andrew, declared he was also joining Newcastle, as player/coach. In no time, we realised Wasps were losing the spine of the team. As well as Rob and Dean, our scrum-half Steve Bates, our centre Graham Charles and the Irish and Lions loose-head prop Nick Popplewell were also on their way to Kingston Park. Not only were we saying goodbye to five of our key players, we were also losing part of our coaching team. Wasps has always been a player-driven club, and while Rob Smith, who's still at the club, was our coach at the time, Rob Andrew and Dean Ryan were important figures in the running of the team. Among the fans, some resentment surfaced because Rob had been the club's heartbeat – it was bad enough that he was leaving, but he was taking four of the best players with him as well. I didn't agree with the fans. Rugby was now a professional game and guys made career choices on the basis of what was best for them and their families. Over time, most of our fans came round to this way of thinking.

Rob's move to Newcastle shook the game. It was as though the club's owner, Sir John Hall, had pushed a big boulder to set it rolling and it was going to smash through everything in its way. Word got out that Rob would be paid £150,000 a year and suddenly every player was asking himself the same question: if that's what Rob's worth, what would I get if I moved? The signing by Newcastle of Rob and four other Wasps players led to a scramble by the other clubs to hold on to their players. If it could happen to Wasps, it could happen to every club. No one felt safe. Wasps being Wasps, we just sat back and watched while all this went on. Of all the professional clubs, we were not in a good position. We had a wonderful but substandard ground in deepest north-east London. It held 5,000 people and it took a big match to fill the ground. Leicester were in the best position, with their huge fan base and their Welford Road ground. Most importantly, they were already making a profit.

Wasps was a ship with the potential to sink. We didn't have Leicester's fan base, we didn't have Harlequins' magnificently located ground nor its corporate muscle, and we didn't have a wealthy backer, such as Nigel Wray, who had taken over Saracens. Unlike Bath, Gloucester and Northampton, Wasps didn't have the support of a particular town. There was no tangible reason to suggest we would be able to survive professionalism. Yet there was no obvious reason why so many good players had come to Wasps through the years. In the old amateur days, it certainly wasn't for the business contacts. There was just something about the place, something indefinable. My first evening at training left me totally confused. 'This,' I thought, 'is an absolute shithole. It's in the middle of nowhere in north London, it's a nightmare to get to and yet the guy I've just spoken to lives in Blackheath and drives from there to here every Tuesday and Thursday evening.' I tried to work out why but could only come up with an 'x factor' that made the place special. Everyone travels with baggage but at Wasps, you naturally left it at the gate and had a great time during the three hours you were there. There was an honesty about the place. You worked really hard and there were no pretensions, no single stereotypical Wasps player. I'm not saying other clubs don't have a similar mix of players but ours seemed unique. You walked out on that training ground and everyone was equal. There was no community around which the club was built, which might have acted as a barrier to some, creating a them-and-us situation. In fact, often nobody had a clue who you were or where you had come from.

I've always wondered what it would be like to play for Leicester or Bath or Northampton, where the team is part of the town. Wasps felt as though it had been dumped in the wrong place, which wasn't exactly surprising considering we would have been one of the RFU's founding members if our representative hadn't turned up at the incorrect venue for the inauguration ceremony. That said everything about Wasps and it was the way we meant to continue – completely disorganised.

Yet the club developed an identity and became known as a place that welcomed the waifs and strays of the rugby world. If you were a Kiwi or Australian wanting to play rugby in London, you felt comfortable in the midst of our ground. People got drawn to the club, spent a few years there and then went back to where they came from. The ethos was straightforward: hard work and no bollocks. What didn't matter was your age or your status in the game – 30 or 22 years old, 82 caps or none, relatively speaking, everyone was treated the same.

It was a genuine rugby club. The bar had the kind of atmosphere that, sadly, you don't often find in the game of today. Now it's corporate thinking and the aim is to make money. Recovery drinks have taken the place of the after-match pint, and the sprint to the bar has been replaced by the warm-down. Afterwards, everyone wants a piece of the players – parents, fans, sponsors, corporate guests – whereas the guys used to end up in the company of their fellow men. Nowadays the only time you are guaranteed to be together is on the pitch.

Of course, it was inevitable that professional rugby would change things and a lot of good has come from it, but I liked the old routine of playing the match and then being off-duty. It was just more fun – you stayed at the club, knowing that Louis would keep the bar open, the pints would keep coming and if you got hungry, you'd all head down to Sudbury Town for a curry. If you had another game the following day, you might end up sleeping in the bar. The next morning there would be a head count and a check to see that everyone was in one piece. There always seemed to be a story, a bit of collateral damage to someone who had drunk too much, and most of us who played in that era have never really lost the thirst for a pint after the game. You'd sit down and talk about it. You may not have played the best game of your career, but over a drink, you'd realise it was not the end of the world, and it's always worth taking the time to enjoy the moment and savour the company of the guys you're with.

However, when the curtain came down on amateur rugby in the autumn of 1995, it wasn't the past that concerned us but the future. Wasps had lost a third of their first XV and the club couldn't afford to give up any more. Players, on the other hand, didn't want to miss an opportunity, and no one had any idea what the RFU's 'moratorium' meant. Word spread that clubs had started to pay their players to ensure they wouldn't leave and whether this was against the rules, no one knew. Lawlessness ruled and, even without a backer, Wasps' management knew they had to do something and agreed to pay the players £250 per game. From my point of view, that was fine because I was still at Kingston Poly and didn't need a lot of money. With Dean's departure, I had a chance to establish myself as the team's No. 8, and the loss of the five of them gave me an opportunity to move up a couple of places in the team's pecking order.

As Dean had been captain, that created another problem for the club, but I didn't give a second's thought to it. If I had been opening a book on the next skipper, I would have chalked myself up as a 50–1 outsider. I had some form, having captained the Under-19s and the second team on a few occasions, but many senior players were still around, who were far better talkers than I was and understood the game better than I did. Even at 50–1, I wouldn't have been taking a punt on myself.

One afternoon I was in the library at Kingston. Note that careful choice of words. I could have said, 'I was working in the library at Kingston,' but that wouldn't have been accurate. The truth is I went there to check out a fellow student, Alice Corbett, whom I knew and quite fancied. In the middle of my afternoon of Alice-watching – and it should be said that she was working quite hard – my phone rang. Shouldn't have had it on in the library, I know, but I was glad I did because it was Rob Smith, Wasps coach.

'Lawrence,' he said, 'would you be prepared to captain Wasps?'

Amazed as I was, I said what I had said to most things in life – 'Yes.'

It is when you put the phone down on something like that that you realise what you've done. I was 23. There were guys on the Wasps team who were 10 years older than that and I wasn't at all sure how well my appointment would go down with them, but clearly Rob Smith, and perhaps some other people at the club, thought I could do the job.

My first game as captain was against Leicester at Sudbury and although we didn't win, we played well and certainly made it hard for them. After that game I was named in the England squad for the game against South Africa at Twickenham, and what would be my first cap. At Wasps, we sat down as a group of players and talked about our target for the season. It was an interesting meeting because not one of us had a contract or any kind of guaranteed future in professional rugby – Wasps just didn't have the organisation nor the finances to do things quickly – but we were determined to be competitive. We spoke about the European Cup, which would involve English clubs for the first time the following season, and decided we had to qualify for that. We didn't know who the club was going to put on contracts but if we were in the European Cup, Wasps would be more attractive to a potential investor and therefore make it more likely that most of the players would be kept on. To get a European Cup place we had to finish in the top four and that became our focus. It was a mature approach from a group of mostly young players and that

← Ah, the classic seventies children-in-the-garden picture. Francesca had just got into the Royal Ballet School, aged eight, one of eight chosen from 4,000 interviewees.

↓ My West End days. Luckily rugby took over or who knows what my dress sense would have turned out like.

↓ Mum and Dad have always been the most supportive parents anyone could wish for, especially after everything I put them through as a teenager.

↓ Despite losing my sister to the Thames, I always felt at home moored at Teddington on *Bardot*.

↑ This plaque was laid in Southwark Cathedral, close to where Francesca died when the *Marchioness* went down, for the ten-year memorial service.

→ Collecting my MBE – a very proud day.

↓ Alice and I got married in Italy in July 2006, with Enzo, Ella and Josie sharing the happy day with us.

↑ Not quite the full international. The 1994 South Africa tour was pretty brutal from the off; me, John Mallett and Victor Ubogu trying to placate the hosts.

↓ Didn't do much good though.

← My first Wasps start in September 1993, with Rob Andrew and me trying to trap Harlequins' Will Carling.

↓ Thoroughly beating champions Toulouse in the 1996 Heineken Cup after a 49–22 thrashing at Munster a week previously. I thought it was the best club game I've ever played in – shame it wasn't enough to take the title.

↓↓ Wasps won the first professional league title – the Courage League – in April 1997, despite my rubbish tackling of Grant Seely of Northampton.

↑ Celebrating with Chris Wright after winning the 1999–2000 Tetley Bitter Cup against Northampton.

→ Despite Danny Grewcock's [right] best efforts by stomping on my groin during the game, we still whipped Bath 48–30 to win the Parker Pen Challenge Cup on 25 May 2003.

↓ A week later we were on form again versus Gloucester in the Zurich Premiership final.

↑ After years of training and building up our team, we finally managed to taste European victory by beating Toulouse in the 2004 Heineken Cup final.

↓ Not keeping up our form following that Cup win. Me, Josh Lewsey and Matt Dawson losing against Leicester at Welford Road the following season.

← Always a pleasure to play on the same pitch as Johnno, but even more so when beating Leicester to take the 2005 Zurich title.

↑ A text-book tackle? Andy Hazell of Gloucester has a go during a 2005–06 Guinness Premiership match.

↓ That makes three Premierships in a row, doesn't it?: 14 May 2005, a proud day for all of us, especially Warren Gatland.

Champions again. Beating Leicester on 20 May 2007 in the Heineken Cup final was a fantastic end to the season.

OFFSIDE

realism helped us through the season. We ended up finishing fourth.

I enjoyed that first experience of captaincy. During my school years, I had been marked down as someone who had the potential to take on responsibility but at that stage, I wasn't ready. The captaincy of Wasps came at the right time. It became apparent that I wasn't afraid to speak my mind before, during and after games. I used to be pretty forthright in spelling out whatever I felt the situation demanded and, with the journalists, I called it as I saw it. Excuses didn't interest me. I would shout and scream at my team-mates if I felt that was what was needed. Whether people responded positively or not was down to them. If you have to be a hard taskmaster, so be it. As captain, I tried to be our best player and was satisfied I wasn't asking people to do what I wouldn't do myself. It was also important I didn't alienate the senior players, who clearly had a lot to offer. I didn't always get that bit right, mind you; I could be a touch hot blooded and hot headed in those early years and tactically, I had a lot to learn. It is only really in the last five or six seasons that I have come to appreciate the importance of getting the game plan right and, similarly, it took me a while to learn how to get the best out of people.

Every time we played Newcastle, it was billed as a grudge match but I didn't buy that. Our players left for Newcastle because they were offered financial deals that secured their immediate futures. They didn't have a problem with Wasps. Dean Ryan spent 10 years of his life at the club and you can't just toss that to one side because he's accepted a very good offer to play elsewhere. Anyway, every match is a grudge match if that's what you want it to be. When we played Harlequins, it was 'the haves against the have-nots'. Saracens were our north London enemy. Leicester were Leicester. You could go on. Now Gloucester are supposed to hate us. But of course, following the departure of those five, games against Newcastle were interesting. My feeling was pretty simple – you don't take our players and then expect to beat us. We won most of the time but Rob Andrew justified his decision to move to Newcastle when he led the club to the first division title in 1998.

After that first season of what was virtually semi-professional rugby, things improved for Wasps. Businessman Chris Wright bought the club in June 1996 for a nominal sum after agreeing to take over the debts. With Chris came financial stability. I'm not sure that he was a huge rugby fan, but he recognised the opportunity of becoming involved with a club that owned its own ground, and had a lot of history and tradition. He saw the possibility of developing a brand in the new era of professional rugby. Suddenly we had a future and everyone was much more positive about it. We held on to the rest of our players, which was a very strong signal. Things changed rapidly. Instead of continuing to play at our homely, but limited, ground at Sudbury, we switched our 'home' games to the Queens Park Rangers football ground at Loftus Road in Shepherd's Bush. Even though I'm a Chelsea supporter, I still appreciated the chance to play on a wonderful pitch in a stadium with a 22,000 capacity, which is more than three times greater than the biggest crowd we could accommodate at Sudbury – not that we ever filled Loftus Road, mind, but with a crowd of 8,000 or 9,000, there was still a great atmosphere. To walk into that ground, having come from Sudbury, was like leaving a Mini Metro for a Rolls-Royce. It was a huge upgrade. We all had our own peg in the changing room and even the showers were more or less warm, provided you got there in reasonable time. There were other advantages. Regardless of the weather, we didn't have to postpone games. The pitch had under-soil heating and no matter how low the temperatures dropped, we knew our game would go ahead. The drainage was excellent, so it didn't matter how much it rained, and even if the surface could be greasy and slippery, the pitch didn't really cut up because the grass, a Dutch variety, was the best that money could buy. We settled into our new 'home' surroundings very quickly, but our opponents found it tough. Knowing that it was smaller and a lot narrower than the average rugby ground, we did our team runs there and made sure our kickers understood the dimensions of the pitch. We were also very conscious of how small the dead-ball areas were – if you went wide, you shouldn't try to take your opposite man on the outside, not unless you wanted to join spectators in the third row of the lower stand. So our wingers always stepped back inside and kept the ball alive.

Our first-ever game at Loftus Road was against Saracens, and we felt as though we had left our comfortable, old world and landed on an entirely different planet. In one respect it seemed complete lunacy. How else could I explain a situation where I was leading Wasps on to a famous football ground to fight for league points against a Saracens team containing Michael Lynagh and Philippe Sella, who happened to be two of the most talented and best-known rugby players in the world? We were amazingly pumped up for the game, because we'd been drumming it into ourselves that to make the move a success, we had to win our first outing. We had to prove to ourselves from the very first match that it was a good place for us to play. That day there was a crowd of about 12,000 or 13,000, and the spectators seemed to be virtually on top of us. We won emphatically. Michael Lynagh won't remember the match fondly because Alex King and I put a double tackle on him early, causing him to fracture his collarbone. To this day, Alex takes the credit for that hit, which set the tone for the game and for our first season at Loftus Road. To Lynagh's credit, he had his revenge on us in the following year's Tetley's Cup final.

We still trained at Sudbury, but it wasn't just the venue for our home matches that changed. Nigel Melville became coach and a very influential figure at the club. He had played scrum-half for Wasps and was a hugely talented player, who would have played many more times for England than he did but for injury. There is a saying at the club, 'Once a Wasp, always a Wasp', and Nigel was proof of that. So am I, I guess. At a time when no one was sure about how often we should train and for how long, Nigel put the first structures of the professional era in place for us. The difficulty was that there was no established way of doing things, no right or wrong way. You just had to find your own path, and very quickly. A lot of clubs were training morning and afternoon, all day, every day, but that wasn't our approach. We worried about generating over-familiarity, because it was a long season and given that we were going to spend a lot of time together, we didn't want to be sick to death of each other by Christmas. The thinking was good but we didn't always execute the strategy correctly. We often did too much but, regardless of that, Nigel deserves enormous credit for the way he set things up. He took on the job when the game was changing radically and Wasps didn't have anywhere near the necessary backroom personnel in place.

Nigel had to be coach, selector, bus driver, groundsman, travel organiser – he was basically running an amateur organisation in a professional league. He must have felt as if he was in charge of a Sunday team, coming in early to turn on the hosepipes so the pitch was watered, then spending half the day on the phone to agents, trying to sign players, and not forgetting to book the coach for Saturday's away game. Maybe he wasn't the best at delegating or maybe he had no choice and had to do everything himself. Other clubs were well ahead of us in terms of their readiness for the professional game, especially Leicester, who were in their kit and on the start line at the very moment the game changed. But with major input from Nigel, a very good group of players and two important signings, we were in surprisingly good shape in that first professional season and actually won the Courage League Division One title. We had Nick Greenstock and Fraser Waters, Paul Sampson, Gareth Rees, Matt Greenwood, Buster White, Chris Wilkins, the old Gloucester hooker Kevin Dunn, Darren Molloy and Paddy Dunston, and most of them had been at Wasps for a long time. We also had the Scottish locks Andy Reed and Damien Cronin, and younger guys coming through, such as Lawrence Scrase, Alex King, Peter Scrivener, Andy Gomersall, Simon Shaw, Will Green and me.

Gareth Rees was a fine example of the kind of person you found at the club. He went to Harrow school and played in the Pilkington Cup final for Wasps as a teenager, and then came back to the club a few years later, playing a big part in our initial success story. Gareth, a great rugby player and a great character, played in four consecutive World Cups for Canada. During what was an uncertain time at Wasps, he was an experienced and cool head. Nigel used to say he was the Peter Schmeichel of rugby because when he played full-back for us at Loftus Road, no one was able to run around him. He won't mind me saying this but if anyone tried, they would have an awful long way to run. Full-back wasn't his favourite position but he played it well and was good under the high ball. He was also a points machine. We used to call him 'the money ball' because in the early years we were playing to win bonuses and if there was a kick to secure a win, Gareth didn't miss. As he was brought up in the amateur days, he knew how to achieve the balance between playing hard on the pitch and enjoying himself off it. I, for one, admired him for that.

As I said, our season was enhanced by two very different signings. Chris Sheasby joined us from Harlequins, which was unusual because 'Quins players rarely came to Wasps, especially someone like Sheasby who had been a lifelong Harlequins player. He proved a great acquisition and played tremendously well for us. Ironically, he returned to 'Quins after one season because they were prepared to offer us a substantial fee to get him back. We didn't want to lose him but it made business sense.

The other bloke who joined us left a deep impression on all who trained and played with him and his legacy remains important to the club.

Early in the season, Wasps announced the signing of Inga Tuigamala, who had been playing professional rugby league with Wigan. His background lay in rugby union and he had played for both Samoa and the All Blacks. Because of what he had achieved in both codes, he was a genuine world superstar and we were intrigued to find out what kind of character he was. While he played well for us, and his presence created space for those around him, he was not at his best. His time in rugby league had taught him to retain possession in the tackle, which left him with a habit that led to the concession of many penalties in union. But it was a small price to pay for the enormously positive influence he had on a club that had just embraced professionalism. He was a role model for everyone at Wasps and I very much include myself in that. We thought we knew what professionalism involved, but we were nowhere near. Inga showed us that you don't train because you have to; you train because you want to and it's your job. Tuigamala had that mentality and he saw the game as a way of life. More than any of us, he understood what being a pro meant.

He brought his own ice-pack to training, he brought his own shaker to mix his recovery drinks and, for us, this attention to detail was from a different world. We were still trying to work out if the club or the players should be providing the ice-packs and recovery drinks. Wonderful talent and a great work ethic weren't the only things Tuigamala brought to the club. He also came with a deep Christianity and a very correct lifestyle. He didn't drink or smoke and, at least in terms of the alcohol, that made him quite different from most rugby players of the time. Life for him wasn't about wine and women. He was a big family man and very committed to doing his job correctly. Few people trained harder and no matter what, he stuck to his values. He would take his bible almost everywhere and was very protective of his beliefs. In a lads' culture, he was a man apart, and as you may imagine, it didn't necessarily make him popular, but no one took liberties with him – partly because of his physical stature no doubt, but also because his faith was so obviously genuine. If you wanted to find out more, he would happily share his experiences with you, but if you didn't, he would never try to impose his views on you.

The thing about Tuigamala was his humility, and the fact that he was a lovely guy. He came to us and showed us a better way to do things. We weren't so backward though – there was a general acceptance that, as professionals, we had to become more scientific about our training and, especially, go on a serious weight-training programme. Suddenly, jobs and futures were at stake and if the coach said you had to get bigger, you got bigger. Having Inga come along, someone who had been a successful professional for a number of years, was like seeing the living example of all the theory our coaches were telling us. If he got a bang or a knock, he did all the right things to ensure it didn't get worse. He also treated his team-mates with respect, as he had always done, and that was great for us. And, of course, he had a winner's mentality. When you've come from the All Blacks and the Wigan Warriors team of that time, you don't go out not expecting to win. His first game for us was Bath away, which must have been bizarre for him because he was facing his friend and former team-mate at Wigan, Jason Robinson, and another rugby league star, Henry Paul. We didn't tend to win away at Bath in those years but we did on that occasion and it gave us a lot of belief that we could go on and claim victory in the league. Due to commitments in New Zealand, Tuigamala had to leave before the end of the season, but his influence carried on for long after he departed.

*

If our league campaign went well, it was a different story in the Heineken Cup. Having worked very hard the previous season to make sure we qualified, we were drawn in a group that included Munster and Toulouse. It wasn't exactly what we'd hoped for but we didn't have a clue what we were getting into. In those days, you played each team just once and we were away to Munster and home to Toulouse.

To us, Munster's Thomond Park was just another rugby ground until we found ourselves on the wrong end of an absolute kicking. They hammered us by 27 points and gave us a real Thomond Park experience. It was one of those games where they started at a hundred miles an hour, went in front early and everything we tried just made things worse. Three of their tries came from interceptions. I threw one of them and if the ground had opened up, I would have been happy to be swallowed. We stayed at the Two Mile Inn outside Limerick and after the match it felt like the ten-and-a-half-mile inn. Munster fans might be surprised at this but I always wanted to go back and have another shot at Thomond Park. Every year afterwards, if we were in the Heineken Cup, I wanted us to draw Munster but it never happened. The only time we met again in the competition was in the 2004 semi-final at Lansdowne Road.

Typically, I'd arranged a little r&r with friends from Carlow and didn't go back home with the team. Instead, I ended up going to Limerick races the day after the match. Not exactly ideal but I'd had no inkling the match was going to be a calamity when I'd made the plans. The day at the races was fun and I justified it on the basis that we had been comprehensively outplayed and there was no point in whinging. And you'll have to agree, it took some courage for a Wasps player to show up at Limerick races after what happened the previous day. I didn't escape. The humiliation continued: 'Jaysus, Dallaglio, you were fucking useless yesterday,' was one of the nicer comments. To add insult to injury, I didn't back any winners, either. But I did learn something from my decision to stay in Limerick. I sensed it at the time and it subsequently became clear to me that I was wrong not to return to England with the team. We'd had a very bad day and, as captain, I should have stayed with my team-mates.

At Loftus Road a week later we played Toulouse, who were the Cup holders and kingpins of European rugby at the time. Having been murdered in the press for our abysmal performance against Munster, there was a lot of soul-searching among the coaches and players. We prepared extremely well and this is what makes rugby such a fascinating game – one week can change everything. Having been thrashed in Ireland, we absolutely smashed Toulouse, scoring 77 points to their 17 and giving them an experience they wouldn't forget. One of their players tried to run round the outside of one our defenders early in the match and ended being battered into an advertising hoarding. That ended his afternoon. French teams don't travel well and before half-time, the Toulouse players were shrugging their shoulders, throwing their hands up in the air, puffing their cheeks, blowing out. Every bit of body language said the same thing – 'This isn't fair.' Everything we tried came off. Chips bounced up into our hands, inside passes found runners steaming through gaps, and in the end, we were running the ball from all parts of the pitch. We did a Toulouse on Toulouse and it was probably one of the greatest performances I've seen from any club team. When I speak to Toulouse players now they still talk about it.

But our extraordinary victory wasn't enough to rescue our European Cup campaign and we were left to concentrate on the league. It came down to a battle between Leicester and us. Getting towards the business end of the campaign, we played them at Welford Road before 17,500 of their fans and, in an amazing atmosphere, they beat us by a couple of points. The narrowness of the defeat convinced us we could go on and win the league, which we did by six points.

One of the more interesting games was a home match against Bath, which ended in a draw. Bath still had Ben Clarke, Phil de Glanville, Jerry Guscott and Mike Catt, and were a class act. Unlike when we beat them at their ground earlier in the season, we didn't have Tuigamala any more, and on a beautifully sunny April afternoon, this was a much tighter game. With time running out, Guscott kicked ahead for Adedayo Adebayo, who appeared to step into touch before scoring. Then immediately some Bath player went off with a blood injury and Jon Callard came off the bench to kick the conversion from the touchline. He went off again straightaway, American-football style. Fair play to them, they bent the rules and got the two extra points. I was subsequently told by a Bath player that no one was cut; they just dabbed a bit of ketchup on a player, rushed him off the field and got Callard on. Hey ho, you do what you have to do to win, and it didn't stop us fighting all the way to the finish. In injury time, when they must have thought the game was won, Alex King scored for us. It wasn't quite at the corner flag but it was definitely beyond the easy zone and, in the circumstances, it was a tough kick for Gareth Rees. But we don't call him 'money ball' for nothing and he didn't miss.

That draw may have felt like a win, but we needed a real one at Northampton in our second-to-last game to become champions. We went up there and on a day when the pitch was wet and the ball greasy, we won well. It was my first major trophy with Wasps and the team's first title under my captaincy, but clinching it away at Northampton felt a little anticlimactic. We made the best of it, though – we've always been a club to enjoy a party.

Nigel Melville did something quite clever and a little sneaky at the beginning of the following week by getting us T-shirts that said, 'Wasps, 1997 Champions'. We had to wear them in the days before our final league game, away to Harlequins. 'Wouldn't it be great to go out as champions and win our last game?' he said. Even though we'd already clinched the league, having the T-shirts made us all think about the egg on our faces if we lost this match, and the thought was enough to ensure we won well. We celebrated with our fans at Harlequins and then all went back to Sudbury for a party. Although we had played our matches at Loftus Road, Sudbury was still our true home and the party was held in the bar upstairs, a place that had so many happy memories for all of us.

To win the league in the first year of professional rugby was tremendously exciting for the club and very reassuring in terms of its place in the new game. Just the season before, there had been real concern about Wasps' future, but we hung on and when Chris Wright took over, the ship was steadied. Great credit must go to him and to his right-hand man at Wasps, Charles Levison, and also to Ivor Montlake for successfully bringing the club into the professional era. From my own point of view, I felt relieved to have been part of a successful team so early on in my career and tremendously proud to captain a side that sat at the top of English rugby for that season.

9

Changing guard at Buckingham Palace

Alice and I disagree on some of the details of the evening we first saw each other, but that's not a bad thing. If you're going to end up with someone long term, you've got to understand you're not going to agree on everything. What's not disputed is that we were on a red double-decker bus. We were both going to the party of a friend, Katie Agnew, at San Lorenzo's in Knightsbridge, and we definitely noticed each other. She wore a black cat suit, had her hair done in a high ponytail and carried what looked like a present. I had a bunch of flowers. Although I'd never seen Alice before, I knew about her from Katie. Whenever I asked Katie if she had any nice friends for me to meet, she'd always say, 'Alice Corbett, you'd like her.' So she invited both of us to her party. But on the bus, we had no idea who the other was. Alice looked gorgeous, I noticed that much, and I was tempted to start up a conversation – 'You're going to someone's party, why don't we swap presents?' – thought about it and decided not to be ridiculous. This was trendy London, not a local dance in the village hall. In any case, I was too shy to take the initiative. And, it should be said, I had a girlfriend at the time.

On that bus journey, Alice says we smiled at each other. I would imagine I was staring at her, making it pretty obvious I was impressed. She knew the right stop in Knightsbridge but was not well acquainted with London, so didn't know exactly where the restaurant was. She says she wondered who the young man with the flowers was and came within an inch of asking me how to get to San Lorenzo's. I got off the bus ahead of her, round by Scotch Corner, and as it was beginning to rain, decided to take a cab the short journey to the restaurant. Unthinking, I left the most stunning-looking girl I've ever seen clicking in her high heels through the puddles. As the taxi moved off, I thought it was a shame I would not see her again. She later told me I looked like Del Boy, jumping into a taxi after travelling four-fifths of the way by public transport.

About five minutes after I got to the party, Alice walked in and growled at me, something about not offering a girl a ride. 'Oh dear,' I thought, 'got off on the wrong foot there.' A few drinks later I looked at the table plan and found my name alongside Alice's. 'Well done, Katie. You've got me a result here,' I thought. Alice was on my left and another girl I didn't know was on my right. I spoke to them both through the meal and when Alice asked what I did, I was sure that here was an opportunity to impress. 'I'm about to go to university and I play rugby for Wasps,' I said. As soon as the word 'rugby' came out of my mouth, I noticed Alice's attitude cool. She had a boyfriend at the time and had come from Devon where a big night out was a disco at the rugby club. It felt like she knew all the stories about drinking games and the exaggerated role of alcohol, and that whole scene didn't impress her. Once she came to London, she wanted to leave rugby club nights behind. Her look said, 'I'm sorry, I don't do rugby players, thanks very much.' I asked her what she did and she talked about studying art and doing a bit of modelling, and seemed pleased with her situation in life. 'Oh,' I said, and then made conversation with the girl on my right. Alice and I did continue to speak through the meal – pleasant, if matter-of-fact, conversation. She had to leave early that evening, which isn't a habit that has followed her through life.

A day or two later, I thanked Katie for the party and asked for more information about Alice.

'Was she seeing someone?'

'Yeah, but it mightn't be permanent. He's almost ten years older than her.'

That was encouraging. Both of us were due to start at Kingston University, so it was likely we would run into each other there. The meeting at San Lorenzo's proved there was an attraction but nothing would happen for years. Both of us were in relationships and while rugby consumed a lot of my spare time, Alice was serious about her course at Kingston. We did meet there, invariably in the bar, where I played table football and she dropped in for a herbal tea and a break from the library. Her course in art and interior design was demanding and based on lots of coursework. After buying her a tea, we would chat for a bit before she had to dash back to the library. Alice says now that when she used to see me, her heart would beat faster, like she was having palpitations. Obviously, I never noticed much of that. Every so often, I'd suggest she should come and see my houseboat. Even if both of us thought it would have been fun, it never happened. Katie would organise different evenings where we were supposed to get together but there would always be something to thwart us – one of us would let her down at the last minute, or I would arrive late on the very evening Alice had left early.

My academic career at Kingston collided with my rugby career. Being part of the England team that won the Rugby World Cup Sevens led to a lot of invitations to play Sevens tournaments in the most exotic places – Dubai, Punta del Este, Lisbon, Amsterdam – and invariably I said yes. These were places I had never been to and, as people were prepared to pay my way, I was prepared to postpone my essays and the like. As at Ampleforth, study wasn't allowed to get in the way of a good time. It did make life a little disorganised. I'd return from a great week away and wouldn't have a clue what was going on in my course. Mostly I spent my time at Kingston going around the campus in search of Alice. She remembers one particular meeting where I was sitting on a wooden seat that went round the trunk of a tree.

'How are you?' she said. 'Haven't seen you for ages.'

I'd been watching her in the library of course, but didn't mention that. 'I'm all right,' I said. 'I've just been asked to be captain of Wasps. It's all changing for me. I never seem to be here and when I am, I'm always on the phone. I don't know what's going on really.'

She says we were ships passing in the night. I wanted something to happen but beyond asking Katie to organise something that got us all together, I wasn't much good. Alice thought we'd be good together as we were both smiley and easygoing, and not too deep. But being easygoing meant we let things drift for a long time. I suppose as the man, I have to take most of the responsibility for that. Then Katie had a baby boy, Joseph, and asked me to be godfather. After the christening in the church, we all retreated to the Chelsea Ram, just off Lots Road in Chelsea. Lots of Katie's friends were there, including Alice, and it was a cracking day. Of course, I got involved with a few of the lads. I've never been good at breaking away from their company when there's a bit of a session on. In this respect, I'm the archetypal rugby player – I love that boys' environment, talking about the game and the gossip around it. Blame Ampleforth and four years of living in an all-male school. That evening, I did at least keep glancing over to where Alice was and noticed she was drinking a fair bit. 'My God,' I was thinking, 'she's still here.'

Alice's view of the entire evening is slightly different. She had just broken up with her boyfriend of three years and hoped something might happen between us. Knowing I would be at little Joseph's christening, she went to the party thinking that if there was to be nothing else, she'd settle for a one-night stand. Alice says she was looking at me through a reflection in a mirror but I looked so vacant, she was trying to work out if anyone was at home. She feared I had the emotional development of a cardboard box. Then, towards the end of the night, she wandered over to me.

'Well,' she said, 'are you going to buy a girl a drink?'

'What would the girl like?' I asked.

'A Jack Daniel's and Coke,' she said, which was my drink at the time.

From there we went to a café on the King's Road for breakfast, then on to a friend's house to play cards and after that I offered to take her home because, by now, my rugby career had earned me a sponsored BMW. I suspect I shouldn't have driven after such a big night out but I was no doubt showing off slightly.

'Where do you live again?' I asked.

'Brixton.'

'Brixton?' I repeated.

'Have you never been south of the river?' she said.

Of course I had, but I wanted to make it sound as though I was really prepared to go out of my way. We got to the flat Alice shared with her lovely friend, Lisa Greenaway, and had another breakfast. Every so often I went over to the window of their upstairs flat and looked down on the road. 'Just checking the car's still there,' I said.

I immediately took to Alice's independence, the fact that she was her own woman and had plenty of confidence. It's not unusual for girls to look with a little awe on sportsmen but she was the opposite. If she'd been over-enthusiastic, that might have put me off but there was no danger there, cool as anything. Her relationship had just ended, I was in a relationship that was ending and, at last, I'd found a woman who'd been in front of my nose for four years. The next day I showed up at her place with a cup of tea and some Viennese biscuits, because she was staying at home to finish some work. We had a big chat and decided to try to make a go of it. We then both spent a little time sorting out our respective relationships, speaking to each other on the phone, seeing as much of one another as my rugby and her work would allow. Then along came an opportunity for us to spend a few days together – an invitation to play beach rugby in Portugal allowed me to take a guest.

This was June 1996. My first season as Wasps captain had ended in that respectable fourth place in the league and qualification for the following season's European Cup. It was now time to enjoy the summer and, even though it was five-a-side, we had a squad of about 15 players. Our Portuguese base at Cascais was beautiful and our invitation side from England included many guys I knew well, including Stuart Barnes and a few of the fellows from Bath. Peter Winterbottom was there, as was Martin Johnson. We arrived on the Friday and didn't waste much time getting into the party spirit. Being the first time on 'tour', it was a bit of an eye-opener for Alice who, heroically, braved the extremely hot sun to watch us in our opening games. As the other girls had been on these trips before, they understood that the rugby was optional for them, so Alice learned pretty quickly. We didn't go far in the competition and were beaten by a team of Portuguese waiters working in Cascais for the summer. It was a great weekend and Alice and I got on brilliantly.

After we came home, we spent another couple of weekends together and Alice then went with Lisa to France to see her mum, who lives in Provence. While there, she began to feel a little unwell and suspected she might be pregnant. After coming back to London, she went on her own to a family planning clinic in Soho and confirmed her suspicions. We had arranged to meet at Mezzo's restaurant/bar in Wardour Street. It was a really hot day and we ordered two Bloody Marys – perhaps not the ideal drink for Alice, but she needed something.

'Look,' she said, 'I'm pregnant.'

After the split second when you realise everything's going to change I said, 'That's brilliant,' and I meant it. 'It's really great news, fantastic.'

I think Alice was worried about how I'd react. It was, of course, all very sudden and we hadn't had much of a chance to be together as a couple but, I've never been one for sitting down and making calculated decisions about my future. Back then I couldn't plan beyond the following week. To be honest, 11 years on, not much has changed on that score. I was genuinely thrilled because I'd instantly known Alice was right for me. You meet a lot of people and you think, 'She's nice, I could easily spend time with her,' but it's different when you consider that person as the mother of your kids. I felt certain Alice and I would be great together and knew she would be a brilliant mother. That's why it didn't worry me that we were going to have a baby so quickly. We would make it work. I mean, she's an earthy Devon woman, the most natural person you could meet, and she was always going to cope well with motherhood. Of course, there were a few little details to attend to. For instance, my parents hadn't yet met Alice and hardly knew she existed. A friend of mine had recently called home and when Mum said I was out, the friend said, 'Ah, he's probably with Alice.' That was the first time Mum heard the name and, of course, she was very curious. A few days after the phone call, I called round to Mum's for dinner.

'I hear there's a new girlfriend on the scene?' she said.

'Really? How do you know?'

'One gets to hear these things. So, aren't you going to divulge her name?'

'No,' and as I said that, Mum began to sing: 'They're changing wives at Buckingham Palace. / Christopher Robin went down with Alice, / Alice divorced her man in the guard, / "A soldier's life was ever so hard," said Alice.'

'How the hell did you find out?'

My mum has always liked to stay ahead of the game.

'You'd have to be up early to get one over on me, son,' she said.

It was probably good news that Mum found out through her own means because I no doubt wouldn't have got round to telling her. And then hitting her with the double whammy that I had a new girlfriend and she was pregnant, well, that might have been a bit much. As it was, telling them wasn't something I looked forward to and, typically, I procrastinated. One evening I was round at their house around tea-time when I broke the news.

'I've got something to tell you,' I said.

'Really, what?' my mother asked.

'Well, pour yourself a glass of red wine first,' I said. Dad got the Barolo flowing.

'You're going to be grandparents,' I said.

'You've got to be joking,' she said.

'I'm not. Alice is pregnant. We're going to have a baby.'

'Lawrence, in my day, we got an engagement ring, we then had a wedding, after that the babies. You're telling me that we've now got the babies first.'

'But Mum, you'll love it. You'll absolutely love it.'

I waited the half-second for their reaction. It was exactly the same as mine. They were thrilled. Once they realised Alice and I were committed to each other, they had no worries. They didn't complain that we'd been together so short a time, they didn't suggest we should get married – they just said they were delighted. It wasn't just talk, either, because Mum and Dad have been the best grandparents to our children, Ella, Josie and Enzo, and have always been there for them.

My view of the world changed as soon as Alice became pregnant. I would wake up in the morning and get that sense of anxiety that comes with a new responsibility. You think, 'This isn't just about you any more, this is about Alice and the baby we're going to have.' Alice's pregnancy changed my life for ever. We could have complained about not having time to enjoy each other as much, or for as long, as we would have liked but it was our own fault. There is a thing called contraception and it does work, apparently. But, on the other hand, the pregnancy accelerated the development of our relationship – it was almost like we skipped the first three stages and went directly to stage four.

Alice's pregnancy went well. We moved into a friend's flat on Cremorne Road, not that far from the Chelsea Ram where we had first got together. It was a downstairs flat, not very spacious, and we obviously needed to get our own place as soon as possible. Thank God for professional rugby as we were able to buy a top-floor flat in Cambridge Gardens, Notting Hill. It was a good location because we had friends who lived close by and with me away playing rugby so often, there would be times when Alice would need her friends. As I'd imagined, she handled the pregnancy brilliantly. She swam a lot, did a bit of yoga and enjoyed getting a cup of tea in bed first thing every morning. She wanted the birth to be as natural as possible and her intention was to have no inducement, no painkillers, no gas, no epidural and spend as little time in hospital as possible.

The baby was due on 12 March but nothing much happened until a week later. Lisa came over to be with Alice. I got back from training with the shopping and, for some reason, decided to make some soup. At the time, Alice was getting mild contractions and was a little surprised at my choice of flavour. 'Why are you doing broccoli and stilton, which I hate, especially when I'm going into labour?' It was time to take the mother-to-be off to the Chelsea and Westminster Hospital. Alice spent that evening and night in the hospital and our baby daughter was born the next day. I tried to ring everybody and got my mum during an interval in a *Marchioness*-related court hearing.

'Well,' I said, 'It's a beautiful baby girl. Ella Francesca has arrived. Both mum and baby doing well.'

'What date is it today?' Mum asked.

'The twentieth,' I replied.

We didn't need to say any more. It had been in the early hours of 20 August eight years before that we lost Francesca.

10

'They don't rate you, they don't respect you.'

Sometimes his passion got the better of him and he would say something that made us smile inwardly. But most of the time Jim Telfer got it right. He was forwards coach to the 1997 Lions and for the previous four weeks he challenged us, bullied us and never allowed us to forget why we were in South Africa. It was as if his sole ambition was to help us discover what it was like to be part of a victorious Lions team. For all the tough things he said, and for all of the brutal training sessions he put us through, it was clear he believed in us and that he was certain we could pull it off. I loved his passion and the way he could get to the heart of things before a big game. When he began speaking to us before the first Test in Cape Town, you could have heard a pin drop.

'The easy bit has passed,' he said. 'Selection for the Test team is the easy bit. This is your fucking Everest, boys ... To win for the Lions in a Test match is the ultimate ... They don't rate you. They don't respect you. The only way to be rated is to stick one up them ... They don't think fuck-all of us. We're here just to make up the fucking numbers.'

You can imagine how we felt going into the first Test.

Having played my first Five Nations Championship in 1996, I got a run of matches at open-side flanker, which was definitely not my best position. Before Jack Rowell picked me there, I think I'd played a sum total of three, possibly four games in what is a pretty specialised position. After South Africa at Twickenham, I started for England against Samoa, also in the autumn of '95. Jack dropped the experienced Andy Robinson, put me at No. 7 and told Robbo to teach me how to play the position. When I thought about how much Neil Back knew about the No. 7 role and how he was being overlooked by Jack, I imagined him up in Leicester making a Voodoo doll with my name on it.

My first 12 matches for England were at open-side and once you're playing for your country, you are a contender for Lions selection. In the summer of 1997, the British and Irish Lions were due to tour South Africa and I was desperate to make the trip. A few months before, 60 of us had received a questionnaire from the Lions management. The aim was to get the players thinking about the upcoming tour they might be going on. One of the questions was: what would it mean to you to be picked for the Lions? Well, how long have you got? Virtually from the moment

I'd fallen in love with the game, the concept of the Lions, drawn from four very different rugby countries, fascinated me. Ray Colham, a friend who owned a bookshop in Fulham, called me every time he came across a book about an old Lions tour and so I'd read a lot about them, especially the '71 team in New Zealand and the '74 team in South Africa. They were both victorious and became an immortal part of Lions history.

After the questionnaires came invitations to meet with the Lions management team of Fran Cotton (manager), Ian McGeechan (coach) and Jim Telfer (assistant coach). Sixty players were at the meeting and all were measured up for the Lions gear they would receive if lucky enough to be selected. It was made clear there and then that the initial 60-man squad would be reduced to 35 and when you looked around the room and saw the quality of players, it brought home the realisation of just how big the Lions were. Who could pick 25 from the 60 and say, 'You lot are not good enough'? I suppose that was the reason we were assembled and it worked for me. I just thought, 'This is something I have to be part of.'

The extent of the change in rugby was shown by the announcement of the 35-man squad for South Africa. Eighteen months before, while driving to Marlow for England training with Jason Leonard and Damien Hopley for company, I'd learned from the car radio that I was going to start my first game for England the following Saturday. Not expecting to be in the team, I swerved off the motorway and had to stop the car to take in the news. 'Guys, did I just hear what I think I heard?' But that was the way it was in the amateur era – you found out you were playing for your country almost by chance – through listening to the radio or by buying a newspaper. How quickly it changed. Sky Sports television had bought the rights to the '97 Lions tour and the announcement of the squad was broadcast live from the station's studio in London, with a satellite link-up to the team captain, Martin Johnson, who was preparing for a game in Leicester that evening. I watched it at Wasps' ground in Sudbury and while it was expected that I would be one of the 35, it was still a relief to hear my name. It's funny the way you catch your name and in the excitement, cannot take in any of the others.

From the start, there was a good feeling about the '97 Lions. No one gave us a chance against the then world champions as the four home countries had not exactly distinguished themselves at the 1995 World Cup, and the fine England team of the early nineties had more or less broken up. Being the underdogs was not necessarily a bad thing and we were lucky enough to have an outstanding management team. Fran Cotton was an astute and likeable manager who had been an important member of the unbeaten Lions in South Africa 23 years earlier. That guaranteed him respect. To his credit, Cotton also understood the manager's remit. Basically, he dealt with all the bullshit and allowed the coaches to get on with the business of preparing the players. He went to all the receptions, negotiated on our behalf behind the scenes, and he knew how to play the propaganda games that are part and parcel of life on tour. His style is direct and forthright and because he had proven himself with the '74 Lions, the South African hierarchy knew he was no soft touch. When you look South African rugby in the eye, as Fran had in four unbeaten Tests, they accept you.

Fran was also a bit of an orator and could hold a room in the palm of his hand. Of course, when you are dealing with a squad of cynical rugby players far from home, the scrutiny is pretty unforgiving and there were a couple of occasions when Fran left himself open to the smart asses and got murdered. When we were in Durban early in the tour, he called the players together and spoke to them about our reason for being in South Africa. In full flow, he was formidable and on this occasion he was looking out at the Pacific Ocean, pointing to the wonderful blue skies and acknowledging that we were in one of the world's most beautiful settings. Outside the waves tumbled on to the sand, people walked dogs or surfed and a few fished. Just then, Fran's point became deadly serious. 'We're not here for this,' he said, pointing towards the windows. 'This is no fucking fishing trip, this is no fucking sun holiday, we're here to do a job.' That was absolutely fine except that he had clearly taken a little too much sun himself over the previous three days and his face was bright pink. We couldn't stop ourselves laughing. The message was spot-on; it was just that the messenger didn't look the part. From then on, Fran's nickname was the Pink Salmon.

Later, before the first Test in fact, he gave us a magnificent talk about the importance of the match. He had every player in the room in a frenzy, ready to do anything to win, when, at the climactic moment, he said, 'As Napoleon once famously said...' Well, not so famously, apparently, that Fran could remember, because he had to look down at his notes to recall good old Napoleon's words of wisdom. We bit our lips to stop ourselves laughing and for days, you'd meet a player and say, 'Did you hear what Napoleon once famously said?' and then look down as if checking your notes – the things we do to keep our sanity on tour!

I liked Fran from the start. He knew rugby players and understood what makes a team tick. Before leaving the UK, we spent a week preparing at the Oatlands Park Hotel near Weybridge in Surrey. Much of the time was spent on team-building exercises, overseen by a company called Impact, and it was all useful and clever stuff. Nowadays, plenty of companies do this kind of thing but back then it was relatively new. For the Lions, it was important. We were a group of people who spent their careers as international rugby players kicking the shit out of each other and suddenly we had to develop a sense of complete togetherness, and we had one week to achieve it, because if we didn't get on that plane feeling part of the same team, we wouldn't have had a hope in South Africa. During the week, we talked about how we wanted to portray ourselves, we agreed our rules of engagement, which became known as the Lions Laws, and basically we sorted out what we stood for as a group. At some point or other during the week, everyone had to get up and say something. Whether you liked it or not, you had to put your head above the parapet and make a contribution.

Fran didn't forget that we were human beings, so towards the end of the week he took us all down to a local pub in Weybridge and bought us a drink. Fran can sup a pint pretty quick and the second round came soon after the first. With the alcohol acting as a lubricant, we had an excellent evening that helped the team-building process. It was like a little reward for the work we were doing, and a reminder that, however tough the rugby, the tour could also be fun. That thought appealed to me.

Once the tour got going, Fran proved an expert at staying out of the way. You never saw him unless you needed to and yet he knew how to keep you in the loop. He made sure there was a senior players' group, consisting of Martin Johnson, Scott Gibbs, Keith Wood, Rob Wainwright, myself and a few others, and invited us to his room every so often for a chat. The principal coaches, Ian McGeechan and Jim Telfer, were also there, a couple of bottles of red wine were uncorked and we talked about how the tour was progressing. It was always relaxed and informal – 'Right lads, how's training going, so-and-so still seems a little homesick, is there anything we can do?' – that kind of stuff and it was just a very sensible way of keeping on top of things. It became especially important when we got to week four or five and our South African base wasn't Durban or Cape Town but somewhere rather less beautiful and less welcoming.

McGeechan and Telfer are both Scots but have very different personalities. Perhaps that's what made them so good as a coaching team, plus the fact they got along really well. McGeechan has said Telfer is 'the most honest man I have known', which is a pretty big compliment, and they were both seriously steeped in the tradition of the Lions. As a player, Telfer toured with the 1966 Lions to New Zealand and the 1968 Lions to South Africa and started eight of the nine Tests played over those two series. He also coached the 1983 Lions to New Zealand. McGeechan's Lions record is possibly the most distinguished of all. He played in all four Tests during the triumphant 1974 tour of South Africa, toured again as a player in New Zealand three years later and played all four Tests, and went on to coach the Lions to a 2–1 series victory over Australia in 1989. When these guys spoke to you about the Lions, you listened. Of the many things that were said, one thing stands above the others. 'To wear the Lions jersey is special,' said

Telfer, 'but to win in a Lions jersey is something completely different.' From all the players who went on that trip, I don't think you could find one who at the end didn't feel anything but total admiration for the coaching staff. They had our respect.

It is, of course, a cliché but they were the archetypal good cop/bad cop combination. McGeechan was quiet, studious, excellent at examining the opposition and pinpointing their vulnerabilities. He also insisted on Telfer being the forwards coach and was always going to allow his fellow Scot to get on with it. I mean, Jim Telfer could bite your head off from 20 yards away and make no apologies afterwards. He was there to produce a pack capable of winning a Test series and that's all that mattered. While he swore and roared at us, pushing us, driving us, Ian would follow the calm route. He might say, 'Guys, Joost Van der Westhuizen is their talisman and the biggest threat to us. But that makes him a threat to himself and his own team, because if we target him and stop him having that influence, they're not going to know what to do.'

I was on McGeechan's side from the start. He had been appointed Lions coach well in advance of the tour and made sure he wasn't involved in any other aspect of international rugby that could have compromised him in some way. Then, the year before the tour, he got himself invited as a guest of the All Blacks to be an observer on their tour of South Africa. That was seriously impressive. Before that 1996 tour, New Zealand had not won a Test series in South Africa and you can imagine how beneficial it was for him to see how the All Blacks dealt with the challenge. They seemed to be well ahead of us in professional development. At first hand, Ian could see where they stayed, where they trained, when they trained, how they acclimatised to playing at high altitude, what food they ate, how much downtime the players were given.

Most of all, it showed the dedication that Ian was bringing to his role as our coach – the fact that he had gone off to South Africa for three weeks to pick up morsels of information that could help us, set exactly the right tone for our tour. In later years, I would sometimes look at the excellent coaches who worked with a very successful England team and wonder why they weren't taking time out to travel to New Zealand or South Africa to learn new approaches to the game. Coaches, like players, need to develop but there were times when I felt the success of the England team made some of our coaches a little complacent.

So much about the '97 Lions tour was right. Martin Johnson was our captain and what an outstanding one he turned out to be. Before '97, I didn't know Johnno that well. We had been team-mates with England for two seasons and we had both been on England's tour to South Africa in 1994. We first spent time together when we shared a room in Johannesburg after the Transvaal game. He had been knocked out during the match and wasn't in the mood for chat. I thought it was me but he wasn't up for talking much in those days and the only people he seemed to speak with were his team-mates from Leicester. They were a tightly knit bunch and seemed to have this 'us-against-the-world' attitude. They were enormously respected in terms of how they played, but socially they weren't very good. I'm not saying that the more free-spirited and cavalier attitude that prevailed among the players from Wasps and Bath was the right thing either, but there were a lot of cliques in the England camp in those days and it wasn't good for the team.

When Martin was made captain of the Lions, he had to come out of his shell a little. He couldn't be a regional guy any more, or even a national guy. He had to become international and I saw a Martin I had never seen before. He was unquestionably the right choice. He commanded the respect of every other player, he had international experience and he had played for the Lions in 1993. As captain, he had to become a bit more open and a bit more extrovert, which he did. He and I played in most of the Saturday teams and when a group went out on those evenings, he was always there. Before then, he wouldn't necessarily have done that with England. When you get to know a player socially, it helps to develop a friendship. Clearly, this person was always there but it took the captaincy of the Lions to bring him out. There was a quiet side to Martin's character, which reminded me a bit of my Wasps team-mate Simon Shaw. You don't imagine anyone who is that big to be at all reserved. We just had a terrific laugh with Martin; we got on very well. On the rugby side, I saw him as a great leader and was very pleased to play under him. He might not have been as expressive or as assured as he would later become in the captain's role, but he was still outstanding as a man. I enjoyed his company very much. The whole squad was well selected, especially Scott Gibbs, Scott Quinnell, Allan Bateman, Alan Tait and John Bentley, who had all played professional rugby league. It was a statement from Cotton, McGeechan and Telfer that they were going to South Africa to win and they knew that these players' experience in rugby league could be put to good use. We all saw that, especially when it came to defence. There were times when our coaches would stand aside and let Gibbs, Tait and Bateman tell us how they defended when playing top-level rugby league. I thought it was clever of our coaches to tap into these lads' expertise. It became even clearer that the selectors had done their homework when Will Greenwood was chosen at a time when he had yet to play for England. Even though we had outstanding centres in Gibbs, Jerry Guscott and Bateman, Greenwood had an excellent tour until he picked up a serious and unfortunate injury in the game against Orange Free State.

For any Lions tour, the choice of players has to be right, but for a series in South Africa, the itinerary is just as important. Where do you play the Test matches and in what order? Pretoria and Jo'burg mean games at high altitude, which are always going to be particularly difficult for the touring side. I don't know if the South Africans cocked up or if Fran Cotton and the Lions committee were very clever negotiators but we got the best possible deal – first two games at sea level, third at altitude. If I was South African, I would have wanted the first at altitude, the second at sea level and the third back at altitude or, at the very least, the venue for the third decided by the toss of a coin. It just seemed to be stacked in our favour. What you don't want is to be pitched in early at altitude, when you're more likely to get an awful, suffocating feeling, like someone has a blowtorch to your throat. With the first two Tests set for Cape Town and Durban, both at sea level, it was clear our best chance of clinching the series was to win both of them.

If South Africa made a mistake in agreeing to Cape Town and Durban, they made an even bigger mistake in deciding that their international players would not play for their provinces against the Lions. They could watch on television but couldn't get first-hand experience of what we were like as a team. The absence of the Springboks also gave us a better chance of winning most of the provincial games and of building momentum.

Given these breaks, McGeechan and Telfer did brilliantly in terms of keeping us on our toes and making sure there was genuine competition for Test-team places. It is normal for the selection to produce one or even two surprises but no one could have come anywhere near guessing the side that would represent the Lions in the first Test at Newlands. Before leaving our England base, we were told the form that got us selected in the squad would not be the form that got us into the Test side. How true that turned out to be. Paul Wallace and Jeremy Davidson came from virtually nowhere to be key players in the Tests and Matt Dawson took the opportunity offered by Rob Howley's injury to become a star of the series. I was picked for the first Saturday game and played every Saturday game after that. By the end, I had played seven out of the 11 games in South Africa, including the three Tests. There was never a 'them-and-us' attitude between the midweek side and the Saturday side because the midweek side played outstanding rugby and it was always a strong possibility that some guys from that team were going to play in the Tests. As well as that, the rapport between the two teams was excellent. For those who played on Saturday, Sunday was a day for recovery but we made a point of joining the midweek team's training to hold the tackle bags, provide opposition where necessary and show our support for them.

Wherever possible, you shared a room with a player from a country other than your own. At the start of the tour, I shared with Rob Wainwright, which was interesting because, as two back-row players, we realised that we weren't both going to be selected for the Test side. We were very polite to each other but it couldn't go beyond that, not at that point of the tour anyway. Rob went on to play blindingly well but didn't make the Test side. The competition for places in the back row was intense: Scott Quinnell, Richard Hill, Rob Wainwright, Eric Millar, Neil Back, Tim Rodber and me were fighting for three places. The battle for the No. 7 jersey was unbelievable as Hill and Back produced a string of extraordinary performances in the midweek matches. Richard would play a blinder on Saturday; Neil would surpass that in the next game and Richard would then produce an even better performance. That's how it went and it was good for the rest of us to see both playing so well.

For the opening game of the tour, against Eastern Province in Port Elizabeth, I was picked at No. 6 in a back row that also included Scott Quinnell and Richard Hill, and was really pleased to be given the opportunity. When you're on tour, the opening game takes on a huge significance because of the importance of getting off to a winning start. While Ian McGeechan appreciated that, he still had the confidence to pick a side that didn't include Martin Johnson. It was highly unusual for the captain not to lead out the Lions in their first match but Martin had come off a particularly long season and had a minor problem with his Achilles. But even given those facts, I still thought it was fascinating they didn't pick him and that it showed the coaches' seriousness. For me, it was a statement from us to South Africa – we can win our first game, even without our captain. In Martin's absence, the captaincy was given to Jason Leonard, who summed things up pretty succinctly in his pre-match speech: 'What you're wearing,' he said, 'people fucking die for.'

The ground at Port Elizabeth held memories for me – three years earlier I'd been battered by an Eastern Province team determined to leave their mark on England, and they had indeed left plenty of marks on me. So I remembered the place well – the train that runs alongside the ground, like at Lansdowne Road, the changing room exactly the same. The only thing that had changed was me. Captain of Wasps for the two previous seasons and an England international with several caps, I was no longer the young deer caught in the headlamps of an oncoming car. But the biggest thing for me about renewing hostilities with South Africa in Port Elizabeth was remembering just how hard those bastards were. If you're not prepared for it, you're going to be battered, as I had been in '94.

This time, it was a very different story. We won 39–11, played some decent rugby and seemed to surprise South Africa with our style. I don't know what they expected but we were prepared to have a go from anywhere and take risks to ensure we had continuity in our play. Our performance wasn't perfect, but it did set the tone for the tour and let our hosts know that we wouldn't be pushovers. From a personal point of view, I felt a bit frustrated at not getting my hands on the ball as often as I'd hoped to, and it would have been nice to be among the try scorers. Rugby is the ultimate team game but that doesn't stop you seeing the match and your performance in a personal and generally critical way.

After Eastern Province, we played Border and realised how straightforward things had been in the sunny and dry conditions of Port Elizabeth. Against Border, the conditions were different and far more difficult, and it became the sort of low-scoring dogfight that doesn't do much for anyone. Still, it was two wins from two games, even if we knew the two sides we'd played were pretty low down in the South African hierarchy. The serious questions would start in our third match, against Western Province. That took us to Newlands and one of the most famous grounds in the game. To walk in there and see the photographs of the greats who have played for Western Province and South Africa is to feel a vital part of the game's history. As a city, Cape Town gives off a good vibe and spreading beneath the splendour of Table Mountain, it has everything going for it. We ended up winning the game decisively but not before a few potential weaknesses had been exposed. Most worrying was the fact that our scrum went backwards. But against that, we'd scored some cracking tries. South Africa's reaction was to give us credit for our attacking game but to suggest that we would be bulldozed into submission by the Springbok scrum. Predictably, our failure to scrum well against Western Province was blown out of all proportion.

As forwards coach, Jim Telfer took that personally and when we lost to Northern Transvaal in our fifth match, he decided the time had come to introduce us to his darker side. He expressed himself with such phenomenal emotion that you couldn't help but be affected by it. He told us we were in our comfort zone, that we came from a part of the rugby world that liked the pub, fish and chips and the sun and that if we were to get anywhere, we had to get into the South African mindset. No matter how hard he was on us, we didn't complain because he clearly had the team's interest at heart. He would be especially severe with some people, and often it was the Scots who had worked with him before who came in for the worst criticism. Rob Wainwright and Tom Smith often took a whipping but no one was spared. He was determined we would improve and believed that would be achieved through hard work. After the Northern Transvaal loss, he had a training session with the forwards that lasted an hour and a half and was devoted to nothing but scrummaging and sprinting. On the scrum machine, we did sets of five and ended up doing well over a 100 scrums. Martin Johnson has said that during that session, grown men were made to cry. I know what he means. But it was that ridiculing of our scrum by the newspapers that got to him most. It was like they insulted Jim's family and he was determined it would not happen a second time.

The difficulty of touring South Africa is that if the wheels start to come off, it can be extremely tough to get them back on track. After losing to Northern Transvaal, we had Gauteng at Ellis Park and everyone was aware how hard it would be to recover from a second consecutive defeat. The guys in that midweek game knew they were playing to save our tour. I watched the match with the rest of the non-playing lads in the stand and have never forgotten the experience. South Africa is my favourite rugby country and I have found its people to be very warm and welcoming, but like everywhere, a minority is anything but friendly. Some of the latter were sitting behind us during the Gauteng game and while we didn't have a big problem with the banter and sledging, it was harder to ignore the bits of biltong hitting us on the backs of our heads. When you're watching your mates playing for you as much as for themselves, you can be easily riled, but we bit our tongues, avoided altercations and concentrated on what was an amazing game.

The match swung one way and then the other and was decided by what will always be remembered as one of the great tries in

Lions history. John Bentley's run was amazing and it drove a stake through the hearts of the Gauteng team. There were other pluses from that game. Neil Jenkins' goal-kicking was again phenomenal, and so important that it became clear he had to be in the Test team. Irish lock Jeremy Davidson was outstanding, and from hardly being a contender, people were thinking, 'This guy can't be left out of the Test side.' Most of all, that victory was a turning point for the team. We all recognised it as such and felt an unbelievable sense of gratitude to the guys who had achieved it. At the final whistle, we rushed from the stand to the changing room and the scene said it all. Everyone was hugging and embracing and no words could have conveyed the mixture of joy and relief felt inside the squad.

Hard work on the training ground and a tough schedule of matches didn't prevent us from enjoying South Africa and, sensibly, our management team understood the importance of the squad having one night out each week. We went out as a big group and then, later in the evening, broke up into smaller groups and dispersed to different bars or restaurants. Jason Leonard and Jeremy Guscott have always been good mates of mine and Scott Gibbs became a very good friend from our time together there. John Bentley was another whose company I greatly enjoyed and Alan Tait was a lot of fun – he invariably ended up at the centre of most things. Tait was a character and on a tough tour, you need guys like him. When you pick a Lions squad you obviously want to take the best players, but in the middle of what was always going to be an arduous few weeks, the people who make the difference are the good tourists. They push the right buttons at the right time, and we're not talking here about what happens on the pitch.

Tait, Gibbs, Bentley, Guscott, Leonard and Keith Wood had been around for a while and understood the demands of touring.

How relaxed the mood was can be gauged from the fact that on the Thursday night before the first Test, four or five of us went to Camps Bay in Cape Town and ate the most amazing food at Blues restaurant. It was full of people, many of whom recognised us as Lions players and couldn't hide their astonishment that we were out 'socialising' two days before one of the biggest games of our lives. We were having a glass of wine (singular) and, of course, a few of the more die-hard Springbok supporters sent us over a bottle of champagne. We politely declined but it was a nice try. I liked the fact that we could go out and relax so close to the Test match. We wouldn't get away with it today. Back then, we didn't care how people perceived what we were doing – nowadays, perception carries more weight.

Ten minutes into the first Test, my lungs burned, my body had been battered and it seemed there was only one thought inside my head: this is more ferocious than any game I've ever played in. Was this the reason the Springboks kept their Test players out of the provincial games? To say to us, 'Look, you thought the lead-in games were tough, they were nothing.' The speed of the match was different, the physicality was very different, but South Africa were not smashing us. Tom Smith and Paul Wallace, our props, did a fantastic job after the trauma of the first scrum when we went backwards and they got the penalty. After that, Smith and Wallace scrummed low, stayed strong and South Africa didn't get the advantage they expected.

The key moment was Matt Dawson's try because it came at a time in the game when the South Africans seemed to be in control. It happened because they didn't know how good Matt was, and didn't appreciate the understanding he enjoyed with his Northampton team-mate Tim Rodber, who was playing No. 8. And, of course, the try also came about because a couple of South Africans bought the most outrageous dummy in the history of the game. Suddenly we were ahead, and just as suddenly, they panicked. You could pick up the vibe: 'We've been on top in this game and now we could lose.' Their fear caused them to push things, to go for passes that weren't on, and that played into our hands because we were able to smash them back. Out of their desperation, we got our second try and the score that clinched victory. They made a mistake, we counter-attacked, Tim Rodber threw an overhead pass to Neil Jenkins and Alan Tait scored. Tait did a brilliant gun salute to celebrate his try and the mood was momentarily ecstatic. We knew the first Test was ours.

In the week that followed, Ian McGeechan talked about what we should expect in the second Test and said that there was only one thing more dangerous than a Springbok, and that was a wounded Springbok. The ferocity of the first five minutes of that game was like nothing I had ever experienced in my life and was more brutal than anything I would encounter in my entire rugby career. They were frenzied, absolutely frenzied, and were intent upon blasting us to pieces. In winning the first Test, we had some-how taken away their honour, their identity as a people, and they had to get that back. So they piled into us. It was a siege that began in the first minute and lasted for the entirety of the match. Rugby is a game of confrontation, not a game of containment, and it's virtually impossible to win if all you do is contain. Virtually impossible – not impossible. That day in Durban, we were forced on to the back foot and all we could really attempt was to contain them. And yet . . .

We tackled unbelievably well but they were so motivated and so powerful, they were always going to score tries. They got three of them but they could never pull clear of us because on the few occasions we got out of our half, we'd win a penalty and Neil Jenkins would get us three points. When you're a forward and you're getting your head smashed to pieces and you're constantly fighting for every inch of ground, the thought that if you can get up there, get some territory, win a penalty, you have a guy who's certain to kick it over – that keeps you going. Neil played full-back in the Test side because he was such an extraordinary goal-kicker he had to be included somewhere. The Springboks didn't have anyone who could kick goals, and in a match where one team had all the possession and virtually all of the territory, the scores were even-stevens. All of our players defended courageously, some were absolutely outstanding and Scott Gibbs was heroic.

My favourite memory from the match was a ball won by Neil Back at one ruck. Neil had come on as a replacement and we were moving the ball wide when it was lost at the breakdown. I was thinking, 'This is going to be dangerous,' when Back suddenly got in there and somehow won the ball back. 'Fair play to you, mate,' I thought. After the game was over, I wanted to watch the video just to see what he had done. From Back's brilliance in getting the ball back for us, Keith Wood kicked downfield and from the line-out came the sequence of play that ended with Jerry Guscott kicking the drop-goal that put us 18–15 in front.

It was a sweetly struck drop-goal and it was immediately followed by a wild celebration as Jerry jumped up and down like a madman. Then you could see Jerry realise that there are still four minutes left and his attitude changed immediately. Suddenly he was marshalling everybody, making sure they were in the right positions to receive the South African kick-off. In hindsight, it's hysterical to remember how the expression on his face changed from euphoria to reality – I mean the guy almost went white. So we had another four minutes of withstanding the siege until, eventually, Neil Jenkins got the ball and we were all screaming at him to kick it out. He did, the final whistle went and every Lion celebrated on the pitch, even those who weren't in the match-day 22. I felt very lucky to have been on the field when the final nail was being driven into the Springbok coffin because this was a series victory created by the entire squad and our excellent management team. Had we not beaten Gauteng two weeks before the first Test, it's hard to see how we could have beaten the Boks.

After winning the series in Durban, it was difficult to escape the feeling that there was not much point in carrying on. We had beaten the world champions in the first two of a three-match series on their home patch – a team that would go on to win its next 17 matches – but there was still the now-dead rubber to play. Our itinerary had us in Van der Bijl Park for the week before the final Test and I imagine it was chosen because it was remote, away from all distractions, and a good place to prepare for a series decider. However, the series was already decided and in Van der Bijl Park there was literally nothing for us to do. After Test matches on consecutive Saturdays, we couldn't train that hard and there was nowhere to go, nowhere to have a drink, nowhere to do anything. The guys who had come from rugby league were especially restless because they couldn't see the point of a Test match in which the result meant very little. So we thought about what it meant to be part of the Lions and we played for our pride. We actually played the best rugby of the series but playing for pride is not the same as playing for your life and we lost 35–16. Defeat is never acceptable to me but it was easier to take on that occasion than at any other time in my international career because it was a battle lost in a war already won.

The heroic defence that allowed us to win the second Test is a cherished memory. I don't think I ever felt more battered after a game and certainly had never been involved in an international where we had to do so much defending. But there are different ways of winning and it was special to be part of a team and a squad where each player was determined not to let his team-mates down. To create that team environment in just eight weeks was the ultimate tribute to the whole group, both players and management. Before that second Test in Durban, Ian McGeechan told us about the significance of what we were going through. 'You'll meet each other in the street in thirty years and there will be a look. And you will know just how special some days in your life are.'

He was right.

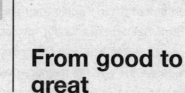

From good to great

The call came in the autumn of 1997. England's new coach, Clive Woodward, wanted me to come round to his house in Marlow. 'Nothing too formal, just a chat, a bite to eat and a chance to get to know each other,' he said. I was intrigued. An England coach prepared to invite a player to his house? That kind of thing just didn't happen.

Clive had taken over from Jack Rowell, who'd had a very different style. 'Who are you?' Jack said to me the first time I was summoned into the squad. A tall, formidable man, Jack challenged you and I liked that about him. 'Well, you should know, you picked me in your squad,' I said. Then he would smile because he wanted players to rise to the bait.

Clive was very different and far more open. He didn't mind ignoring the barriers that divided player and coach and wanted you to get to know him. At the time, I wondered if any other player had been invited (later, I would learn that many had). It showed how comfortable he was about his home and family. Knowing Clive now, I reckon he would have enjoyed introducing me to Jayne and have her give me the once-over. 'So, what did you think of him?' he probably asked her afterwards. Clive was yet to choose his England captain and while Martin Johnson was the favourite, it was speculated that I was the alternative.

I knew very little about Clive, apart from the facts that he had played for Leicester, England and the Lions. From the things you heard, he was a talented player who had been part of England's Grand Slam-winning team in 1980 and had toured with the Lions that summer but not played very well. After that, he had gone to Australia, played a little in Sydney and then disappeared off the radar only to return a few years later as a coach at Henley and later at London Irish. He then spent a short time at Bath and suddenly he was England coach. For a time, he was in charge of the England Under-21s and when the senior side was preparing for a game, we would sometimes have them as opposition. Andy Robinson worked with Clive and you definitely got a sense of that particular twosome's ability and ambition from the way they fired up the youngsters for the sessions against us. They'd surprise as with a number of little tricks and once they started causing a few problems, Martin Johnson or Jason Leonard or Gareth Archer would say, 'That's enough from these little fuckers, 'cos they're doing my head in.' And that would be the end of it – blood everywhere, practice session cut short. I remember Joe Worsley, then an Under-21, getting under Neil Back's skin and copping one for his trouble. Nine years later, the same thing happened in a Wasps v. Leicester Premiership final. Joe was on the receiving end of another Neil punch but that day Wasps smashed Leicester and the dig wouldn't have cost Joe a second thought.

The Under-21s had something about them and you associated that with Clive. There were some intriguing stories. Once Clive got his players to put pillow cases on their heads, turn their backs to the ball and at the sound of the whistle, they had to whip off the pillow cases and react as a ball was thrown among them. It was Clive's way of showing the players they had to adjust to what was in front of them and it was probably a clever way of making the point. Watching from the touchline, it must have seemed bizarre. Imagine what it looked like to the parents, wondering what sort of religious cult their sons had signed up to. If you spoke to people about Clive, you got the same line – 'Well, he's different,' the implication being that he was a bit of a maverick. I liked the fact that he was different and brave enough not to want to do the job in the way all his predecessors had done it. If that made him a maverick, so be it.

It was, of course, flattering for me to be invited to Clive's house. I was 25 years of age, beginning my third season as an England player and still relatively inexperienced by the standards of international rugby. The first thing I noticed on my arrival was that Clive had a beautiful house, an M3 convertible in the driveway and a smashing family.

'What would you like to drink?' he asked and I hesitated, wondering about the impression I might create. He could sense what I was thinking and said, 'Why don't you have a beer?'

'Yeah, perfect,' I said.

Jayne had prepared a lovely dinner, the kids strolled in and out of the room where we ate – they were still young then – and I was very impressed by the ambience. Given the welcome and informality, you couldn't help but like the bloke. He was a guy with whom you could have a normal conversation and I struck up a good rapport with him. We had some wine with dinner and everything seemed pretty cool to me. Towards the end of the conversation, we talked about the team and his vision for how he wanted England to play and where he wanted the team to go in world rugby. I talked about what I saw as my role within the team. Eventually, he brought up the subject of the captaincy.

'I'm thinking of making you captain,' he said.

'If you did, that would be great,' I replied.

Before meeting with Clive, I had decided to stay cool about the question of who would be named captain. Two years earlier, when Jack Rowell made Phil de Glanville captain, a number of media people had suggested I should have been given the nod and, being young and probably too excitable, I had allowed the possibility to get inside my head. When Phil got it, I was a little disappointed, which was stupid, so when it came to Clive's decision on the captaincy, I protected myself. 'Do you know what, Lawrence,' I told myself, 'you weren't captain when you got into the England squad and you probably won't be captain when you leave it. So what?' If it came along, great, but I wasn't going to chase it. I wasn't even going to think about it too much. I'd been there, done that. While I would never diminish the honour of captaining England, I felt that Will Carling, not all through his own making, had elevated the captaincy to a level it did not warrant and resulted in too much attention being focused on him. He did take England forward and the team did achieve a lot of success but it seemed to me that the captain's role was too high profile and it lessened the attention given to others on the team.

Most commentators felt Clive would choose either Martin Johnson or me. Had Martin been made captain, no one would have had any complaints, especially not me, but Martin wasn't the person then that he is now. He was a great player and, primarily because of that, he was a great leader. The Lions tour was a one-off situation that he had handled really well but he still had this sort of angry look all the time – the furrowed brow was pretty constant back then. Martin used to hide behind those dark eyebrows and there was no getting past them. The sign said 'No Entry' and that was it. Over the last six or seven years, Johnno has shown a side he wasn't prepared to show in the early years. He is incredibly witty, and once we got to know each other properly, there's been a lot of warmth between us.

When Clive first brought up the captaincy, I said it wasn't an issue for me, and I wouldn't feel I was treading on anyone's toes. Johnno had been a wonderful captain of the Lions. I had captained Wasps to the league title and played a small supporting role in the leadership of the Lions. In the end, the decision may have come down to the fact that Clive is different. Martin was the safe choice, the guy people may have expected to be captain, but as was his wont, Clive went against the grain. Perhaps he liked the fact that I was a lot more talkative than Martin. That was more Clive's style. In the early years, he was full of ideas and I think he liked to feel he could discuss them with his captain. If an idea struck him, he'd pick up the phone and say something along the lines of, 'What do you think of this? What if we tried this player in that position? Should we bring X into the squad?' At the time, Martin wasn't that type of person. He would just say, 'Yeah, that's all right, whatever you think,' but wouldn't engage. Over the years that aspect of his nature changed and I believe he became a better captain because of it.

I'm not suggesting you have to be a talker, because you don't. Christ, I talked far too much. I engaged too much with people and ended up saying more than I should have. To my cost, as it turned out. Probably the ideal was somewhere between the two of us. Whenever people speak about Martin, they say, 'He's a bloke who doesn't say much, just gets on with the job.' His quietness in the early days was, I think, due to shyness. That's the way he was naturally, but as he grew into the captaincy, he knew he couldn't remain like that. With Clive, talking was the preferred option.

What I particularly liked was Clive's vision. He didn't want England to be the best team in just Europe, he wanted them to be the best in the world. That meant beating the southern hemisphere countries and doing so regularly. It meant winning the World Cup, and even though I was young and didn't know much, I could see we were never going to do that without a radical change of attitude. And Clive definitely wanted to be the man to bring about this change.

Perhaps the first indication that he was going to be different came with a phone call a few nights after I'd been to his house. 'I've made up my mind,' he said. 'You're captain.'

*

When I was a kid in the England squad under Will Carling and Geoff Cooke, we were the team to beat in the northern hemisphere. Every so often, we achieved a notable victory over one of the big southern hemisphere teams but we could never consistently beat them. In terms of how we viewed ourselves, we were a good international team but in terms of how the rest of the world saw us, we were underachievers. Our ambition was to win the Five Nations Championship and every so often to pick up a Grand Slam. Geoff Cooke's England won two Grand Slams and got to a World Cup final and were rightfully regarded as success- ful; Jack Rowell's team won one Grand Slam and got to a World Cup semi-final and, by the standards that existed at the time, Jack's reign was successful. But in many respects, the environment around the England team was still steeped in the amateur era and we had a long way to go before getting anywhere near the standard of New Zealand, Australia and South Africa.

What happened at the end of the 1997 Lions tour was madness, but I wasn't about to complain. I was a 24-year-old who had captained Wasps to win the English championship in the first season of professional rugby and who had then had a nine-week adventure with the Lions. Although the tour to South Africa was great fun and hugely satisfying, it came at a tough time because eight weeks before departure, little Ella Francesca Dallaglio had come into the world – not an ideal time to leave Alice and the baby. At the end of the Lions tour, I was physically exhausted but had to fly off to Australia straightway to play for England in a one- off Test against the Wallabies. When you've just won a Test series for the Lions, the last thing you need is another Test match on the other side of the world. How nice it would have been to have flown home and had a bit of time with Alice and Ella and to savour what we'd achieved in South Africa. Anyone who has taken a flight from Johannesburg to Sydney will know that it's a horror in terms of jetlag and that's the thing I will always remember – far worse than anything I've experienced travelling from London to Sydney. But you don't argue when your country needs you.

Since I had not seen Alice and Ella for almost nine weeks, we arranged for them to come to Sydney where we would spend two weeks together and then travel on to Bali for two weeks' holiday. We wanted, and needed, to spend time together. Given my state of exhaustion, another Test match seemed like a piece of the jigsaw that didn't have a place. All I wanted was to be with Alice and Ella and recover from the jetlag, but I had to train every day. The game itself was a decidedly average experience. A gashed head in the first couple of minutes didn't exactly help, and although we held Australia up to half-time, we were well beaten in the second half. Jack Rowell was still in charge but everyone, especially Jack, could see the end was nigh. His body language made that clear, and it got to the point where he didn't know what to say to the players any more. He knew and we knew it was his last game in charge.

Given that Clive Woodward's aim was to make England the best team in the world, he certainly started in the right place. On the last three Saturdays in November 1997 and the first Saturday in December, we played Australia, New Zealand, South Africa and then New Zealand for a second time. Any normal coach would have thought, 'This is not where I want to start,' but Clive thought it was just fine. He wanted to see what he had and four tough games against the three best sides in the world would tell him a lot. According to him, if you aspired to win the World Cup, you had to have the ability to win big Test matches on consecutive weekends. We lost two of the games and drew two, made tons of mistakes and, most of all, learned what we were lacking. We drew the first game with Australia and thought, 'We're not that far off the pace,' but then lost badly to New Zealand at Old Trafford. In that match, Martin Johnson famously lost his rag and punched Justin Marshall, the New Zealand scrum-half.

At the time, I thought it was a fair cop. Marshall knew exactly what he was doing, winding Johnno up because he had a short fuse, and he could hardly complain when Johnno reacted the way he did. But the nature of the game was changing and Martin was cited for punching Marshall and banned from the following week's game against South Africa. That incident was a turning point for Martin, who evolved into a more disciplined player, although he never lost his hardness. I mean, you've got to change because if you continue punching people's lights out, as Danny Grewcock seems to have done through the years, it's going to hurt your career.

Another incident from that New Zealand game at Old Trafford is notable because it was the first demonstration of how ruthless Clive could be. And this was something he never lost. As he was to demonstrate in similar circumstances years later in the 2003 World Cup. In Manchester we started with a back row of Richard Hill at 7, Tony Diprose at 8 and me at 6. Clearly, Clive felt the back row hadn't performed in the first half and at the interval he came into the changing room, looked at Diprose and said, 'Right, you're off.' Turning to Neil Back he said, 'You're on.' It was brutal. Rugby substitutions didn't happen like that, at least not in an England dressing room. That was the start of the successful back row of Hill, Dallaglio, Back.

The attitude of the New Zealand coach, John Hart, was also memorable. As we were making our way to the changing room at half-time, we saw John banging on the referee's door and then giving the ref a very hard time. Although they were winning the game, Hart was still making sure his team got a better deal from the referee in the second half. It opened my eyes to the way professionalism was changing the game and how far off the pace we were. Clive was seriously pissed off, more by the fact that there was a game behind the game that we knew nothing about than John Hart's lecturing of the referee.

To crown a bad day, the New Zealanders got on their high horses and ridiculed us for what they saw as 'a lap of honour' by a losing team. At the end of the match, Clive had innocently asked the players to thank the fans for their support, solely because we were playing in front of northern fans, in a very famous football stadium, and it was clear from the noise and passion that it was a different crowd from the one we get at Twickenham. We did a little half-lap of the pitch, from the dugouts to the tunnel, and thanked the crowd on our way. Big deal! I thought it was typical bloody New Zealand the way they claimed the moral high ground.

After losing badly to South Africa in our third game, the series ended with another tilt at the All Blacks, who had won every match on their tour and for whom this was the final game. The match provided another interesting insight into Clive's mindset because it was clear beforehand that he'd had enough. OK against Australia, poor against New Zealand, dreadful against South Africa – he just wanted a performance from us. In the team talks before the game, he dispensed with logic and measured tactics and the coach's favourite, 'playing the game in the right parts of the pitch'. Instead, he spoke from the heart. 'Let's just have a fucking go at this fucking New Zealand team. Let's just tap everything, fuck 'em, we've lost the last two games anyway. We don't have much to lose, so let's absolutely go for it. Let's go for the jugular with these guys, let's not fucking piss about here, let's get some fucking pace into the game.' He then wrote 'three tries' on the board in the team room and told us that was the target for the game.

It was a brilliant approach, almost as if Clive was saying, 'Do whatever the hell you want.' We went out and just blew them away in the first half an hour. Phil de Glanville knocked someone over, the ball fell loose and I hacked it to score. Then our wing David Rees got a beautiful try when he chipped over Jonah Lomu's head, raced past him, re-gathered and had his teeth smashed in the act of scoring. De Glanville got a third and we were in the extraordinary position of being 21 points clear of the best team in the world. We had them completely shell-shocked, rattled like I've never seen the All Blacks rattled. They had thought of us as a forward-dominated team that played boring rugby and suddenly we were scoring tries left, right and centre.

Of course, they regrouped and before half-time we were defending desperately. Richard Hill made one fantastic try-saving tackle on Jeff Wilson but we were still well ahead as we received a standing ovation from the Twickenham crowd on our way to the changing room at the interval. But even after that magnificent effort, you only had to look at the scene in our changing room at that point to realise why we were miles away from the best countries in the world. After playing at the higher tempo that Clive demanded, we were physically shattered after 40 minutes. I felt sick and was retching, other guys were in an even worse mess and it was plain that 40 minutes of rugby at that pace was more than we could cope with. We knew we couldn't sustain that level of performance through the second half and Clive must have looked at us and thought, 'We're not fit enough, we're not strong enough, we're simply not good enough.' He knew, as we knew, that to win a World Cup you've got to play back-to-back Tests at the level we couldn't even sustain for 40 minutes.

It was carnage in the changing room. No one could speak. Players were sprawled on the floor, others were vomiting into the bins and it was simply a question of allowing players to regain some semblance of physical normality. We should have gone out and closed the game down, but instead we started falling off tackles and allowed them to get into our territory. One try came, then another and, at the end, we were happy to hang on for a 26–26 draw. After my first four matches as England captain there was nothing in the win column, although the games had had their moments. As captain, you've got to make a speech after every game and already I'd grown tired of congratulating the opposition. And this was no different. Even though we had drawn against the All Blacks it felt like a defeat because we had been in such a strong winning position. The reason why things were not as bleak as the results suggested was Clive Woodward. His vision for England was more ambitious than anything I'd known and he knew what was needed to make us consistently competitive against every opposition. At first, he tried to change the structure of the game in England but that approach ended up in various political battles with the clubs and even the Union itself, which was his employer. It took time, but Clive eventually realised he was not going to win that battle, so he settled for changing and improving the environment around the national team. Famously, he once said that during the early years in the job he felt like he was skiing uphill. Things evolved slowly but the first two seasons under Clive, from 1997 to 1999, were an enormous learning experience. I don't know what Clive would now say, but I felt he was simply trying to clear up the mess he'd inherited. It wasn't until 1999 that we were anywhere near where he wanted us to be and even then, when you lined up England against any of the big three from the southern hemisphere, those teams were much better physically, especially their backs. What Clive and the rest of us knew was that if we were serious about becoming the best team in the world, it was going to be a hell of a long journey.

At the end of 1997, the rugby writers presented me with the Pat Marshall Memorial Trophy for being their player of the year. The decision was based on Wasps winning the league, the Lions winning in South Africa and then my being made England captain. It had been a good year for me and the rugby writers' banquet is always well organised and a fun evening. I had attended it four years previously when Ben Clarke was player of the year and was blown away by the experience. Ben was a back-row forward, as I was. He had played in every back-row position for the Lions, he played No. 8 for England and at that time he was the player I wanted to be. To be at the same banquet just four years on, receiving the same trophy, was a great thrill.

On the evening of the banquet, England's four autumn internationals were fresh in everyone's memory and in my little speech I reworked an old story told by the late and great Scottish forward, Gordon Brown.

'When I first got the England captaincy, the ex-captain, Phil de Glanville, handed me three white envelopes. "Look," he said, "it's going to be a tough job, and as someone who has been through it, I'd like to help. So here are three envelopes, to be opened during the bad times, and there will be bad times. The messages inside will offer a little bit of inspiration." I thanked Phil and kept the envelopes safely. In my first international as captain, we drew with Australia and I thought that was an OK result – no need to use the envelopes. Second match, we were hammered by the All Blacks, so before going to the post-match press conference, I opened the first envelope. Inside, it said, "Blame the goal-kicker." That was fine. Mike Catt was our goal-kicker and not always reliable. "The score looks bad," I told the press afterwards, "but if we had actually kicked our goals, it would have been a different game and quite possibly a different result. Of course, I'm not blaming Catty, but the goal-kicking was decisive." The following week we were thrashed by South Africa and the message inside the second envelope said, "Blame the structure of English rugby." In the press conference, I said, "Our structure just doesn't give the England team a chance to compete at the highest level. The players give one hundred per cent but we're not competing on a level playing field." Then we played New Zealand again and blew a big lead before scrambling a 26–26 draw. I needed a little more inspiration, but the message inside the third envelope just said, "Start writing three new white envelopes." '

And that was my acceptance speech. After the most recent four internationals, the award had to be taken with a pinch of salt.

The wheels of progress turned slowly. My first Five Nations Championship as captain began at the Stade de France on the first Saturday of February 1998 and ended in a defeat more clear-cut than the 24–17 scoreline indicates. We won our remaining three matches, scoring 60 points against Wales at Twickenham, 34 against Scotland at Murrayfield and 35 against Ireland at Twickenham — victories and points totals that were generally dismissed as unimportant by most commentators. 'England,' they said then, and would continue to say, 'failed to win the match that mattered.' Yet we knew that it meant something to score 60 against the Welsh, and to beat Ireland and Scotland so decisively.

That Clive Woodward was a very different kind of England coach became clear in the lead-up to the 1998 tour to the southern hemisphere, where England were due to play Test matches against Australia, New Zealand and South Africa. It was a murderous schedule, including two Tests against the All Blacks, and to have any chance of decent results, England needed its best players. But Clive had already formed a plan. He recognised that because of the previous year's Lions tour, England's top players hadn't had a proper break from the game for almost two years. In the Lions season, I played 52 matches, the last three but one against the Springboks in the most punishing series I'd ever been involved in. I was desperately in need of a long break. Team-mates Jason Leonard, Martin Johnson, Richard Hill and Neil Back couldn't have felt any better than I did.

Previous England coaches would have looked at that schedule of matches in the southern hemisphere and decided they needed all the senior hands. Clive looked at the schedule and thought it was exactly what his senior players did not need. Instead, he looked ahead to the 1999 World Cup and thought the only way to have his best players fresh for that tournament was to ensure they had a proper break in 1998. In what was an incredibly far-sighted approach, he decided to break the cycle. He started the process by talking to me.

'Look,' he said. 'I'm thinking of not taking you on tour. You're England captain, you'll be disappointed, but I believe you need to get some rest.' He was right on both counts – I did need rest and I was disappointed that he didn't want me to make the summer tour. What Clive didn't know at that point was that I had been playing with a worsening shoulder injury through the second half of the season. By the time we played Saracens in the Tetley's Bitter Cup final, I was struggling to make tackles and Saracens produced one of their greatest performances to smash us. François Pienaar, Richard Hill, Tony Diprose, Kyran Bracken, Michael Lynagh, Philippe Sella and their team-mates took us to the cleaners.

Although I wanted to go on the tour, it was obvious that I needed to get my shoulder sorted. It eventually needed surgery and God knows what state it would have been in if I'd gone. Clive encouraged most of the other senior players to rest and get their injuries cleared up. From the outside it looked as if senior players were pulling out of a particularly arduous tour, but every decision followed a conversation with the coach that ended with Clive telling the player to stay at home. Other coaches thought short-term whereas Clive was brave enough to think longer term.

A press conference was organised for Twickenham to announce the squad with Matt Dawson as captain for the summer tour, and Clive asked me to come along too. I met with him and the RFU press officer, Richard Prescott, at Rugby House in Twickenham an hour or so before we presented ourselves to the media. Our meeting was to ensure that Clive, Matt and I would all be singing from the same hymn sheet. It wasn't complicated. Clive was going to say I needed to get my shoulder fixed and would not be touring with the team to the southern hemisphere. In my absence, Matt Dawson would captain the side and, presuming I returned to form and fitness, I would be back as captain in the autumn.

At the press conference, I'm a bit of a dead man, sitting back, as I know what's going to be said and so I'm not paying much attention. Suddenly, something sparked and I am sitting up and listening to every word. 'So Matt Dawson is the new captain and although Lawrence wasn't considered for the tour, I have to say that he hasn't been playing that well and if he was fit and I was picking the England team today, I'm not sure he would be in it.' Clive went on to speak about Saracens' Ben Sturnham, who had played so well against me in the Cup final two weeks earlier, and I'm just sat there thinking, 'What about the bloody hymn sheet?' I could see the glee on the faces of two of the more experienced rugby writers, Terry Cooper and Barry Newcombe, because this was a little story they hadn't expected. I was asked questions and gave diplomatic answers, reserving my annoyance for Richard Prescott afterwards. 'Look mate,' I said, 'I'm not very fucking happy about that. That was out of order.' Typical of Clive, he had the good grace to ring and apologise that evening, said he hadn't meant to deviate from the script. But that was Clive, if he made a mistake, he was big enough to admit it.

England set off on what would become known as the Tour of Hell without 15 or 16 front-line players. While I agreed with Clive's thinking, it was still sad to see that 76–0 scoreline against Australia, which still crops up today as England's heaviest-ever defeat. Some of the guys who played on that tour shouldn't have ever played for England. Afterwards we heard stories about how the coaches treated some of these lads and we knew that wouldn't have happened if six or seven of the senior players had been there. To make a bad situation worse for me, I stayed at home to get my shoulder right and did the rehab suggested by people at the club. The summer came and went but my shoulder got no better. To discover at pre-season training that I needed an operation I could have had two months before was demoralising but it's what happens in sport. Eventually the job was done by Paul Calvert, a surgeon based in Wimbledon, who has sadly since passed on. It wasn't a major operation but Paul did a super job and for the first time in almost nine months, I was able to lift my right arm over my head without pain.

I was 25 when Clive asked me to captain England. Then, as now, I was in love with life and loved playing for both Wasps and England. About the only plan that Clive and I had for the captaincy was that we would make it less high profile. Clive's feeling was that the captain had to be a world-class player, but overall leadership had to come from a number of players in the team. As a young captain in 1997, '98 and early '99, I was headstrong and didn't shirk from saying tough things. I didn't tolerate failure, didn't tolerate people pissing around and I hated losing. It never dawned on me that I should temper my style, or try in any way to be somebody I wasn't. Rather than tiptoeing my way round a problem, I would bash my way right through it.

I had always been like that and that side of me became even more pronounced after my sister died. To me, it felt like I was on this treadmill with my finger on the accelerate button – I had to go forward all the time, I had to feel we were progressing. I didn't spend much time thinking things through before acting. Whatever felt right, that's what I did. Afterwards I would think about it and be concerned that I had overstepped the mark in terms of apportioning blame. I am a compassionate bloke, I'm very sensitive, but if you had been there on some of the losing days, you wouldn't necessarily have thought that. Other times, I just wouldn't realise it was best to say nothing, but these are things you can only learn with experience. There is no doubt that my judgement has improved with age. What people have to understand is that there is no manual telling you how to captain the England rugby team, and I wasn't the kind of bloke to go away and read books on leadership. Over the years, and especially at Wasps, I proved to be a reasonably successful captain. When I look back on those early seasons as England captain, I think there were a lot of things I did well, but there were many things I could have done better – I wince at some of the things I did and said.

The most important thing was that England were improving. The '98 tour of the southern hemisphere was disastrous but only because Clive didn't have his best players available. Five months after losing so heavily to the Aussies, we fielded our best side against them at Twickenham and lost 12–11, which was a far more realistic measure of the difference between the teams. A week later we beat South Africa 13–7 and we went into the 1999 Five Nations believing we were good enough to win every game. We beat Scotland at Twickenham, Ireland at Lansdowne Road, our biggest rivals, France, at Twickenham and went into our final game against Wales odds-on favourites to win the Grand Slam. With the Millennium Stadium under construction at the time, Wales were playing their home matches at Wembley and that seemed to play very much into our hands. Technically, it was an away game, but how can England be deemed to be the away side when the game is in London?

Wales's first achievement was to ensure Wembley was packed with their fans, which turned the ground into a cauldron of Welsh support. On a very warm Sunday in April, the atmosphere was brilliant. We played well in the first half and sliced open their defence on a number of occasions, but it wasn't clinical and although we were by far the better side, we couldn't make it count on the scoreboard. Too many times we conceded penalties in our own half, which was madness as we knew their kicker, Neil Jenkins, simply wouldn't miss. They played well in the second half but we were always winning. Then came the moment that would be relived countless times after the game. Deep in the half we got a penalty that was kickable but I chose to go for the corner, aiming for a try that would have clinched the Grand Slam. At the time, we were six points clear but I was a disciple of Clive's have-a-go philosophy. Both of us were naturally opposed to the lack of adventure traditionally associated with England. Another factor in my decision was that Jonny Wilkinson was not the kicker then that he subsequently became and taking a shot at goal was no guarantee of three points.

I remember the moment vividly. It was quite a long way out, on the left-hand side of the pitch, which was the wrong side for Jonny. I turned to the players close to me before speaking to the referee.

'Come on,' I said, 'let's go for the corner.'

Johnno and I looked at each other for a second.

'Are you sure?' he asked.

'Yeah, why not?'

'OK, fair enough.'

The key mistake was my belief that at that point in the game, Wales weren't going to go down to the other end of the field and score a try. I should have known better. In hindsight, it was a big mistake. An important decision went against us when referee Andre Watson gave Wales a penalty following a Tim Rodber tackle that touch-judge Alan Lewis deemed to be illegal. It was a borderline call as Watson saw nothing wrong with the tackle, but from the ensuing line-out, Wales scored a terrific try through Scott Gibbs. The conversion to win the game would have been tough for any kicker other than Jenkins. It was halfway out but he kicked it like it was under the posts. We weren't finished yet though. The Grand Slam could still be ours. We had two minutes left and tried to create a drop-goal opportunity for Mike Catt. This was four years before we would win the World Cup with a similarly late kick and, in truth, we were about four years away from the kind of cohesion and organisation that enables you to execute the moves that create the chance. We had the ball, Wales stepped forward, just as the Aussies would do in Sydney 2003, but that's where the similarity ends. In the Telstra Stadium we were composed, forcing the Australians to step back, giving Jonny the time he needed – at Wembley we were rushed and unplanned, we didn't create those vital few seconds for Catty and his drop goal attempt sailed wide of the right post.

I've always considered myself gracious in defeat (although many one-eyed supporters would disagree) and, despite feeling as though I was in the middle of a nightmare, I shook Welsh hands, said the right things and was one of the last English players to leave the field. Walking down the tunnel, Welsh supporters spat down on us as we went through, and I remember wiping spittle away from my eye and feeling nothing but contempt for the people who would do that. Inside my head, a voice said, 'Bottle this feeling, mate, and I guarantee it will help you in the future.' The changing room was like a morgue – complete silence. Guys sat in stunned bewilderment. How did we lose that? We had blown it and we knew it. If you looked around, some guys were quietly shedding tears. What hurt most was that we had contrived to lose a match when we were the better team. I blamed myself for the decision not to kick for goal. Over the following years we would learn how to build a winning score, brick by brick. Scott Gibbs became a hero in Wales because of the try but he was already a hero to me because of how he played for the Lions in South Africa. The day after the match he called and left a message on my answer machine: 'All right Lol. Scotty here. Just wanted to apologise for the try yesterday.' It was a nice message from a great bloke, a fellow who had been on the losing side a few times and knew what it felt like.

For us, it was one of those crushing defeats that stays with you.

It drained my morale, left me feeling really down. Normally I bounce back pretty quickly because there's another match to think about, but on this occasion, the bad vibes hung around. You go to the supermarket or a restaurant and someone innocently asks, 'What happened to you against the Welsh?' and it gnaws away at you. At the time and for the following three or four weeks, it felt like the end of the world.

12

A web of deceit

I could tell something was wrong. The way people were looking at me wasn't normal. When you play rugby for England and your face is constantly on television, you are going to be recognised. It's never bothered me. If you treat people normally, they will treat you the same. Sure, there was an element of the 'There he is,' that I'd experienced before, but on this Sunday morning at the beautiful Woolley Grange Hotel in Bradford-upon-Avon near Bath, it was different. This was 23 May 1999. As soon as I walked into the breakfast room, people's eyes were fixed on me and everyone's expression was sombre. Even though I'd no idea why, there was a whiff of disapproval in the air. It seemed as if they knew something I didn't.

Alice and I were spending the weekend at this 400-year-old Jacobean manor with our two daughters, Ella and two-week-old Josie. A few days later I would be on my way to Australia with the England rugby team. Coming at the end of another long rugby season and before the short tour to Australia, we needed the break. Alice and I had particularly enjoyed the previous day, Saturday, just relaxing with our daughters and savouring an ambience very different from what we were used to in London. I'd gone down to breakfast before Alice and the children and turning on my mobile phone, I discovered a couple of missed calls from my then agent, Ashley Woolfe. I called him back straightaway.

'Hi Ash, mate, what's up?'

'You're all over the front page of the *News of the World*,' he said. 'The headline's pretty bad – they're saying you were a drug dealer. Those two guys we thought were executives from Gillette were *News of the World* reporters.'

I felt numb and panic-stricken. Ashley explained what was in the story but only bits and pieces registered with me. I went straight back to our room. Alice listened as I gave her a short account of the situation. Having had Josie just weeks before, it was a terrible time for her to have to deal with this and she was traumatised by the news. 'We've got to pack up immediately,' I said. 'We've got to go.' At the reception desk, I apologised to the owner of the hotel.

'We've had a lovely time but something's cropped up and we've got to head for home if that's all right,' I told him. It was clear from his sympathetic reaction that he had heard about the *News of the World* story.

'I understand,' he said. 'I hope you've enjoyed your stay and you're welcome to come back any time and enjoy a full weekend.'

As the implications of the story began to sink in, I despaired at my own stupidity. I'd landed myself right in it but that wasn't the worst thing. I landed everyone around me in it. The hurt caused to Alice and my parents, the embarrassment felt by friends and team-mates bothered me far more than the personal consequences. I would lose the England captaincy because of this but that wasn't my overriding concern. What would Alice and my parents think of me? What would Clive Woodward, who had made me England captain, think? I'd let everyone down. I thought especially about what Mum and Dad had been through following Francesca's death and now I was causing more pain and grief.

On the journey back to London, I rang my parents and told them that what was written was not true and that before anyone started reading too much into it, they should know the circumstances. The press were camped outside my parents' house in Barnes and also outside my house in Ladbroke Grove. Clive Woodward was the next person I phoned. I wanted to put him in the picture. He was going to have to answer a lot of questions about this. I wondered how he would react? Would he just cast me aside? 'Sorry mate, you've cocked up, completely blown it, you're out.' But Clive was very good about it.

'Look, where are you?'

'Just left Bath, we're on our way back to London.'

'Where are you going to go?'

'I don't know, mate, there's press outside my house.'

'Well, why don't you come here?'

'Are you sure? That would be very kind.'

'Of course I'm sure. We can talk about it.'

'I've got Alice and the kids.'

'That's fine. Jayne's here, she'll take care of Alice.'

We stopped at a service station on the way back and, again, I could feel everyone's eyes on me and was certain they were judging me. Whether this was paranoia or actually happening didn't really matter. It felt like the walls were closing in on me. Around 10 o'clock that morning we arrived at Clive's place in Marlow. Ridiculous as it sounds, it felt like we were on the run and had reached a safe-house. Jayne immediately took Alice and the kids under her wing and I sat down with Clive to tell him the full story of what had happened. He listened intently and at the end, he said, 'Well, you've been a bit of a prat, haven't you?'

'You could say that,' I replied.

A lot of things were happening in 1999, World Cup year. Rugby with Wasps and England, life with Alice, Ella, and the arrival of Josie, were enough for one family to deal with but as England captain, there were extra demands that meant I hadn't a spare moment. I wasn't complaining. I was the one saying yes to the optional stuff. To every request that came along, my inclination was to go for it.

'Yeah, why not?'

'Yeah, I can do that.'

'Yeah, I can help this guy with his charity night.'

'Yeah, I don't mind meeting with the MD of a potential sponsor.'

I can say now that it's sometimes better to say no, to disappoint people so that you protect yourself but that wasn't my style. I wanted people to like me and to know I would put myself out. Whatever it cost in terms of time or a helter-skelter lifestyle, I would deal with that. This is how I was before I became England captain and I didn't see any need to change. There were good reasons for saying yes to commercial opportunities. Rugby careers are short and you've got to take advantage while you're playing because the offers dry up after you retire. Although I've never been driven by money, I am pretty good at spending it.

In early 1999, Ashley Woolfe was considering an offer from PhysioSport, a subsidiary of Fabergé. The deal was for a one-off campaign involving advertising that would use images of me. Contracts were agreed but not signed and I remember they were going to pay me around £30,000. In mid-February, a few days before our opening Five Nations match against Scotland at Twickenham, Ashley's lawyer, Andrew Morris, heard a rumour that a newspaper was planning an entrapment story in which I would be the victim. Ashley took it seriously enough to tell me about it and he also told Clive. The possibility that someone might be prepared to do something like that was a bit surreal but nevertheless worrying – surely no one would try it, but if they did, would we recognise it for what it was? The news didn't do much for my performance against the Scots. We scraped through 24–21 and I played poorly. As the Five Nations Championship played out and nothing happened to back up the rumour, the threat receded and we more or less forgot about it.

PhysioSport's offer was still on the table, awaiting my signature, when on 14 April Ashley received a faxed letter from the creative director of an advertising agency, the CSR Partnership:

Dear Sirs,

We are a design and advertising agency who have been recently commissioned to launch a new range of male toiletry products into the European market place by a major American multi-national client. Anticipated launch date is November this year at this moment.

Our client is very interested in using major sports stars in the ad campaigns, both as an image and on personal appearance basis.

I understand that you represent Lawrence Delaglio's commercial interests, and we would be particularly interested in talking with you and your client at the earliest possibility about this contract opportunity.

Best regards,

Yours faithfully,

Peter Simmons

Creative Director

The fax came on letter-headed writing paper and was cleverly put together. For example, they spelt my name incorrectly, but then under Peter Simmons' name at the bottom, there was a line that said, 'Dictated but not read by Mr Simmons, ref Gill/2351'. The 'Gill/2351' reference implied that the client was the brand-leader in toiletries, Gillette.

Five days after receiving the fax, Ashley met Peter Simmons at Oriel's brasserie in Sloane Square. Simmons was a well-built man, around 5ft 10in., in his late 40s, who looked like a former prop forward and said he had played for Northampton in his early years. Affable, well spoken and seemingly trustworthy, he didn't arouse any suspicion in Ashley. He talked about his career in advertising and how he started CSR Partnership. His company, he said, had a niche client base in the toiletries market and acted for the leading brands – Gucci, Burberry, Armani, Hugo Boss and Ralph Lauren. He went on to tell Ashley that Gillette saw me as the ideal sportsman for a promotional campaign that would involve advertising in all rugby-playing countries. The campaign, he said, would involve billboards, men's magazines, radio and television advertising.

Of course, the figures were attractive. Peter told Ashley that Gillette would pay me £250,000 per annum for two years with an option to renew for a further one or two years after that. Ashley was impressed and asked Peter to provide written confirmation of the offer, mentioning the fact that there was another deal from a toiletries company on the table. Both agreed it would be preferable to get things moving as quickly as possible. They spoke for an hour and later that day, Ashley and I met so he could outline the proposal. Two days later Peter sent a fax detailing the offer. I didn't read the note at the time, and I'm sure I wouldn't have picked up on this even if I had, but in hindsight, the most telling part of that second fax, dated 21 April, was the following:

As you are aware I am presently trying to arrange a 'get-to-know-you' evening with the UK managing director and possibly a member of his PR team. This looks good for Thursday 22nd April at 7.30pm-ish. I suggest that the three of us meet prior to this for me to be able to give you a briefing on the philosophy and nature of the client (!!).

At this moment in time, I have not managed to confirm any

arrangements but will speak to you later today with regard to this. I suggest that you and I exit 'stage left', leaving Lawrence with James for the rest of the evening.

Ashley spoke with Peter a number of times later that day, and Peter indicated he wanted me to meet the UK Managing Director of Gillette, James Tunstall, the following evening. I was due to attend the testimonial dinner of my Wasps team-mate, Damien Cronin, and Ashley said it would only be possible if we met either before or after the dinner. Peter thought that wasn't a problem. We could meet after the dinner and he hoped I was prepared to have a good time as James liked to party. He reiterated he would like to meet with me earlier in the evening, before the testimonial dinner, so he could explain what kind of person James was.

Ashley, Peter and I met at the Kensington Hilton, Holland Park, at 6.30 on the evening of 22 April. It was the first time I'd met Peter and, like Ashley, I thought he was a nice guy. The notion that he was a con artist working for a tabloid newspaper wasn't even a dot on my radar. He talked about the Gillette executives I would meet later that evening, Tunstall and his colleague, Louise Wood. Louise, Simmons said, had been hired by James and was Australian. She would be my day-to-day contact for Gillette-related personal appearances. According to Peter, she was 'very important' to James. Peter's opinion was that the deal would go ahead if James and Louise hit it off with me. Peter banged on about how James and Louise were the kind of people who 'worked hard and played hard' and how they wanted to have 'a good time' with me. He made it clear that it would help if I played along and joked that I should be prepared for a big night out. But as I was going to have to drive to Langan's restaurant in Mayfair for the meeting, I told Peter I wouldn't be drinking. If only I'd stuck to that resolve.

At around 7.15, I left for the testimonial dinner. Ashley and Peter went to dinner and Peter said the contract, which would be drawn up by Gillette's in-house lawyers, would be ready for signing by the time I got back from England's tour to Australia. He apparently once again emphasised to Ashley that my meeting with the Gillette executives would work best if he and Ashley disappeared before it got going. We all met up in Langan's at around 10 p.m., and James spoke about the MACH 3 razor campaign and how £1 billion was to be spent on advertising but that the outlay would be recouped four times over. (These figures all sounded reasonable and were confirmed in newspaper articles a few days later.) At 10.30, Ashley and Peter said their goodbyes while James, Louise and I headed upstairs to a private room for dinner.

It was a very intricate web of deceit and neither Ashley nor I twigged a thing. Should we have? Maybe, but clearly the biggest mistake was mine in being so open with people I didn't know. I should probably have stayed out of the picture altogether at that stage. Until the deal was nearer completion. I could have said, 'Keep me out of this until further down the road,' but I have always been easy about that kind of thing and if I felt it was the right thing to do, I would willingly meet anyone.

The rumour of an entrapment story that we had heard about in February had come and gone and, now, as we were into rugby's close season, it just didn't seem possible that a newspaper would be looking for a sensationalist rugby story. How wrong we were.

Ashley and I hadn't discussed his leaving early but he was doing what he thought was best. To be honest, I wasn't bothered that he left because the two Gillette people were outgoing and seemed good fun. Over the years, I've turned this over and over in my mind, and I still don't understand how I was taken in so easily. I've always considered myself a fairly savvy and streetwise character and yet I walked into this completely. When they said they had booked a private room, I thought that was because they wanted us to be able to speak privately. Over the meal there was a lot of alcohol on offer but, as I was still planning on driving home at this stage, I didn't get stuck in. That was the only thing holding me back in the early part of the evening. Although I'm not a big drinker, I am a social animal and if I thought my having a glass or two would help the evening along, I would usually drink to that. As I proved wholeheartedly within a couple of hours.

With the benefit of hindsight, my behaviour could have been a lot better as the evening progressed but I presumed I was dealing with honourable people. I would soon pay dearly for my naivety. In the back of my mind was Peter's advice that James and Louise were party animals and expected to have a good time with me. Was I delivering at that stage? I wasn't sure. What I didn't realise was that they were trying to use alcohol to make me more talkative and less guarded in terms of what I told them. And I wasn't yet playing along. But how willing I was to please was obvious from the fact that I had eaten a full meal at Damien's testimonial dinner and, rather than explain this to the Gillette people, I ate a second evening meal in the space of three hours. Over dinner we spoke about the sponsorship deal and how Gillette were going to become involved in an inner-city rugby project. After eating, they suggested we all go back to their suite in the Park Lane Hilton for a nightcap and I agreed. From there on in, it all went pear-shaped.

It wasn't just one nightcap. We ended up having many drinks at the hotel and the conversation became livelier and more outrageous. During my childhood in Barnes, I'd hung out with guys who knew a lot about gangs and the recreational drug scene, and as the chat shifted in that direction, James and Louise gave the impression they found this stuff fascinating. So I took what I knew, exaggerated it, put myself into various stories I'd heard and tried to be the guy they wanted me to be. When it comes to bravado, I can give it with the best of them. Because of the presence of the woman, some of the newspapers would later claim it was 'a honey trap', but it wasn't. There was no offer of sex and I wasn't trying it on with the so-called Louise. I didn't find her attractive and, in any case, we were hardly ever alone.

The next day I felt the evening had gone well but that I had drunk far too much. As well as that, I'd had to get back to the Hilton for my car because I'd got a taxi home. Ashley phoned Peter to see if the Gillette people were pleased and whether everything was going to progress as we hoped it would. Peter reported back that the evening had been very successful and all that remained was for the deal to be given the go-ahead by Gillette executives in the US. To help this along, they needed to organise a photo-shoot so they could show the US people exactly what I looked like. The shoot was arranged for 21 May, more than four weeks after the initial get-together in Langan's. In the meantime, I arranged two tickets for Peter and James to attend Wasps' Tetley's Cup final against Gloucester at Twickenham but

Peter pulled out, saying that a colleague of his had been arrested for possession of cocaine in France and he had to go to Paris to bail him out.

Ashley and I then invited Peter to the Professional Rugby Association's end-of-season dinner at Shoeless Joe's Bar in Temple. We met for a drink in Essex Street beforehand and introduced Peter to various business friends of Ashley's – Phil Collins from Golden Wonder crisps, Gordon Baird from Timberland, Bill Nathan from BMW – and also to Ashley's lawyer, Andrew Morris. All four men spoke at length to Peter and not one had the slightest suspicion about him. In telling lie after lie, Simmons managed to come across as perfectly plausible.

Prior to the photo-shoot, which took place at the Conrad Hotel in Chelsea Harbour, Peter suggested there was no need for Ashley to attend. The photographer preferred to have as few people around as possible. He suggested Louise would be able to take care of things. Having done photo-shoots in the past, I was surprised it was to take place in a hotel rather than a studio, but the room was decked out properly, and there were two make-up artists and a designer as well as the photographer – elaborate enough to convince me everything was normal. The photographs were typical promotional shots, with me holding a razor in various poses.

We had been told James and Louise wanted to join me for drinks afterwards and my plan was to have one or two and disappear. They urged me to stay on and were very persuasive. I stayed far longer than I'd intended and had been talking non-stop, regurgitating stuff I'd already said. It was about 9.30 when I left, having pre-arranged to meet a few friends up in town. When I got there, I felt really bad. Not so much drunk as out of it, all over the shop. My eyes were glazed and I felt nauseous and uncomfortable, in a bit of a daze. Chris and Simon, two of the guys I met up with, asked if I was all right. To this day, I suspect that my drinks were spiked with something. People might think that is an excuse but I believe that's what they did. I can't prove it, of course, but it's what I think. Up in town, I couldn't recall precisely what had happened after the photo-shoot.

When it was revealed that Peter Simmons, James Tunstall and Louise Wood were all working for the *News of the World* and that every conversation had been taped, I felt sick. And it all made a different kind of sense. Having got me into a situation where I felt obliged to consume a lot of alcohol, they steered the conversation into the gossipy and titillating areas. They wanted me to dish the dirt on all sorts of things relating to rugby. What did I know about Will Carling and Princess Diana? No more than what I had read in the newspapers but you try to give a better answer than that. Had I ever taken recreational drugs? Like most teenagers, I had experimented in my late teens but that wasn't going to impress them, so I embellished the stories. You sense what people want to hear and you give it to them. Yet, even now, I look back on my meetings with these people and wonder how I let it happen. Why would I, even when trying to impress two potential backers, talk about drugs and those sorts of things? They set the trap and I didn't so much get caught as throw myself headlong into it.

That's part of the reason I've never been too bitter about the hassle that followed because I certainly wasn't blameless. At any moment in the evening, I could have got up and left. I could have said, 'Look, whoa, whoa, whoa, this is not for me.' At one point in the Conrad Hotel, the thought struck me that I was saying some pretty outrageous things to people I hardly knew and what if they were undercover journalists. That thought did actually cross my mind but as soon as it did, I told myself to stop being paranoid. James and Louise seemed exactly what you would expect young executives to be and they got me to be incredibly cavalier in my conversation. It's what can happen when you're involved in what you believe is a totally private conversation. Think of a similar situation you've been in, with people you trust and drinking a lot of alcohol, and imagine that conversation being made public the next day. I'm not looking for sympathy, though, because everyone's responsible for what comes out of their mouth. I am just embarrassed that I was stupid enough to have said the things I did.

The morning after the photo-shoot at the Conrad Hotel, Alice and I and the kids headed west for our weekend at the Woolley Grange Hotel. Idyllic on Saturday, the picture changed drastically the following day.

After arriving at Clive's place on that Sunday morning and telling him the details of how I ended up in the *News of the World*, I began the process of defending myself and my actions in this 'so-called story'. I use that expression quite deliberately because the whole situation was totally contrived by the newspaper. They tricked me and it didn't matter to them that the stories were greatly exaggerated and mostly drawn from a period in my teenage years when I wasn't playing serious rugby. Alcohol was one of the reasons that I'd allowed my guard to drop so low. Rank stupidity was the other.

My neighbours at Ladbroke Grove told me journalists were sniffing around, trying to get them to say all sorts of things about me, all negative of course, and press people were still at my parents' house. I could lie down and die, or I could come out fighting. The former wasn't an option.

On Monday morning, Ashley Woolfe and I travelled to the RFU's centre of excellence at Castle Croft, near Wolverhampton, for a meeting with Clive, Fran Cotton and some senior RFU people. They needed to know what had happened and how it impacted on my rugby career. Gradually, the implications were becoming clear. I would not be able to travel to Australia with the England team because my presence in the squad would be too much of a distraction and, in any case, I needed to stick around and face the music. As Clive would have to appoint a new captain for the trip to Australia, we felt it would be better if I resigned first rather than be replaced. I underwent a drug test to make the point that I hadn't been using drugs. Two days after the publication of the story, we held a press conference at Twickenham so that I could explain how I was set up and the lengths to which these people went to catch me out. It was a difficult situation because, however you phrase it, you are always going to look like a fool when you pipe up with something like, 'I did say it but I was lying.' Better just to accept that I had been foolish and very naïve and that as a consequence of my stupidity, I was resigning as England captain. The journalists wanted to go into the specifics of what was in the story but beyond admitting that I had experimented with recreational drugs when younger, I didn't say much. There was the possibility of litigation or an RFU enquiry further down the road and more detailed explanations would come then.

With journalists still waiting outside our house, Alice and I just wanted to get away from it. Jayne Woodward had been a star in how she took care of Alice and the girls, and on the Wednesday morning we went to Portugal to stay with a friend, Chris Thompson. I wanted to be somewhere quiet, where nobody could pester us, and the English newspapers weren't in our faces. As well as that, I'd spent two days trying to put out fires and wanted a break from it. Portugal worked, but only up to a point, because once the tabloids get their teeth into you, they don't easily let go. The *News of the World* was determined to follow up with more of the same and furthermore, on that following Sunday, the *Mail on Sunday* wrote a front-page story that accused me of snorting cocaine in a bar. You think you've been through the worst newspaper experience of your life and then something else happens.

People see the *Mail on Sunday* as somehow more believable and less scandalous than the *News of the World*. The reality, in my view, is that it's probably worse, or certainly on a par. The difficulty was that while a lot of people take the *News of the World* with a pinch of salt, they half-believe the *Mail on Sunday*. What astonished me was that they could publish a sensationalist and untrue story about me on their front page on the weekend that British troops went into Kosovo. From a personal point of view, it's pretty horrific when a newspaper writes that you snorted cocaine. You tell family and friends it's a load of bollocks but what do you do with the millions of people who have read it? At least the *Mail on Sunday* piece had the effect of making the previous week's story old news, and because it was such complete nonsense, it was easy to deal with. They claimed that after a Wasps match, a number of the players, including me, ended up at a bar in Battersea, staying after closing time as guests of the owner. We were in the bar, and we *did* stay on after closing time. But they also claimed that, during the after-hours drinks, I snorted cocaine off a mirror in the bar. Now that was totally false.

The newspaper said it had two witnesses, one a chef at the bar, the other a barmaid, and that these witnesses had signed affidavits swearing they saw me do it. Of course, this story managed to keep Lawrence Dallaglio and drugs in the news for one more week. Where my reaction was deep embarrassment at having been so stupid with the *News of the World* reporters, anger was my response to this second story. The guy who ran the bar was devastated by what appeared in the *Mail on Sunday* and fully accepted it wasn't true. Since this alleged incident took place after a Wasps match and in the company of my team-mates, I rang Wasps owner Chris Wright to reassure him the story was fabricated and to apologise for the fact that Wasps' name was being dragged through the mud. Chris is a level-headed bloke and fairly tuned in to how the media works. He was very much on my side.

'Lawrence,' he said, 'I'll help in whatever way I can. First, let me give you the name of a good solicitor. There's a chap at Harbottle and Lewis, Gerard Tyrrell, who you should speak to.'

Gerard immediately suggested that I sue the *Mail on Sunday*, which I did. Their witnesses, a Kiwi and an Australian, had disappeared back to their own countries after signing the affidavits. Our information was that they had been well compensated for their stories but we couldn't put that to them because they had disappeared. In many ways, it would have been laughable if it hadn't been so serious. The downside to litigation is that it takes for ever, costs a fortune and is just more trouble than it's worth. After it had dragged on for a long time, we settled for an apology from the *Mail on Sunday* and their agreement to pay my costs. The apology conceded that the story about me snorting cocaine was not true and, in typical newspaper style, they put the apology on page 11 or thereabouts, even though the original story was all over their front page. It took two years to get that. We thought about suing the *News of the World* but it would have been messy because they were going to play all their tapes in court and even though I believe we would have won, it would have been painful. Would it be worth it? No was the answer.

In the weeks that followed the publication of the stories, my concern wasn't so much the newspapers, but the Rugby Football Union, who felt they had to investigate the allegations. After an initial gathering of evidence, they decided to charge me formally with bringing the game into disrepute. The Union believed it had to be seen to do the right thing and I wasn't the first rugby player to be a victim of the Union's desire to play to a media agenda. Why did they need to charge me? There was no criminal case. Very tenuous amounts of truth were involved in one story and none at all in the other. The latter case, such as it was, would have been thrown out of a court of law. Yet the RFU still had to have its internal enquiry. Roy Manock, a retired solicitor from Yorkshire, was the disciplinary officer at the time and he was intent upon pursuing it. On the other hand, there were others in the Union who felt I was a key member of the England team that would compete in the World Cup, and they wanted it out of the way. A number of people were very supportive and helpful, especially

Damien Hopley, chairman of the Professional Rugby Association, and Tom Walkinshaw, Gloucester's owner. He said the clubs considered I was important to the image of the game in England and they wanted to stand by me in whatever way they could.

Gerard Tyrrell thought we should arm ourselves properly for the RFU's enquiry and in going for the late George Carman QC, he opted for some heavy artillery. Regarded by many as the best in the country, George was the QC Mum wanted to use in her battle for justice following the *Marchioness* disaster but he was tied up with another case. We spoke about that and he explained that he was very sorry not to have been able to help Mum, but it had been impossible for him given his on-going commitments at the time. Having worked with George, I can't speak highly enough of the bloke. At the time of our first meeting, at his house in Wimbledon, he must have known he was suffering from cancer. I'd read about many of the more famous cases he had undertaken and was honoured just to be there, let alone have him on my side.

'So, talk me through precisely what happened,' he said. 'From start to finish.' I told him the full story, from Peter Simmons to James Tunstall and Louise Wood.

'Well,' he said, 'we are in a bit of bother, aren't we?'

'Yeah,' I said, 'I think I might be.'

I couldn't afford to retain George Carman but, having listened to my account, he decided it was a case he wanted to take on. He worked for much less than he was used to earning and having him in my corner meant I was going to defend myself vigorously. Even turning up at the enquiry with George alongside was a statement of intent. The message to the RFU was, 'I may be just a player, but I'm not going to be pushed about.'

Not only did the RFU hold an unnecessary enquiry, they also invited the press along. If a player is before the RFU Disciplinary Committee for throwing a punch or stamping on an opponent, the press are not permitted to attend. They changed that rule because the RFU wanted to be seen to 'try' its own captain. So along we went to a room in Twickenham. It was actually quite funny as George Carman, Wasps rugby director Nigel Melville, Gerard Tyrrell and I showed up at exactly the same moment as the Union's disciplinary officer, Roy Manock. Arriving together was bad enough but we all ended up in the lift at the same time. I'm sure Roy is a really nice bloke and I don't mean him any ill will but, at the time, he was the enemy. So, there we were, all together in this confined space, everyone feeling uneasy until the ice was broken by Roy and Nigel, who knew each other from Nigel's playing days with Yorkshire, where they're both from.

'Nigel, how are you?'

'I'm fine, Roy. You?'

'Fine. And how is that lovely mother of yours?'

'Well, actually, she died five years ago.'

'Oh, I'm so sorry.'

I was trying not to crack up, because this was not an occasion for comedy, but I was barely able to stop myself. Thankfully, the lift soon opened and we were on our way again. The hearing lasted about an hour, and George was brilliant in highlighting the dishonesty and fraudulent tactics of the *News of the World*, all in the name of selling more newspapers. I don't want to minimise the seriousness of the mess I created because, as England captain, I had behaved irresponsibly in talking in such a stupid and cavalier way with people I believed to be sponsors. Perhaps I felt bullet-proof at the time, and thought I could get away with saying anything, no matter how outrageous. Yet no one had been hurt by the affair, except my own family, and as time passed, resentment at the way I had been stitched up just increased. It was a concocted story and I wasn't going to be brought down by it. They set up the trap, lured me into it, gave me plenty of alcohol and then asked the right questions. With the media present, the RFU enquiry looked to me like a bit of a show-trial, their way of saying, 'Look, we're taking this seriously and it doesn't matter that Lawrence is one of the best players in the country.'

At the end of the hearing, the RFU decided I did not deserve a ban but should be fined £15,000 and ordered to play £10,000 costs as well. At any time, to a professional rugby player that's a lot of money but it was a small fortune back in 1999. Bizarrely, I got refunded the £25,000 about six months later. It was paid by the EPRUC, the umbrella organisation that runs England's top clubs, but from what I was told, the money came from the RFU and my sense of it all being a bit of a show-trial did not lessen. All through, I felt like I had no choice but to play along because that was the way to get back in the squad for the World Cup. 'Keep your head down, do as you're told and this will all blow over,' was the message. As well as feeling hard done by, I fully accepted the mistakes I had made and the fact that I had let people down. When journalists are constantly waiting outside your parents' home and outside the home of your father-in-law, and are pestering your partner, that's hard, especially when it's your fault. Alice remained incredibly dignified and through the slurs and the accusations, she was incredibly supportive.

Losing the England captaincy wasn't that big a deal for me. I had been captain for almost two years, things were going well and I enjoyed good relationships with both the players and Clive Woodward. But while I was desperate to play for England, I didn't set out to be captain of the team. That happened because of the way I played, the position I played in, the passion I brought to the game, my fierce ambition to see England do well and, also, because Clive Woodward had weighed up the pros and cons and had initially chosen me over Martin Johnson. The extra responsibility didn't bother me. I was captain at my club Wasps, and I was the kind of rugby person who tended to say what was on his mind – something that happened whether or not I was captain. When the team departed for Australia with Martin as the new captain, the disappointment for me was simply not being able to travel with the team. When you are all in that group, each contributing in his own way, it doesn't matter that much who is or isn't captain. Martin knew that, when I was back in the team, I would give him the same 100 per cent support he had given me. It wasn't complicated – what mattered was being part of the team; the rest was peripheral.

But do you know what? In comparison with what I'd experienced after Francesca's death, the pain I felt then and the sense of crisis in my life for the following 18 months, the *News of the World* story didn't even scratch the surface. It was nothing compared with what our family had been through, and were still going through, over Francesca's death. How could I be upset about a stupid newspaper article when, eight years after my sister's death, I could still see how much her loss affected all of our lives, especially Mum's?

*

I returned to rugby for England's World Cup warm-up games in August and September. We played Canada and USA and had two games against Premiership All Star sides. After the controversy, I was a man on a mission and that was to repay the support I'd had from so many people, not least Clive Woodward and all my team-mates. This was also my first World Cup and I was really keen to perform well. I don't know if it's still there now but in one of the rooms we used at Twickenham, there was a dagger on the wall. We called it the dagger of honour and awarded it to the man of the match for our home games. The dagger wasn't actually presented but you became the holder if the coaches named you. You wouldn't believe the amount of rivalry it generated and with Jonny Wilkinson and Martin Johnson competing, to name but two, it was hard to win the award. I got my 'hands' on it twice, both for World Cup warm-up games in 1999. That tells you something.

As well as family, friends and team-mates, it should be said a lot of people at the RFU were very supportive during the bad times. I felt sorry for Peter Trunkfield, a good man whose year of presidency happened to fall in the year when we lost a Grand Slam to a late Welsh try and two months later the team captain caused all sorts of mayhem. Through it all, Peter worked behind the scenes to get me back into rugby, and I remain in his debt.

We went into the 1999 World Cup believing we could win it but, in hindsight, we were never going to. Most of the team hadn't played in an England side that had beaten the All Blacks and we had to play them in a pool match of enormous significance. If we won that game, we had a pretty good route to the semi-finals.

Lose it and we were virtually on our way home. They beat us 30–16 at Twickenham, although it was a closer game than the score suggests. We played reasonably well, won a lot of possession but struggled to break their defensive line. By contrast they had Jonah Lomu and at a critical moment in the game, he ripped our defence to shreds and scored an outstanding try. Late in the game, they switched Lomu to No. 8 and he drove forward off their attacking scrums – just what the opposing No. 8 wants in the last 20 minutes of the game!

As disappointed as we were, the New Zealand players were chuffed with themselves, although that didn't manifest itself in any bonhomie towards us. I've always found the All Blacks pretty distant after a game, but that has changed slightly in very recent years. That day we were all in the Rose Room at Twickenham and none of them was interested in any sort of conversation. Maybe they just didn't like us, I don't know. I found it strange, though. They had just beaten us, fair enough, and they thoroughly deserved their win, but surely you can sit down and speak to your opponent afterwards. We just shrugged and let them get on with it. A few days later I saw photographs of them surfing in the south of France. That didn't look right to me. 'Oh dear,' I thought, 'they don't look like champions.' I read afterwards that their coach John Hart thought he lost the team mentally after the trip to France.

Our World Cup was on a bad course after the New Zealand game. We put on 101 points against Tonga in our final pool match, but instead of progressing to the quarter-finals as you do now, we had to take on Fiji in a play-off match at Twickenham on the Wednesday. The quarter-final was due to be played four days later at the Stade de France, and the opposition was South Africa. It was ridiculous scheduling. The Springboks had double the amount of preparation time we had, and Fiji actually gave us a punishing game in the play-off. We won 45–24, comfortable enough in the end, but a World Cup-winning team is not going to concede 24 points to Fiji. What with travelling to France and trying to recover from that game, we had virtually no time to prepare for South Africa, and I was further puzzled by Clive's team selection. I expected him to play Jonny Wilkinson at fly-half and on the evening before the team was announced, Clive gave a few of us the definite impression that Jonny was going to play. Then the next morning, he named Paul Grayson at 10 and Jonny was on the bench.

Someone said Clive had had a dream and decided to go with Paul on that basis, but I'm sure he just woke up in the morning and thought, 'I'm going with Grace,' as he was entitled to do. Paul was a good player. In any case, the No. 10 wasn't the reason we went out of the World Cup, or if it was, the No. 10 in question was South Africa's Jannie de Beer, who kicked five drop-goals. He killed us. You could tell they had worked it out – England defend well, so let's set up drop-goal chances. What really annoyed me was the fact that none of us could get near de Beer, who sat so far back in the pocket that he was untouchable. Of course, he couldn't have done that unless he had such a big boot. South Africa and their coach Nick Mallett were clever in other ways, too. They noticed in earlier matches that I was taking the opposition kick-off and making a lot of ground running the ball back. At the restarts, they positioned their No. 8, Bobby Skinstad, on the opposite side to where I stood, forcing me to decide whether to stay or go. I was really annoyed with myself for taking the bait – I followed

Skinstad and they kicked it to the other side. As a team, we didn't have enough ability to think on our feet.

Even though we had a long way to go we were improving, but that's not how we saw ourselves at the time. Losing to South Africa devastated us. Through our preparation and during the tournament itself, we'd worked really hard, behaved professionally and hardly had an evening out. Nevertheless, we found ourselves in Paris on the Sunday evening, out of the World Cup and all feeling pretty miserable. We made a decision to drown our sorrows as a squad — a release valve at the end of an intense campaign. Joe Worsley had got his first cap against Tonga earlier in the tournament and we hadn't had a chance to celebrate that milestone in Joe's career. Even Jonny Wilkinson came out with us that evening.

During the early part of the evening we all stuck together, but as we moved from place to place, we split up. I ended up in some bar or club on the Champs Elysées with Leon Lloyd, Neil Back, Johnno and a couple of others. It was about two in the morning when an England fan, who was obviously the worse for wear, came up to Neil Back and began telling him how badly the team had played. This guy had the Cross of St George painted on his face and the red was beginning to run down on to his chin and neck. Completely ignoring him, Backy kept talking to Leon and me. Then the guy started having a go at me, which I also ignored, so he turned again to Backy, tapping him on the shoulder. 'Mr Persistent,' I thought, 'I wouldn't push it if I were you.' He didn't see the danger, though, because he then got personal. 'You didn't play with any passion today,' he said. I knew where this was heading — Mr Persistent was about to meet Mr Angry. After losing a World Cup quarter-final, no player will easily accept being told he didn't play with passion. Dropped a pass, missed a tackle, you could accept, but not that you played without passion. Especially not if your name is Neil Back. 'Mate,' I thought, 'you're barking up the wrong tree here.'

When the guy made his 'without passion' comment, Neil looked up for the first time and offered him a way out.

'What did you say?'

I thought, 'Son, do yourself a favour, say nothing and move on.'

'I said you didn't play with any fucking passion and, and . . .' and he was clearly intent on saying more, except that Neil felt this had gone far enough.

'Lawrence, hold that,' he said, handing me his drink, and he just turned round and whacked the guy. He went down, his mate came and helped him away and that was that. Neil took his drink back and we continued talking. It was a priceless moment.

We stayed late, drank a lot and by the very end, we were all dribbling. Jason Leonard and I put Johnno in a cab and I can still see the driver protesting that he didn't want Johnno in the car. Jason and I were having none of it. 'Look mate, you're taking him,' we said. Getting Johnno into the back seat of a relatively small taxi, when he hadn't full use of himself, wasn't easy. In the end, we sort of wedged him in the back seat, gave the cab driver lots of cash, a key card from the team hotel and told him to get Johnno there.

Next morning we were on the Eurostar bound for London and, even though we had tried, the previous night's drinking hadn't got rid of the depression. It was just that everyone now had a hangover to go with the misery that comes after a big defeat.

Even Jonny was suffering. That was probably the last time I saw him a bit worse for wear as after that night out he wasn't one for the post-match drink – until the Sunday after the 2007 World Cup final that is. The team-bonding the night before to get over our sorrows had been essential, but it took its toll. It was a sad end to our 1999 tournament. Our challenge fizzled out and the World Cup continued without us. That's the hard part and you can try to find all the positives you want but you can't get rid of the feeling that you're leaving and the big boys are getting on with it. We wanted to be among them but we weren't good enough and that hurt. You learn from experiences like that and over the following seasons, Clive never let us forget how we felt on the journey home from Paris. Any booklet he produced for us carried photos of us at the end of that game and there was one wonderful shot of Backy crouching down on all fours, utterly distraught. If Mr Persistent had seen that, he might have thought twice about having a pop. Another photo showed Johnno and I looking hopelessly over our shoulders at a de Beer drop-goal as it flew between the posts. Clive touched a raw nerve and when he saw us wince with pain, he touched it again and again.

Gradually we realised that as a bunch of guys, we didn't do losing very well.

13

Club England is born

After our exit in the 1999 World Cup quarter-final, Clive Woodward talked about the team moving on and progressing from good to great. Teams change slowly, though, and it can be hard to pinpoint any one moment and say, 'There, that's when it happened.' But there was one such moment for me, when it was obvious that something had happened and that we had moved up a notch. I was standing in the South African changing room at Loftus Versveld in Pretoria on the evening of 17 June 2000. We had lost a tight Test match and yet what I saw in that Springbok changing room convinced me that everything was shifting.

The match had been intensely physical, as they tend to be

when you play South Africa. On this occasion, we'd given as good as we got. That's saying something because the Springboks, especially when they play at home, expect to win the collisions. They had Rassie Erasmus, Andre Venter and Andre Vos in their back row and those guys played every game with sleeves rolled up. At one point my opposite man, Vos, got some kind of blow to the head and was knocked unconscious.

In these situations, you expect a guy to regain consciousness quickly but Vos's injury was a little more serious and he was put on to a stretcher and taken from the field. As far as I could see, he was completely out of it. I hoped he would be OK and wondered who would be brought on in his place. About 15 minutes passed and, suddenly, there was Vos again, thundering into a ruck. 'What are you doing here?' I thought. His return was either the medical miracle of the season or the medical disaster of the century. It had to be risky but I admired Vos's determination. 'Unless you've got a serious spinal injury or you're completely knocked out, I expect you to be in the defensive line,' our Wasps coach Shaun Edwards would say to us. Shaun came from Wigan, a background as different as you could get from the Afrikaner's but he had the same mentality. Over the years I got to know Vos and what he did that day was typical. He was incredibly tough, a great player.

I'd gone to the South Africa changing room because I wanted to swap shirts with him. Sometimes you might send the kit man round with your jersey but on this occasion, I went myself.

After-match changing rooms are the same the world over. Losers sit there, physically shattered, mentally drained and demoralised. Down the corridor, winners laugh and joke. At Loftus Versveld that day, it was different. We were disgusted to have lost and thought we deserved to win, but that's not the same as being demoralised. We knew we had competed fiercely and perhaps shaded it. The game turned on what I regarded as a bad decision by the video referee, who refused to give us a penalty try when Tim Stimpson was clearly pulled back as he attempted to control and then ground the ball over the Springbok line. It was the first year of video refereeing and given the atmosphere in the stadium, I don't suppose I blame him for making the call he did. But it cost us seven points and we ended losing by five. We were pissed off and everyone in our changing room knew that we had to win the second Test in Bloemfontein. No ifs and buts, we just had to do it. That was the general feeling. Then I went off to give my shirt to Vos and I couldn't believe what I found in their changing room. It was like a scene from *M.A.S.H.*, bodies everywhere, bandages being taken off, ice-packs on knees and heads, players having wounds checked and everyone too shattered to talk. Their wasted bodies were a joy to behold, their silence music to my ears. They were completely gone whereas I felt we still had 20 to 30 per cent of our energy left. At that moment I knew we would take these guys the following week.

I also knew that in their bruised and smashed state, they now respected us. With that thought came the certainty that we were no longer the old England.

Our failure to get past the quarter-final of the 1999 World Cup was an eye-opener and made us realise we had a lot of things to do to get to the top of world rugby. We had to improve the overall leadership within the team. Martin Johnson was a great captain but he needed more help than he was getting. Jonny Wilkinson says that he wasn't ready in 1999 to be the leader that the No.10 must be and it wasn't until he began to play regularly with people such as Mike Catt and Will Greenwood that he received that support. Jason Leonard and, later, Phil Vickery would become influential in the organisation of our scrum; Ben Kay would take responsibility for our line-out; a lot of players would end up making important contributions. But for the team to take off, Clive Woodward had first to create the right environment.

One thing was sure – we were growing tired of losing. After the ignominy of being well beaten by the Springboks in the World Cup, we put that defeat behind us and, in 2000, went in search of the Grand Slam in what was the first Six Nations Championship. We played good rugby in the first four games: scoring 50 points against Ireland at Twickenham, beating the French in Paris, scoring 46 against the Welsh at Twickenham and then 59 points in our first-ever championship match against the Italians. It all came down to our final game against the Scots, who had lost all four of their matches to that point. No one was giving them much of a chance but we knew they had Ian McGeechan and Jim Telfer behind them and that meant the Scots would turn up believing they could beat us. We expected a big match but didn't prepare for the foul conditions. Even though it was the first Sunday in April, it turned out to be a wet, windy and miserable day. Instead of rethinking our tactics, we stuck with the predominantly running game that had served us well up to that point. It wasn't a day for running out of your own 22 metres but that's what we tried to do – and we paid for it.

Maybe the decision to play our normal game in such lousy

conditions was, in part, down to naivety. Clive also decided to go with the second rows who had played in the early matches when Martin Johnson was injured. Martin was fit again and had played the previous weekend for the England A team in Italy. He could have been put into the side against Scotland but Clive's feeling was that Simon Shaw and Gareth Archer deserved the chance to see out the tournament. Was it a mistake? Perhaps, but few were complaining at the time. What is certain is that the Scots deserved their victory and, as sick as we felt afterwards, we had no right to complain.

Clive's great strength was his ability to see the bigger picture. The loss of a second Grand Slam was something he could live with because European domination wasn't the ultimate aim. Two months after Murrayfield came the summer tour to South Africa and, probably for the first time, Clive had more or less everyone fit and available. He would have seen the tour as being a much better barometer of our progress than the admittedly abject performance in Scotland.

The tour to South Africa showed Clive's seriousness. Firstly, he was determined the tour would be different from any other trip we'd made to the southern hemisphere, and if a lot of feathers were ruffled in the process, that wasn't going to give Clive any sleepless nights. In a general sense, tours are organised by the host country for the visiting team. Clive wasn't having that. He wanted a short tour, just two Tests, and because three weeks meant there wouldn't be time for people to play themselves into the Test team, Clive basically picked his Test and midweek teams before we went. People outside of the squad questioned it but that didn't bother Clive, who told the guys in the Test 22 that, barring any injury, they would stay in that 22. You might imagine the midweek squad being disgruntled but they weren't, probably because they knew where they stood from the beginning. Clive didn't make any bones about the situation. Had someone played very badly in the first Test, he might have been dropped for the second but Clive wasn't planning to make changes. It was a policy that wouldn't have worked for a seven-week tour, but it was sensible for this much shorter trip.

Clive also decided we wouldn't waste time moving from one hotel to another, figuring he wouldn't win a Test series with players exhausted from travelling. Our South African hosts would have preferred us to move from one city to another, changing hotels every few days, because that's the way it was always done. Instead, Clive booked us into the Westcliff Hotel in Johannesburg and told us that this was it, we wouldn't be moving. The Westcliff is an amazing hotel. Built on a hill, it consists of a series of very plush separate buildings with golf carts on hand for guests to travel within the hotel grounds. The lads particularly liked the way you pressed a button in your room and a television appeared at the bottom of your bed. You could argue that by setting up camp at one hotel, we weren't touring in the proper sense, but those days were coming to an end with the arrival of professional rugby. What I liked about Clive was the way he seemed to enjoy upsetting officials who wanted to organise everything in the way that suited them. For Clive, getting the logistics to our liking was a victory in itself.

Even though I wasn't on the Tour of Hell in 1998, I heard the different stories that filtered back. There was one where Clive checked the squad out of a hotel in Cape Town and moved them to a better one, producing his own credit card to guarantee payment. The South Africa Union originally had England in a hotel with the Springbok Under-21 team, who played their game, went out on a big night and made a lot of noise when they returned. England had a Test match to play a few days later and, understandably, Clive was furious. He believed our squad should not be sharing with any South Africa team, and especially not a young side with guys making a nuisance of themselves. In any case, Clive didn't think the hotel was up to scratch so, typical of him, he contacted the best hotel in Cape Town, the Mount Nelson, and booked all the boys in there. That's not the kind of move that's going to make you unpopular with the players and Clive did a lot for his standing with them at that moment.

Graham Cattermole, the accountant on that tour, must have been having kittens and no doubt didn't share Clive's enthusiasm for the move, but he wouldn't have stood a chance. I can imagine Clive's response if Graham wondered about the cost – something along the lines of, 'Graham, I've got a Test match to win in three days and I'm not going to piss about.'

By the time 2000 came around, Clive was sure of how he wanted to organise things. As both of our Test matches were at altitude, in Pretoria and Bloemfontein, it was going to be hard enough without any extra difficulties caused by bad planning. Making the right decisions was key for Clive. When my tour report arrived with assessments from the various coaches after losing that Pretoria Test so closely, Clive wrote that he wasn't happy with the decision-making between Nos. 8, 9 and 10. I felt fairly sure that criticism was directed at the choices we'd made at the series of scrums close to the Bok line.

When we came off the pitch at Loftus Versveld, we felt a deep frustration. Yeah, we felt robbed over the Tim Stimpson incident but the sense of injustice was backed by a determination to win the second Test. On the way to the dressing room I stopped to do a flash interview with one of the people from Sky television. Clive didn't believe we should do interviews until we'd showered and cooled down after matches, and it probably is better to wait, but on this occasion I had forgotten our protocol. 'We feel we should have won that game and now we've just got to win next week. We will have a good week's preparation and then we've got to come out and win in Bloemfontein.' As soon as the interview ended, I had second thoughts. 'God, I hope that didn't sound too gung-ho, and I hope it doesn't come back to haunt me.'

That's how I felt, though, and back in the England dressing room, everyone felt the same. Deep down, the South Africans knew they had won a match they shouldn't have won. They were aware that we'd had no Jonny Wilkinson, who had been ill on the morning of the game, and although Austin Healey played well in his place, Jonny's all-round kicking game would probably have made the difference.

With one week between the Tests, recovery was what we most needed and we weren't able to do much on the training ground. Yet it was a fantastic week for us, both in terms of our preparation and also in the way we were starting to come together as a group of players. Although we were scattered round in the Westcliff's different buildings, meal times were fantastic, and when we had free time, we would all gather around the swimming pool and have a lot of fun. It was noticeable that the little cliques you normally got in the England camp weren't operating any more. It was probably just the natural integration of a group that had been together for a while now. We'd prepared for the 1999 World Cup, we'd been through the bad days against Wales at Wembley, against the Scots in Murrayfield and we were stronger for them. I had been touring with some of the guys for what felt like an eternity – Mark Regan, Simon Shaw, Kyran Bracken, Mike Catt, Will Greenwood and I had been in Australia together as Under-21s in 1993.

In terms of ferocity, the second Test was no different from the first. Towards the end of the first half, their fly-half, Braam Van Staaten, tackled one of our guys close to their line and Jason Leonard was the next player to arrive on the scene. As Jason went to get Van Staaten out of the way, he caught him with a proper knee in the back. Referee Stuart Dickinson saw it and, in one of those classic refereeing moments, said, 'Jase, sorry mate, I can't let that go. You're off to the bin. Ten minutes.' Jason didn't complain – 'Fair enough. Can't argue with that.' He got a bit of a bollocking from Clive at half-time but when the game was over and England had won by five points, he said to me, 'Hey, did you see that Van Staaten come out for the second half? Me neither. Poor thing. And they didn't kick much after that, did they . . . ?'

We won the match by the same margin they achieved in the first Test, and it was a huge victory for us. For Jonny Wilkinson, it was a seminal moment. Clive had messed with him at the 1999 World Cup, although that might be a harsh way of putting it. In any case, Clive didn't believe he was ready to face the Springboks then. Only nine months had passed and Jonny controlled the game in Bloemfontein, scoring all of our 27 points. Of course, the kicking opportunities arose because the pack performed superbly and overall it was a very good team performance in a match we had to win.

Without doubt, it was a turning point in the development of the team. We had come to South Africa and drawn the Test series 1–1 but we all knew we should have won it 2–0. Still, in a really important game, we had beaten them in one of their favourite backyards, Bloemfontein, and you couldn't overstate the importance of that in terms of our confidence. It was the first time we had won away against one of the southern hemisphere's big three and it actually started a run of 14 consecutive victories home and away against southern-hemisphere opposition. The last in that run, coming in Sydney, was probably my favourite but when I look back on what Clive's England team achieved, those 14 victories rank right up there with winning the World Cup.

That South Africa tour convinced us all that Clive was the right man. For one thing, his attention to detail meant that the logistics of the three-week tour could not have been better. We felt like we were part of an élite group and had someone at the top who wasn't going to be messed around. Clive also showed a huge amount of common sense in the way he dealt with various situations that arose. For example, the tour schedule was unusual in that there was a midweek game after the second Test, and you had to feel sorry for the guys who were playing in that game because it came after the ball was over. Seeing the potential difficulty, Clive got the first-team squad together. 'Look guys,' he said, 'I don't care what you do. You can fly from here to Cape Town for all I care. You can enjoy yourselves as much as you like because you deserve it. We've had a great tour. But the one thing you can't do is distract the other guys as they prepare for their final match.' That was fair enough. The midweek team, to its credit, won that last game and went home unbeaten – another sure sign that the bar was being raised in the England squad.

The first-team squad went out every night through those last four days and we had a fantastic time together. It was so unusual to end a tour and not be travelling home the next day. Guys who wouldn't normally socialise that much had no reason to stay in and the team-bonding process was taken a stage further. The hardcore would always find a way to have a night out whatever the circumstances, but there were others who would venture out only if the time and place were right. We'd had our big night out in Paris after the World Cup defeat but that was a good night for the wrong reasons. This was different. And important. Take my relationship with Martin as an example. We'd got on really well in South Africa on the '97 Lions tour when the team was winning and we had the opportunity to socialise. After that, he went back to Leicester, I went back to Wasps. The night out in Paris was a one-off. In South Africa we rediscovered what we'd had with the Lions three years before. That kind of coming together happened throughout the squad. For me, South Africa 2000 was where Club England was born.

We were slowly realising how clued-in Clive was. For instance, you would be working out in the hotel gym when someone would mention that our fitness coach, Dave Reddin, had been in South Africa three months earlier and checked the facilities before Clive committed to the hotel. Examples of that kind of planning were everywhere. Clive should also get praise for the way he handled players. During the tour, there were a few hairy moments, a few situations where he could have lost his rag but didn't. A golf cart went missing at the hotel and what might have developed into a major controversy ended before it began because Clive quietly sorted it out with the hotel manager. Perhaps if we had been spanked 2–0 in the Test series, more would have been made of the mystery of the missing cart, but those things can get overlooked when you win. And Clive always struck me as a person who hadn't been afraid to enjoy himself when he was a player and therefore didn't resent us having a good time, as long as we delivered!

Believing that the 2000 tour to South Africa was the moment when England walked on to the world stage was one thing, but the proof would be in our results. Five months after that tour, we played and beat Australia, Argentina and South Africa in our autumn internationals at Twickenham. We won all three matches but they were overshadowed by an embarrassing battle with the RFU over pay. From the players' point of view, it was a PR disaster. We were portrayed as not prepared to play for our country because we weren't being paid enough. How do you win that argument? You can't – simple as that. The truth is that the players were unhappy with what they were getting from the Rugby Football Union – I think £6,000 was the match fee at the time. Twickenham was getting bigger and bigger and was full to its 75,000 capacity for virtually every England game. As well as that, the corporate boxes were overflowing and the whole show was based on the 30 guys performing on the pitch. We felt that in percentage terms, the match fee did not reflect our contribution to the occasion. So the players appointed Martin Johnson, Matt

Dawson and me to negotiate. We dealt with Francis Baron, chief executive of the RFU, and we found him a tricky negotiator, but I'm sure if you were seeing this from the Union's point of view, you would say Francis was tough and able.

We looked at how sportsmen in golf, tennis, football, any major professional sport you care to mention, were paid and knew that compared to them, we were being very badly treated. We weren't asking for anything ridiculous but there were issues that just had to be dealt with. For example, you would have 30 players in the England squad in the week of an international but by Saturday afternoon, the squad was reduced to 22. The eight people left out had to cope with the disappointment of not making the match-day 22 and they weren't getting anything for their time with the squad. We argued that they had to be paid. At some clubs guys were being docked wages for the time they were away with England and in a few cases, the international match fee wasn't as much as the player was being docked. In effect, it was costing him to play for England. There were arguments, too, that worked against us. Some people felt that England players were doing extremely well because they were being paid twice when on international duty – that is by the RFU and by their clubs.

I found the negotiations with Francis Baron a nuisance. As I've said, I have never been motivated by money and arguing about pay is not one of my favourite pastimes. When I started in rugby, I played for a pint, a pie and a good yarn. The negotiations were like a game – we asked for this, they offered that and we would end up settling for something in between. But when Francis Baron came back to us, he was offering less than what was agreed a few days before. I mean, the amount of money was small, £250 or something ridiculous like that, but it became a point of principle. When we went back to our players with the various deals, a number of them had very strong views about them. Withdrawing labour was the last resort, the option no one wanted, but it almost came to that. We had a vote about whether we would go on strike. Even now when I use the word 'strike' in relation to the England team, it makes me uneasy, but that is what we voted for. It was a very difficult situation. Some people, including Jonny Wilkinson and Richard Hill, didn't want to go on strike, no matter what, but they made it known they would go along with whatever the group decided.

Clive's role in the dispute upset me a little because I felt he shouldn't have got involved. A few months earlier, he had invited Alice and me round to his house for lunch and it was clear he was agitated about something. When we had a chance to speak privately, he told me his contract negotiations with Francis Baron were taking longer than they should and they were arguing over money.

'If you're not getting what you deserve,' I said, 'just go on strike. Then they'll pay up pretty quick.'

'You're right,' he laughed, 'maybe I should.'

When the boot was on the other foot and we were the ones arguing with the RFU, I thought Clive should have stayed well clear. Instead, he took our threat to strike personally, as if we were letting him down. We could have done without Clive weighing in against us because we were already being hammered by the RFU's PR machine. They were issuing statements, briefing journalists, and there was an unhelpful photograph of Matt Dawson driving away from a meeting in a top of the range car. What did help us, though, was that Martin was on the three-man players' committee. Matt would have been seen as trouble and I was regarded as a bit militant, but if a solid guy such as Johnno believed in the cause, it had to have some merit.

Clive's interference drove a wedge between the players and the coaching staff. A lot of things were said that didn't need to be said. It got to a ridiculous point where all the other coaches weren't talking to us, as if they had to support their head coach by not communicating. Clive told us that going on strike would be the biggest mistake we would ever make because he would pick an England team to replace us. What he didn't understand was that every professional player supported us. As can happen in acrimonious disputes, players who were known to have major reservations about the threat to strike were targeted. Clive telephoned some of them and asked, 'Are you with me or with the guys going on strike?' Fair play to them, they didn't buckle. 'Look Clive, I'm sorry but I'm with the guys,' was their answer.

In the days leading up to the Argentina game, the players were scheduled to attend a dinner in London. We reckoned we'd be crucified if we didn't show up, so even though RFU people were going to be there, along we went. As it turned out, when we all got together, things began to progress. We didn't want to pull out of the game, the RFU didn't want a strike, and even though an important point of principle was at stake, it wasn't worth the strife it was causing. So we reached a compromise that we could all live with. On the Saturday at Twickenham, Argentina proved as tough an opposition as the RFU, and even though we got through 19–0, we felt the same as we did after endless rounds of negotiation with Francis Baron – it hadn't been much fun. Both the RFU and ourselves had taken a hammering in the media and it is still hard to believe it got to a point where we voted to strike. From a team point of view, the controversy played a part in binding us even closer than we had been before. No one enjoyed it, no one wanted to go through it again, but at a time of serious adversity, we stuck together.

I was impressed by the way Clive regained the trust of the players. The row had the potential to damage the coach/player relationship. Clive was upset by the experience and felt let down by his players who, in turn, felt the dispute was none of his business. Clive regained lost ground by talking about the situation, and we all accepted that he genuinely believed what he was doing was the right thing. I thought some of the players would have given him a wide berth but everyone seemed to realise it had been a strange, one-off situation, and should not be allowed to destroy what we were trying to achieve. So we shrugged our shoulders and said, 'Ç'est la vie.' Once we put it behind us, a new respect became evident in the relationship between all the parties. Through the tears and grief we had seen how strong we were. Pistols at dawn had ended in kisses and hugs in the evening.

Results proved the dispute didn't hurt the performance of the team. A week after it ended, we beat South Africa at Twickenham and then two months later we produced some of our best ever rugby to beat Wales, Italy, Scotland and France in the Six Nations Championship. We played France at Twickenham in April, when you expect them to be strong, and scored 48 points. Iain Balshaw was playing with tremendous confidence at full-back, Mike Catt was passing the ball beautifully and some of our running was exhilarating. I have no doubt we would have beaten Ireland and won the Grand Slam if an outbreak of foot and mouth disease had not caused the postponement of the game. That match went ahead the following October but, by then, lots of things had changed. The Lions tour to Australia had taken place and taken its toll. My slightly torn cruciate didn't hold up in Australia and I returned home early for major surgery. That ruled me out of Dublin for our Grand Slam match. Martin Johnson was also injured and Iain Balshaw returned from the Lions less confident than he had been for us in the spring.

Clive played his part in our loss by not organising a warm-up game before Dublin. Ireland had played their postponed matches against Scotland and Wales in the weeks before and on the day of our match they had the sharpness that we lacked. Clive stuck with the players who had performed well for us the previous spring but who weren't on good form at the time of the Lansdowne Road match. Working for radio, I watched the game in Dublin from the press box and the occasion was memorable for the fact that Pete McCarthy, who wrote that very funny book, *McCarthy's Bar*, came and sat beside me during the match. I had met Pete a few times and liked him a lot. He has since passed on and it is nice for me to recall that we spent a very pleasant afternoon together – 'the day Ireland hammered England 20–14,' as he would have said.

Losing to Ireland was hard because it was another Grand Slam we had let slip through our fingers – the third in two and a half years. Those losses might have undone a lesser coach but because he was so focused on the bigger picture, Clive quickly put them behind him. Three weeks after losing in Dublin, England had

Australia at Twickenham and I think, although he might never admit it, that mattered to him more. We beat the Wallabies, then the Springboks two weeks later with a 29–9 victory, more comfortable than was expected. There was no doubt England was moving forward all the time in a gradual but definite progression towards the top. Along the way there were a number of one-off defeats that were hard to take but, ultimately, played a significant part in making the team strong. One of them occurred at the Stade de France in March 2002, when we deservedly lost 20–15 to the French. Through Serge Betsen, they managed to put Jonny Wilkinson under a lot of pressure and we didn't deal with that very well – probably because the French had us on the back foot in plenty of other areas as well.

However, our general improvement was obvious from the 2002 autumn campaign. We played New Zealand, Australia and South Africa on three consecutive Saturdays, won all three matches, and yet didn't feel like we had done anything fantastic. In fact, we didn't play well against the All Blacks and kind of scraped home in the end, 31–28. A week later we played great rugby when we needed to against Australia and just won, 32–31. In our final game that autumn, a dirty match against the Springboks, we beat them 53–3 and didn't have to play extraordinary rugby to run up the record score. Nevertheless, any team that defeated the All Blacks, Australia and South Africa on successive weekends had to have a serious chance of doing well in the World Cup – we were starting to believe the ultimate prize was winnable.

My own memories of those three games are not as good as they might be because after the New Zealand game, I was dropped. As this had never happened before and as the Australia match was to be my 50th cap for England, it was a hell of a shock. I thought that perhaps there was a slight element of rotation in the selection of the back row for the three matches because Neil Back was left out of the All Black game, replaced by his Leicester team-mate Lewis Moody, but then Neil was brought back in and I was dropped. It would have been hard to drop Lewis, who had taken his chance well in the New Zealand game and scored a good try, but I still felt a little harshly treated. Sure, I didn't have my greatest game against the All Blacks but that was true of most of the team and I was the only one who carried the can. I asked Clive and Andy Robinson why I'd been left out and they said I hadn't got my hands on the ball often enough against the All Blacks. I didn't think much of that reasoning because the stats showed I was England's top tackler and the effort involved in that might have had something to do with the amount of times I got my hands on the ball.

Privately you feel disappointed, and even a touch let down, when you're dropped, but you can't reveal that in public. Both to the media and within the group, I said exactly what a responsible member of the squad should say. On the bench against Australia, I came on as a blood replacement when England were winning and left the field 10 minutes later after the Aussies had scored two tries. 'Well done, Dallaglio,' this big West Country fan boomed out as I returned to the bench, 'we were winning before you went on.' I couldn't argue and in fairness to the fellow, he said it a bit tongue in cheek. Thank God, though, England played a magnificent last 10 minutes to turn the game back in our favour and Ben Cohen got the decisive try after some neat work by James Simpson-Daniel. Lewis Moody picked up an injury and was struggling through the following week but, like anyone else would have done, he said he was OK to start the Springbok game. He lasted about 15 minutes and I was again off the bench, this time for the remainder of the match. As Richard Hill and Neil Back both scored against South Africa, I was keen to get one, too, and late in the game, I touched down for a pushover try. It didn't involve much on my part but when the two other back-row players have scored, you'll take whatever you can get.

When the dust settled after those three games and the disappointment of being dropped faded, I decided to try and make sure it never happened again.

14

The best of times

Early in 2002, Wasps' owner Chris Wright called me in a bit of a panic and said our director of rugby, Nigel Melville, was leaving to join Gloucester. Chris wanted to know my reaction and my thoughts on what we were supposed to do. At the time we had a horrendous injury list (I was still recovering from a knee operation after sustaining an injury on the Lions tour), we were at the bottom of the Zurich Premiership and generally things were not in good shape.

Nigel had been coaching and organising us since 1996 and had done a tremendous job in helping the club establish itself in the professional world. He had been an outstanding scrum-half who finished his playing career at Wasps. Some part of Nigel would always be Wasps, and you couldn't write the history of the club without giving him a lot of credit, but six seasons is probably enough to be coaching any team if the players don't change and Chris Wright's call didn't exactly shock me. A couple of months earlier, a friend from the West Country had told me the Melvilles were looking at houses in Cheltenham and I thought perhaps Nigel had received an offer from Gloucester. We had been successful under Nigel, especially given the resources, having won the Courage League title in 1997 and then twice winning the Tetley's Bitter Cup (1999 and 2000), but we needed to progress. To do that, we needed a stronger squad with the emphasis on improving its depth. It wasn't Nigel's fault that we weren't bringing home more trophies, but my hope was that a new coach might be better able to bring about the changes.

The mark of Nigel's quality was that he wanted to leave Wasps in good shape and his offer to help in the hunt for his successor was accepted. New Zealander Warren Gatland was always going to be a contender because he had just parted company with Ireland and was available. His record was impressive and the failure of the Irish Rugby Football Union to renew his contract in November 2001 was a mystery. Ireland won 7 of the last 10 games they played under Warren and the October 2001 victory over England, to deny us a Grand Slam, was one of the best Irish performances for many years. It was no surprise to discover that Warren had eight or nine job offers in front of him and the fact he chose to come to Wasps had a lot to do with Nigel's promotion of the club to him. It also had something to do with Kiwi pragmatism. Warren looked at our league position, then looked at our list of players, and reckoned there was only one way things could go. He said yes to working with Nigel, and after Nigel moved on a short time later Warren told the board they shouldn't feel they had to give him that job. The board, however, had already come round to the view that Warren was the man to take the club forward.

Many fundamentals needed to be changed at the club. Facilities and staffing levels at the training ground were two obvious examples. Warren's belief was that unless the facilities were improved and more coaches were employed, the club wouldn't progress. He said he wanted to create a structure that would enable Wasps to be successful, and one that would survive long after he departed. When I heard he was considering issues that went far beyond winning the next game, I thought, 'Here's a guy with a lot of confidence in his own ability – and a lot braver than the average.' At one of Warren's early meetings with the board, he produced a list of things he wanted to change and although none of them was hugely expensive, collectively they added up to quite a bit of money. So the board politely said there wasn't the money to implement all that he requested. 'OK,' said Warren, 'in that case, what I'm going to do is sell Joe Worsley and use whatever transfer fee we get and the money we save in wages to fund the changes I want to make.' The board said, 'Hold on, he's one of our best players, we can't sell him.' But Warren wasn't backing down. Faced with the prospect of losing Joe, the board sharpened up its act and found the funds to help Warren.

He first brought in Craig White as fitness coach. Craig had his own team working under him and so instead of having one guy looking after our fitness, suddenly we had six. We also got in sports science students on a gap year from Bath University to do a lot of the prep work – weighing players, sorting out the ice-baths, making up the recovery drinks, getting all the equipment ready. Having these jobs taken off their hands left the senior fitness trainers with more time to work with players. Warren understood that coaching wasn't just about winning but also about creating an environment in which players will improve. And he was sensible in his attitude to the game in the northern hemisphere. Our rugby has its weaknesses when compared to the best in the southern hemisphere but it has its strong points as well, and Warren appreciated that. A lot of guys come from the southern hemisphere and see nothing except what is wrong with our rugby. Buck Shelford was a classic example. One of the greatest No. 8s to play the game, all he could find to say about the English game was negative – 'You're not hard enough, you're not fit enough, you're not good enough.' Warren had a very different approach. 'You know,' he would say, 'we're not as good as we think we are in New Zealand.'

Warren wasn't working on his own at Wasps. In Shaun Edwards, he had a fantastic partner. Nigel Melville might not thank me for saying so, but I think his bringing both Shaun and Warren to the club was as great a contribution as anything he did for Wasps. Shaun has the same common-sense approach to life that Warren has. A legend in rugby league, Shaun won God knows how many trophies at Wigan, whom he joined as a teenager. Like Warren coming from the southern hemisphere, Shaun didn't come from the north of England shouting about how much we had to learn from rugby league. Instead he would point to the ball and start talking – 'Same oval shape in league and union, same green grass, same posts, same objective of grounding the ball over the other team's line.' They say an open mind is the definition of intelligence and if that's true, Shaun must be very bright. He made no secret of the fact that he had much to learn about union and when we came back to Wasps from an England tour to the southern hemisphere, he was the one saying, 'OK, anything happening down there I need to know about? Anything they're doing that we should try to take on board?'

There is so much about Shaun that players respond to. The thing I noticed immediately was that most of what he did on the training ground was relevant to what you would do on the Saturday. You weren't doing bullshit drills or moves that bore no relation to the reality of a match. Neither did he waffle on or use corporate jargon to make a point. His approach was, 'Here's the ball, here's the tryline, you know what you need to do and I can help you improve some of the skills necessary to do the job.' He would then show us something as basic as putting the ball down correctly when scoring a try and have us do a drill that reinforced this technical aspect of the game. Every player can relate to that. We've all seen tries vanish because a guy loses control of the ball in the act of scoring. Shaun worked on teaching us how to pass the ball properly, how to use the hand-off, how to step and how to tackle – even if players think they have already mastered these skills, Shaun has the ability to improve them. Then one morning you'd ask where Shaun was and someone would say, 'He's away on a coaching course' – the humility that made him always want to learn was a key part of his character. Down through the years, I've worked with a lot of coaches in the England set-up who seemed to believe they knew it all. That belief stopped them learning anything new, or at least their humiliation was as apparent.

Shaun was already at the club when Warren arrived and I like to think that Nigel saw how effective they might be together. From day one, Warren and Shaun got on very well. One came from Waikato on New Zealand's North Island, the other from a working-class background in the north of England, and although they were from such very different places, they were two peas in a pod. Neither sought the limelight and when they walked into a team room, players quickly realised these guys weren't there to promote themselves. One of Warren's first tasks was to make Wasps' defence more aggressive, something that tallied with Shaun's belief in a blitz defence. Warren also said he thought Wasps were too reliant on a few big-name players and that he hoped to lessen this dependence. I knew I was one of the players he was thinking of and I couldn't have agreed more. It wasn't something I enjoyed, this feeling that 'unless Lawrence plays, we're in trouble'. Warren and Shaun were similar in other ways. They both enjoyed a drink and an occasional bet on the horses, and they had no desire to put themselves above the players.

Perhaps more important than any of the technical stuff was the human energy the duo brought to the club. They interacted with the players in a way that earned them respect. Warren came to us after Ireland had shafted him. We knew that, most people in rugby knew that, but he never said a thing about it. If you tried to draw him on it, he would just say, 'I'm not going to let one or two people spoil my good memories of the years I spent in Ireland.' I had a lot of admiration for his dignity. Shaun is a very human, blue-collar sort of bloke. He would have the backs in early one morning and have them work incredibly hard on one aspect of their play, and then at the end of the session, he'd invite them to a diner in Ealing, have breakfast with them and pay the bill. It was his way of showing the players that he was more than a coaching machine, he was also a human being and he enjoyed the craic and a bit of banter.

After Nigel left for Gloucester in the spring of 2002, Warren and Shaun took the reins for the last two months of the season. We were bottom of the Premiership at the time but, with players returning from injury, we improved rapidly and won six of our last seven league games, just missing out on qualification for the Heineken Cup. For the future, the signs could not have been better.

Without a doubt, the three seasons under Gatland/Edwards stand as the most glorious chapter in the history of Wasps – three championships, one Heineken Cup and one Parker Pen trophy. The time just flew by and we had a lot of fun along the way. Things happened – bad things, serious things, sometimes crazy things, often good things – but through it all we went to work with a smile on our faces. There were many great moments, remembered for different reasons.

OH, DANNY BOY!

To get to the 2003 Parker Pen final, we beat a very useful Stade Français side in Paris and saw off Pontypridd in the semi-final. Nick Mallett, the Stade coach, predicted we would win the final and lamented his team had to meet us at the quarter-final stage. We were hitting top form going into the final against Bath at the Madejski Stadium. Our plan was to start at a high tempo and blow them away in the first 30 minutes, which is pretty much what we did. Although we were well ahead, the forward exchanges were still ferocious. Our pack always enjoyed battling with Steve Borthwick and especially Danny Grewcock. When I came up against Danny, I knew that something was going to happen – a stamp, a knee, a punch – and invariably I was going to be the one on the receiving end. Sometimes, the stamp would get me in a place where you would really prefer not to be stamped. I'd look up and say, 'Danny, what are you doing?' And he'd sort of say, 'Well, you know what you get with me, Lawrence,' which is true, I did know. 'Yeah, fair enough,' I'd say as he walked away. It never really bothered me.

On this occasion, our little altercation took place late in the game when we were more or less playing out time. They were attacking our line and I'd got hold of their ball in a ruck, at first legally but then I lost my footing and it was no longer legal. Danny was pissed off because I was slowing their ball and he came in stamping and punching and generally showing his frustration. Unfortunately for him, the touch judge was watching, a mere two yards away. Fortunately for me, my head was buried and he ended up punching the back of my skull, something more likely to damage his knuckles than me. I know this from experience. The ref sent off Danny, but with the contest already decided, it didn't seem a big deal. It was only afterwards that we understood the implications. Any kind of ban would rule Danny out of England's pre-World Cup tour to the southern hemisphere and mean him missing games against New Zealand and Australia. As I was enjoying a celebratory drink at the Madejski, a Bath official tapped me on the shoulder.

'Lawrence,' he said, 'Danny's hearing is going on downstairs. Any chance you'd go and speak on his behalf?'

It may sound bizarre but of course I agreed because Danny's a good guy and I love him to bits. Some of his antics on the pitch bear no resemblance to the smashing bloke we know off it, and if I'm honest, there have been many times with England when I've been pleased to have him on my side.

So I left the post-match reception and headed downstairs to the room where the hearing was taking place. The referee and Danny were there already. The ref gave his version of events, Danny gave his, I gave mine, and the only thing that was clear was that someone was not telling the truth. At least Danny and I were singing off the same hymn sheet – 'Look chaps, it was handbags. Storm in a tea-cup. Much ado about nothing. My head was buried, I didn't feel anything, certainly didn't feel like I was being punched.' But they didn't fully accept our stories because Danny got a two-week suspension that ruled him out of the England tour. And the lesson? If you're going to get involved in a punching incident, it's dangerous to pick a high-profile game.

STEVE STAYS COOL

Winning the Parker Pen was the first of two victories that we wanted at the end of that 2002–03 season. We had also reached the play-off final in the Zurich Premiership and that was at least as important to us as the Parker Pen.

Gloucester were our opponents and most rugby fans hoped they would win. This was the first season that the winners of the play-off final would be acclaimed as champions – up until then, a club won by accumulating the most points through the season –

and ordinary rugby people didn't like the change. Gloucester were a record 15 points clear of us at the end of the regular season and were seen as victims of the new system. Gloucester themselves seemed to think they were being hard done by. The rhetoric coming from them was nervous and carried traces of self-pity. I felt they weren't in the right frame of mind for the game against us. They should have been saying how much they were looking forward to playing us and that it was going to be a great game instead of moaning about the play-off system. They even tried to make it a grudge match against us. I'm a big one for feeding off stuff like that and my attitude to the whinging was unsympathetic. Were the play-off rules in place at the start of the season? Of course they were. Did we all know what the rules were? Of course we did.

We had other little sources of motivation. Head coach Nigel Melville and assistant coach Dean Ryan were both ex-Wasps, and even though they were brilliant at Wasps, we didn't want them putting one over on us. Player contracts were among the million and one things Nigel did during his years at Wasps and while they worked out fine for some players, they were problematic for other guys. Often players blame the personalities involved when it's actually got nothing to do with them. I could see a few of our players had issues with Nigel and I imagined it would have been easier for him to face any club other than Wasps.

In addition to all that, our preparation for the game was excellent. In anticipation of a warm day, we trained with black plastic bags under our shirts so that we would be ready for the discomfort of playing in hot weather. It turned out to be sweltering and with around 55,000 people at Twickenham, the atmosphere was electric. Gloucester brought a huge following with them and all their wonderfully loyal fans seemed to be in the team's colours. What made the occasion even better was that it didn't feel corporate. Our fans were outnumbered but they're pretty colourful and passionate too, so it was a perfect setting for the first winner-take-all final. The mood inside our changing room was perfect – confident, but also fiercely determined. We had hit form at the right time and we knew it.

Shaun Edwards is good mates with the former world champion boxer Steve Collins, and he invited Steve into our changing room before the match. I could tell Shaun wanted Steve to say a few words to us because Steve (a true warrior) had been in a lot of tight situations in the ring and had handled them brilliantly. Steve observed our build-up and then spoke with Shaun, basically saying he didn't think there was anything he could say that would improve our mind-set going on to the pitch. Steve could see we were ready. Two minutes into the game, we were seven points up and we ended it winning by 36. Gloucester caught us on a red-hot day and while it was unfortunate that the team who had finished the season 15 points clear at the top of the table should have been smashed in the play-off final, that wasn't our concern. Our first full season working with Warren Gatland and Shaun Edwards had ended with us winning two major trophies.

PREPARING TO DIE

I have always loved playing in arenas that are full of passion and against teams that are truly up for it. In January 2004, Wasps travelled to Perpignan in the south of France for a Heineken Cup pool match that would determine whether or not we progressed to the knock-out stages of a competition we were desperate to win. For some reason, Warren and Shaun decided we should travel over on the Wednesday before the Saturday game. 'We're here a bit early, aren't we?' was the comment from the players the evening we travelled, but our mood changed the next morning when we woke to blue skies and the freshness of a spring-like day. We stayed in a hotel on the edge of Perpignan and, being there 72 hours before the match, we had a chance to immerse ourselves in the build-up to a game that meant as much to the home side as to us. They needed to win and pick up a bonus point to be sure of going through, whereas we just needed to win.

This was a hot bed of French rugby, so of course the local papers were full of stories about the game, and although I don't speak brilliant French, I can sort of read it. What was perfectly clear from the newspapers was that the pressure was on their coach. The previous season, Perpignan performed brilliantly to reach the Heineken Cup final in Dublin, where they were narrowly beaten by Toulouse, but they hadn't reached those heights this season and the coach was being blamed. In the circumstances, it was understandable that he would shift the pressure on to his players. We translated his quotes as best as we could and his message was clear. 'There's going to be murder on the pitch,' he said, 'and we have to be prepared to die.' It was a little strange and, if we're being honest, a little scary. When Warren discussed it with us, we agreed the Perpignan guys were clearly on the edge and their under-pressure coach was winding them up for one thing and one thing only. We decided it was going to be a brutal battle and we had to be ready for it.

A siege mentality can often help a team on the pitch and we felt like Christians about to be thrown to the lions. Before the game, the mood in the changing room was unbelievable as we worked ourselves up into a frenzy of emotion. You know that scene from *Gladiator*, when Russell Crowe and the others stand around before they walk out into the arena? Well, that's how we felt. Outside, the jam-packed stadium was full of passionate Perpignan fans. Drums were beating, flares were lighting up the sky and as we came out on to the pitch, quite a number of us were in tears, something I hadn't seen before – tears of joy at being so together, tears of defiance at knowing we wouldn't roll over. We just loved it. 'This is it, lads,' I said. 'This is everything we have wanted in eighty minutes. This is beautiful.' As you would expect, the game began at 100 mph, they got penalty chances but chose instead to run and there were bodies everywhere. They wanted an early try and I thought, 'Guys, you're being silly. Take the two penalties, get 6–0 in front and force us to chase the game.'

They were hitting anything that moved, punches going in everywhere, head-butting, stamping all over anyone lying on the ground. We weren't innocents as we killed the ball and slowed their possession in whatever way we could. Alan Lewis, the Irish referee, had an almighty job on his hands. Trevor Leota was making some horrendous hits, Simon Shaw got himself 10 minutes in the sin bin and I had 10 minutes in the second row. Then Simon came back and our other second row, Martin Purdy, got the sin bin and I had another stint in the engine room. But all the time, we were more clear-headed and better at actually playing the game. The points mounted and long before the end, we were clear. But, my God, it never felt like a 34–6 game and the scoreline was a gross distortion. That match will stay long in the memory. I loved it, loved every minute of it. In a typically French way, the Perpignan fans made it the most hostile arena I've ever played club rugby in and then, at the end, they stood up and applauded us off the pitch.

That night we went into the centre of Perpignan and found a small restaurant where everyone, players and coaches, enjoyed dinner together. It was simple French food but beautiful in its way and we stayed at the restaurant all evening. Martin Purdy got out his guitar and started playing, some of our supporters turned up and we had the most fantastic night. Martin is an extraordinary gentleman. He had been at Wasps for a long time, the club his father had played for in the eighties. Martin is also a Cambridge graduate, with a double first in engineering, and he plays the guitar like nothing I've heard. I always thought he was far too bright to play second-row forward. He could sing as well as strum and he got the singsong going that night. The club, entering into the spirit of the evening, picked up the tab. It was one of the great nights in the history of Wasps and probably the kind of night you can only have with your club team-mates.

Afterwards a list was put together of the potential instances of foul play committed by the opposing players. I think it ran to something like 39 separate incidents and, as a result, 12 of those were deemed citable offences and action was taken in five cases. Their captain, Bernard Goutta, was given a six-week ban for head-butting Joe Worsley, which is some achievement given the size of Joe's swede, and their hooker was banned for punching and stamping. Being honest, they actually got off lightly. None of our players was cited. We were all innocent, of course!!!

HOW MANY FINGERS?

Gloucester were our opponents in the Heineken Cup quarter-final and after smashing them in the Premiership grand final at Twickenham the previous season, we expected a backlash. The press billed it as a chance for Gloucester to take their revenge but we had home advantage and felt comfortable about the fixture. The record books will tell you we won the game fairly decisively, 34–3, but there isn't much I can tell because there isn't much that I remember. I think it was 15 minutes into the game that my team-mate Paul Volley and I went to tackle the same guy. As we did, our heads collided and a lot of lights went out. Both of us were knocked unconscious for a short time. Even though play continued, the Gloucester prop (and now my Wasps team-mate) Phil Vickery thoughtfully went to Paul's assistance and removed his gum-shield. As I came to and realised what Phil had done, I said, 'What about me and my gum-shield? You didn't take mine out.'

'I was happy to see you off the pitch, you bastard,' said Phil with a smile.

Such was the impact of the collision that Paul and I were completely out of it, but at least we regained consciousness on the pitch. Mind you, I hadn't much of a clue where I was or what was going on. But I did at least realise that Paul seemed worse off and if the two of us had to be replaced, it would be a disaster. Medically speaking, it wasn't the right thing to do, but I said I was fine because you know that if you leave the field with concussion, they'll say you can't go back on. I knew it was concussion because I'd had it before – the luminous yellow flashes were back again. In today's game there is a very strict protocol that determines whether a player is concussed, whereas a few years ago the team doctor came on and asked how many fingers he was holding up. But just because you could tell it was three, didn't mean you weren't concussed. I certainly didn't mention the flashes, nor the splitting headache and dizziness. And Paul Volley was saying the same thing. 'I'm fine, I'm fine, I'm fine,' he said, then he wobbled and the doctor said, 'There's no way he can carry on.' But both of us did stubbornly play on.

At half-time one of the lads told me we had scored two tries (one of which I got) since the collision, but I couldn't recall us scoring anything. Apparently, we were in complete control of the game but that was news to me. I probably should have come off at that point, which would have been the logical thing to do. Hardly my style, though, and as it turned out, everything was fine. We won the match and Paul and I suffered no serious effects. In fact, I made just one mistake that day – choosing to smack heads with probably the hardest one in the game.

THIS ONE'S FOR YOU, MATE

When we knew we had to travel to Lansdowne Road to play Munster in the Heineken Cup semi-final, I immediately thought the match would have a special significance for Warren Gatland because of the way he had been ditched by Ireland. I didn't know the specifics and in the lead-up to the game, I asked him.

'What was the story over there?'

'Look mate, you don't need to know. Suffice to say, I want to fucking win this game.'

'Yeah,' I said, 'I'm sure you do.'

I wasn't the only one thinking about Warren going into this

game – other Wasps players felt the same and I let it be known in the changing room that this was an ideal match for us to repay some of the faith the coach had shown us. I really don't know what happened with Ireland but Warren's record over there should not have cost him his job. Later, I went on the 2005 Lions tour and spoke to a number of the Irish guys. Nearly all the players got on well with Warren. In fact, a lot of them spoke very highly of him, although I don't think Keith Wood and he were exactly a match made in heaven. Given Keith's standing in Ireland, that was perhaps a slight problem, but it all remains a bit of a mystery to me.

As for the game itself, although I always wanted to get back to Thomond Park, I wasn't unhappy it was being played at Lansdowne Road. I'd won every game I'd played at Lansdowne Road and agreed totally with Martin Bayfield's philosophy that if you're going to lose a big game, Dublin is the place to do it because an hour afterwards, no one is going to remember the score anyway. But this was one we were desperate not to lose – it was our first time in the last four of the Heineken Cup and we were playing a team who were perennial semi-finalists. For Munster, the tournament seems to begin at the semi-finals. I was an admirer of theirs and went as a fan to the 2001 semi-final against Stade Français in Lille, and like everyone else, felt Munster were so unlucky then. On the train back to London, I drank with a lot of Munster fans and the great thing about the journey was that by the time we pulled into Waterloo, you would have thought Munster had actually beaten Stade Français.

Warren put us in a hotel in the heart of Dublin, with Munster fans everywhere – the build-up was amazing. When we went to do our line-out practice, a couple of thousand people were watching us. If the desire to make sure Warren left Lansdowne Road that afternoon with his head high was one part of our motivation, Trevor Leota was another. A Samoan, Trevor had been with us for a good few years and at that time was dealing with serious personal problems so, basically, we became his family during that time. We felt we had a duty to look after him. That's the way it's always been at Wasps. The nice thing about a Heineken Cup semi-final is that both teams walk out together and as we emerged from the tunnel, the scene was like nothing I had ever seen before. It was a record crowd for a semi-final, an estimated 51,000 packed into the stadium and it seemed like 50,000 were wearing Munster's red shirt. You couldn't help but be inspired by it. I'd love to have been a Munster player performing in front of that. Jesus, they must have felt like they were being spoon-fed adrenalin.

When the game kicked off, we were much too wound-up and were giving away silly penalties at every turn. Trevor was responsible for a few, and I gave away my share. Ronan O'Gara kicked one, missed another and we were lucky to be just three behind. Then, from our first proper attack, we put together sequences of play that just obliterated their defence and created the chance for Josh Lewsey to score. You could see the Munster lads' reaction: 'Fuck, we're playing a bloody good side here.' And so began a memorable game of rugby – the lead kept changing, we got guys sin-binned, they got guys sin-binned, we looked in control, they looked in control and with 10 minutes to play, we were 10 points down. In spite of the gravity of the situation, we were calm because we felt we would win. We were dominating despite the scoreline, and we were all saying the same thing – 'We're not going to lose this game.' I don't remember many grounds having a stadium clock in those days but Lansdowne Road had one.

'Is that right, ten minutes to go?' I asked the ref.

'Yeah,' he said, 'that's the time.'

It was a help to know that because it told us there was no need to panic, but we did need some points sharpish. Alex King obliged with a penalty and then Tom Voyce weighed in with a try, which we converted to level the scores.

That gave us the confidence to attack straight from their kick-off and we went right down the other end of the pitch. After two or three rucks, Trevor Leota went over in the corner. It wasn't certain Trevor got the ball down properly – and even after seeing it on a video replay, I still wasn't sure – so we needed a little luck and fortunately this was one of those 50–50 decisions that the video ref gave to us. Even after Trevor's try, Munster came back at us, Christian Cullen made a good run and we were scrambling to hold on. It was a fantastic game – without doubt the best club game I've ever been involved in. People will say it's easy for me to say that because we won, but the truth is that we just happened to be ahead when the music stopped. That's the only way you can describe it. It had the build-up, it had the stadium, it had the sense of occasion, it had great weather, it had two teams packed with internationals who played great rugby, some of the best we've ever played in my view, and it definitely had the crowd.

After the game, I gave Warren a bit of a hug and, for a guy who normally has a slight poker face, it was strange to see the permanent smile that evening. 'Good on you, mate,' I thought.

There were plenty of things I would like to have said to him but we don't always say the things that matter the most – until now. 'Gats, you left Ireland with dignity. You got sacked, it was unfair but you didn't moan about it, you didn't go whinging to the Irish press. You went away, considered your options and picked a fucking good one, frankly, in Wasps. You came to us and you made it work. Now you've returned to Dublin and without saying a word, you've made your point. You've told them everything you needed to tell them, which was that they made the wrong decision. As much as I think Eddie O'Sullivan is a very good coach, you had a lot more to give Ireland and they never discovered it. But their loss, mate, was our gain.'

TWO WEEKS, TWO FINALS, TWO TROPHIES

After the victory over Munster came the hangover. Funnily, this was a hangover in which alcohol played little part. We were physically and emotionally drained after the Lansdowne Road match and to have to travel to Kingsholm to play Gloucester six days later wasn't ideal. As well as that, we were already assured of making the Zurich Premiership play-offs and the game at Gloucester wasn't life or death. Still, we wanted to keep winning and our coaches opted to go with more or less the same 22 players who had featured against Munster. We didn't play well and were deservedly beaten. A week later we lost at home to Leicester in another Premiership game that didn't change anything except that it created a little bit of doubt in our minds. Here we were, two weeks before the three most important weeks in the history of the club and we had just lost two consecutive matches. First we had to face Northampton at home in the Zurich Premiership play-off semi-final, a week after that we had Toulouse in the Heineken Cup final and, provided we beat Northampton, we would then have Bath in the Premiership final.

One of the things about Shaun Edwards is that he's odd, but interestingly odd. You meet him, he talks a lot of sense and he makes you want to know more about him, but he doesn't reveal everything. It's not like you're going to know him after three or four meetings. What makes him fascinating is that he looks at situations his way and although he is a very humble bloke, he's not afraid to call things as he sees them. Before our game with Northampton, he was absolutely brilliant. He came into the changing room with *The Racing Post* on the day of the game, opened it towards the back and found the preview of our game. Then, in his strong northern accent, he began.

'Graham Woods, the bloke who wrote this, don't know him from Adam. All I know is that he does this for a living and if he doesn't know his stuff, he doesn't have a living. So what does he say? "*Wasps were trounced at home by Leicester last weekend but that is no reason to oppose them in today's play-off semi-final against Northampton. Warren Gatland's side have been so successful this season because they hit their peak in terms of performance at the right time.*" This guy can't afford to get it wrong. He hasn't got it wrong.'

That was all Shaun said, and all he needed to say. Our doubts were lessened and although we started with understandable caution, we began to play really well after Tom Voyce scored an outstanding individual try in the first half. In the end, we won 57–20 and put ourselves in the right frame of mind for the Heineken Cup final six days later. It was our first European Cup final, and the biggest day in the club's history. The signs were good. The fact that the game was at Twickenham was a huge factor in my mind, and not just because it was like a home from home for us. For all Toulouse's quality, and they had plenty of it, they often struggled when playing outside France, especially when they came to England. You couldn't deny their pedigree in the Heineken Cup. They had won the first staging of the tournament, won it again in 2003 and, in between those two victories, they were always there or thereabouts. But their record in England was fairly abysmal – three victories from 11 matches, and when we played them at Loftus Road in 1997, we beat them by 70 points.

During the week before the game, the Toulouse captain, Fabien Pelous, came to London for a press conference and while he said all the right things, you could tell he was conscious of the impact Twickenham would have. They actually played superbly on the day. It was a cracking match and if we got through in the end, it was only by the skin of our teeth. They went 6–0 up through two penalties, we got a penalty, and then Simon Shaw made a great run, and Stuart Abbott produced a lovely step to score a fantastic try. With Mark Van Gisbergen's conversion, we went 10–6 in front. They then got a try back and would have got two or three more if we hadn't defended so well. At the break we led 13–11.

'We're playing a worthy opponent here,' said Shaun during the interval, 'we've got to be totally on our guard.'

We picked up the pace in the second half. The 'Evergreen Everbald' Alex King made a terrific run into the heart of the Toulouse defence and linked with Van Gisbergen who scored. The conversion made it 20–11. Midway through the second half, I got sin-binned for slowing down their possession (standard!) and they began to claw their way back. Three penalties later, the scores were tied at 20–20 and we were looking at extra time. It was backs-to-the-wall stuff for us and we put Joe Worsley on the powerful and dynamic Isitola Marka. His instructions were, 'When he gets the ball, Joe, you just smash him every time.' Then in the dying seconds, Rob Howley chipped the ball forward, their full-back Clement Poitrenaud tried to usher it into touch but the ball bounced back into play and Rob was there to capitalise on what had been a monumental mistake by Poitrenaud. Mark Van Gisbergen struck a fine conversion from the touchline, the ball bouncing over off the crossbar, confirming it was our day.

A week later we had Bath in the Premiership final and another tumultuous occasion at Twickenham. They'd had three weeks to prepare for us and they used it well because they knew our line-out moves better than we knew them ourselves. No matter where we threw the ball, and Trevor Leota's throwing wasn't at its best, Bath were ready. They stole enough of our balls to control the match for long periods but played a very basic and unadventurous territorial game. Against our defence, that approach wasn't going to get them many tries. We defended well. The turning point came 16 minutes from the end when a Paul Volley tackle led to a loose Bath pass, Tom Voyce scooped up the ball and sent Stuart Abbott sprinting to the corner. That put us ahead for the first time in the match and although we were better in the second half, it wasn't a vintage Wasps performance. At the end, we were just happy to have won. When you remembered it was our second consecutive Premiership title and that it had come one week after our first Heineken Cup victory, the actual performance on the day seemed pretty irrelevant. Two seasons under Warren Gatland and Shaun Edwards had delivered four major trophies and when memories of the individual games had blurred, the record books would show these to be the two best seasons in Wasps' history.

It's not until you win something like the Heineken Cup that you realise the significance of the achievement. That victory over Toulouse put us up there with the top clubs in Europe and yet when you compared us with Toulouse, it was chalk and cheese really. In terms of financial resources, support, history, our respective places in our cities, it was a bit like David and Goliath. They're like a giant corporation as opposed to our cottage industry. Yet we compete at their level and pretty successfully. In the playing sense, we have always seen ourselves as a big club. I have often been given credit for spending my entire career at Wasps but, in a sense, the praise is undeserved. If Wasps had allowed standards to fall and I'd felt we were not going to be competitive in the future, I would not have stayed. Any club can have a fallow year, when there are too many injuries or the coach and players don't quite gel – you can live with that. But not when a club loses the ambition to win the biggest prizes. That never happened at Wasps and I never left.

My belief has always been that if you're one of the best players in the country, you should be playing for one of the best clubs, be it Wasps, Leicester, Bath, Sale or Gloucester. This puts me at odds with my England team-mate Jonny Wilkinson because he is clearly one of the best players of his generation and as yet he is not at one of the best clubs. I understand his reasons for joining

Lions Tours

→ My first taste of Lions and of victory. Winning the first Test in Cape Town in June 1997, with the help of legend Gregor Townsend and despite the best efforts of the inimitable Joost Van der Westhuizen.

↓ Jerry drop goals us to our second Test win in Durban to clinch the series. At this point it wasn't quite over yet, but we soon sorted that.

←↓ My following two tours weren't quite as successful: a knee injury ruling me out of the Tests in 2001, and fracturing my ankle in 2005. That injury did make me reassess my life's priorities though, and what was important to me – silver lining and all!

Internationals

↑↑ I didn't get much of a chance to win anything against Campese but we managed it in the World Cup Sevens final at Murrayfield in 1993. You can see what the Scots thought about England being in the final by their turnout.

↑ A moment never to be forgotten. My first cap, 18 November 1995 against South Africa. Eighteen minutes of just trying to keep up.

← Not going to get it, am I? A home win at Twickenham against South Africa in 1998.

↑ Think the heading should have instead been '*News of the World* sets up a story, gets someone drunk then records their exaggerated ramblings as fact'.

↓ and → The turning point for English rugby? The international series in June 2003 where we beat New Zealand and, for the first time ever, Australia on their own turf.

Five and Six Nations

↑ Part of the winning 1996 Five Nations squad, and one of my first matches in the tournament.

↓ Captaining England two years later to win against Ireland.

→ and ↓ Ooh, this is painful. Losing to Wales at the last possible moment in 1999, costing us the trophy. 'Dejected' just isn't the word.

← On the other hand, scoring a try against Scotland in the 2000 tournament helped us to win the championship.

↓ How many Welsh players does it take to stop me getting over the line? Making sure we beat Wales this time, also in 2000.

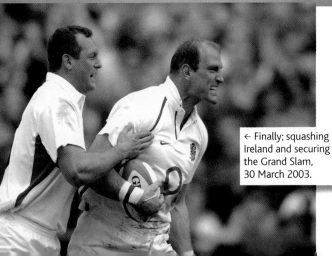

← Finally; squashing Ireland and securing the Grand Slam, 30 March 2003.

World Cup

← Making sure I get my point across. But Jonah and the All Blacks had the last laugh in my first World Cup in 1999.

Victory in 2003

↑ A general lie-down against Samoa in a pool match. Think Backy's just scored a try under all that.

↓ Getting to grips with the French in the semi-final. Their coach, Bernard Laporte, might like to note we could win games which really mattered.

→ And the Australia game to end all games. David Lyons trying his best to keep hold of the ball.

→ Reasonably pleased with the result, I'd say.

↓ Relief. Very happy relief.

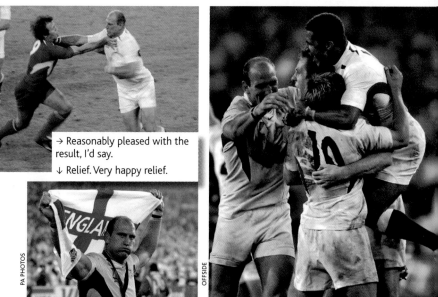

Heading to the 2007 final

↑ Nobody gave us a chance against Australia but we always believed. A magical moment with fellow Wasp Paul Sackey.

→ Battling against the hosts in the semi-final and coming out on top. Martin Corry and I realise that England are only one step away from a historic defence of our world crown.

↓ Keeping the ball in play during the final with Mathew Tait. But retaining that crown just wasn't to be.

Newcastle when he did – it was an opportunity to link up with his old school teacher, Steve Bates, and he believed he was going to a club that would grow into one of the very best in Europe. But so far that hasn't happened. Newcastle hasn't yet fulfilled its potential – I think they've won two Powergen Cups during Jonny's time there – and I believe that, as the best fly-half in the country, if not in the world, he should be playing for one of the top clubs.

After we won the World Cup, I read an article in which Jonny talked about wanting to win the Premiership and the Heineken Cup with Newcastle and I thought to myself, 'He's either kidding himself or we're blind to what's happening at his club.' To win anything, they would have to improve dramatically. To improve enough to win a Premiership or a Heineken Cup would take a number of years. Of course, Newcastle is a progressive club, but to become a dynasty, to become a club that is successful year on year, that takes a long time to achieve. When Martin Johnson was in his prime, he was captain of a dominant Leicester side and I felt at my best in the years when I captained a successful Wasps team. Farther afield, the outstanding New Zealand No. 10, Dan Carter, doesn't play for Southland, he plays for the top province, Canterbury. Jonny's had extraordinarily bad luck with injuries and because he has missed so many matches, he probably feels a huge loyalty to Newcastle, but his first loyalty has to be to himself. Would he have had as many injuries playing behind a pack that protected him better than Newcastle's forwards can?

Perhaps I'm wide of the mark here and Newcastle will soon become a consistently powerful force at the top of English club rugby but I know if I was England coach, I would prefer Jonny playing in a squad that had 20–25 internationals, rather than for a club where he is very much the main man. If I had been in Jonny's boots, I would have considered leaving a long time ago – but then, as I've already indicated, I think you've got to be more selfish than he has been. As much as Jonny values his privacy and appreciates the lifestyle he can have in the north-east, I think that can become an excuse. I know that at the end of my career I will look back and feel pleased to have been part of a team that won two Heineken Cups, four Premierships, three domestic Cups, and one European Challenge Cup. It's not about ticking boxes or collecting medals but being part of a club that has a realistic shot at the biggest prizes.

Finally, it would be wrong to leave out London's role in my loyalty to Wasps. While I've always enjoyed being in the country and feeling the open spaces, London is where I belong. I used to joke when we turned up in a new city how the stench of urban life made me feel at home. Bars, restaurants, casinos, lots of things to do and plenty of places to go – 'If you're tired of London, you're tired of life', as Samuel Johnson said. I go along with that. I do understand why the big city is not to everyone's liking and Alice and I love to take the children down to Devon or off to France and Italy but after a while, I'll begin to miss home. I was born in London, brought up in London and the city's in my blood now.

15

Unfinished business

I n the end, the Grand Slam became our personal toothache. It didn't hurt all the time but it flared up in the cold months of January, February and March. The only way to get rid of the pain was to win the damn thing and stop all the nonsense. Even though it was World Cup year, during the early weeks of 2003 we thought about nothing other than beating all of our rivals in the Six Nations Championship. Clive Woodward's reign as head coach began in the autumn of 1997 and under him, we had spent five years chasing the clean sweep. Each year we won all but one of our championship games and in three of those years we fell at the final hurdle. It always intrigued me that we could win four of our matches and the only one anyone talked about was the one we lost. We're England and we should win the Grand Slam every year, so when we lose one game, it's a calamity. As for the ones we did win, they didn't matter, apparently. And because we kept losing this one final game, we were thought of as a team that couldn't close the deal. We would play France in the World Cup semi-final much later in the year and before the game, Bernard Laporte offered his tuppence worth. 'England,' he said, 'can never win games that really matter.'

Really?

Through those early months of 2003, we decided not to talk about the World Cup and, as much as possible, not to think about it. We had the Grand Slam to occupy us and even though Clive kept saying we shouldn't hark back to the ones we missed, it was hard when everyone else was reminding you. We came through our first four matches against France, Wales, Italy and Scotland well enough but hadn't played particularly strongly. There were periods when we were good but they weren't sustained. The game that mattered was the final one against Ireland in Dublin. As they had also won their first four games, it was winner-takes-all. That suited us because with the trophy at stake, Ireland had as much to lose as we had. That affected the psychological balance of the game and meant they were under as much pressure as we were. You suspected Ireland would have been more comfortable if they were simply trying to spoil the English party.

As it was a Sunday game, we didn't fly over to Dublin until Thursday evening and we were happy enough about our match preparation for the coaches to give us Friday off. I felt we were as focused as for any England game I had been involved in. Mentally, we were ready for a fast tempo, and tactically, we targeted their midfield of David Humphries, Kevin Maggs and Brian O'Driscoll. If we hit them hard and made sure they didn't get any space, we would be able to deny them momentum. If they weren't going forward, the crowd would eventually grow quiet and it would then be easier for us to gain an edge. Clive didn't hedge his bets. He told us straight up that losing this game would seriously hurt our World Cup chances.

From the moment we arrived in Ireland, I felt this was one match that was going to go our way. The bond forged between the players three years previously in South Africa was now incredibly strong and we were as united as you could imagine. We had been through a lot together, including personal tragedies that were shared by everyone. Ben Cohen had lost his father in tragic circumstances; Will Greenwood had lost his baby, Freddie; Martin Johnson had lost his mum and we were all affected by the unexpected death of the Harlequins scrum-half, Nick Duncombe. Some of the lads had played with him, most of us had played against him, and Dan Luger was one of Nick's closest friends.

The game could not have gone better for us. We soaked up the early waves of Irish pressure and when we got into their half, Matt Dawson made a slashing break, I followed him and was in the right place to take his pass and score beside the posts. We had a lot of defending to do in that first half but we did it well and even though they had a fair bit of the ball, Ireland didn't look like scoring a try. When we went to the other end of the field, Jonny Wilkinson would drop a goal or kick a penalty and stretch our lead. Ireland had to chase the game in the second half, which made it easier for us to pick them off. Mike Tindall got our second try and Dan Luger put us out of sight with another one. As he scored, Richard Hill, Neil Back and I got in a huddle and had our own little back-row celebration. I liked the fact that we had grown so close. We were three very different characters, and in the early years, we were wary of each other. Neil was always very intense about his rugby and was probably a little bit too serious at the beginning. Not getting selected for England by Geoff Cooke affected him badly and it was ironic that things started to happen for him when he became less uptight about it. It wasn't that he mellowed or became any less competitive, he just concentrated on doing a great team job for Leicester and let his England case rest on that.

When we came together as England's back row, I think we could see that we had potential as a unit. My trust in Richard and Neil was 100 per cent. In very different ways they were two fantastic players and as we began to play regularly together, our personal relationships developed. Before matches, after we were changed and all strapped up, we would go out for our pre-game warm-up together, do a couple of laps of the pitch and sort out little things about strategy in our heads. We became much closer than I ever thought possible. At the start of my career I was headstrong and not as understanding of my team-mates as you need to be. Sometimes, that would have come across as arrogance and, even though I don't honestly believe I was arrogant, people say that I became more humble as I got older and more experienced. I think it was down to playing alongside Richard for so long, because for a man who was always such a good player, he was unbelievably modest.

After the match, in the dressing room at Lansdowne Road, when we were all drenched with champagne that could surely have been put to better use, I had a quiet cup of tea with Neil and Paul Grayson. To give the often-maligned officials credit, the post-match dinner was actually an enjoyable affair. It hit exactly the right note – lounge suits rather than black tie, speeches done and dusted before grace, Irish and English players sharing tables. 'Ah,' we all thought, 'this is how it was in the good old amateur days,' when in fact the speeches used to go on for ever and we would all be dying of boredom. But the amateur spirit was revived later in the night as both sets of players and their partners partied into the early hours.

A match that mattered duly won by England. Point made.

Clive's decision to make a short tour of New Zealand and Australia three months before the World Cup was interesting because it was an ambitious undertaking. To use a favourite expression of Shaun Edwards', it was 'high risk, high reward'. No matter what we had tried to tell ourselves afterwards, if we had lost Test matches against the All Blacks and Wallabies so close to the World Cup, it would have reduced our confidence going into the tournament. But Clive doesn't think negatively and he saw only the benefits of beating our two greatest rivals in front of their own fans, not just in terms of the boost to our morale, but the equally important effect on their confidence. The quality of Clive's management was apparent in the vision but also in the execution of his plan. Before we left for New Zealand, we had a squad meeting in which Clive again asked us to forget about the World Cup and just concentrate on the three-week tour we were about to embark upon. That was hard because we all knew the one-off Tests against New Zealand

and Australia were part of our World Cup preparation. Clive anticipated this problem and had asked our excellent video analyst Tony Biscombe to prepare a presentation that highlighted the significance of the midsummer Tests.

In a short and to-the-point video, questions were posed about England's record of playing New Zealand and Australia in their own countries. Thirty years had passed since England last beat the All Blacks in New Zealand. Even as I thought, 'But we don't go there that often,' I suspected the reason for that was that we didn't fancy our chances. Clive was basically asking us if we wanted to do something no England team had done in New Zealand for 30 years. Of course we did. Then there was Australia, where no England side had ever won a Test match. I listened to that statement in disbelief and nudged the guy alongside me, no doubt Jason Leonard, who'd been around so long he had probably played in every England/Wallaby Test, and asked him if it was true. Had we never beaten the Aussies on their own patch? 'Never,' he said. Everyone in the room was feeling the same: 'For God's sake, this can't be right.' But it was true, and Clive was standing there, inviting us to create history by changing that statistic. As we listened, the World Cup did seem irrelevant, which was the object of the exercise.

Of course, it was the slickness of the presentation as much as the message itself that won us over. Tony Biscombe had done a tremendous job. There were quotes from former England captains saying how hard it was to win in the southern hemisphere but that, ultimately, it was the place to succeed. As a group of players, it got us talking and it dawned on me that I had never even been to New Zealand. Ten years in professional rugby, nine seasons in the England team and I had never once been to the world's number one rugby country. How stupid was that? Jason said he'd been there in 1993 with the Lions and had played against the All Blacks but he had not played a Test match for England in New Zealand. Martin Johnson said he had never played in an England shirt there.

'Boys,' I said, 'this is incredible. We're almost at the end of our careers and none of us has taken on the All Blacks in their own backyard. Well, we're not going to get another chance. I mean, if we don't go there and win, there will be something missing from our scoresheet, and every fucking Kiwi you ever meet is certain to tell you that.'

We arrived in Wellington on Wednesday, leaving England's early summer sunshine for the freezing cold of winter in New Zealand. Martin Johnson tells a story about a few of us going for a coffee together that evening, determined to stay awake and get our body clocks tuned in to Kiwi time. As well as Johnno and me, Dorian West and Neil Back came along. It was around nine o'clock at night and downtown was pretty deserted. We found a place that was still serving and were sitting in a corner minding our own business when a guy approached us. 'Are you the England team?' he asked and when we told him that we were, he said, 'Oh, great! I can give you some shit then.' He didn't mean much harm, and he probably thought he was being funny, but the joke was lost on us. New Zealand is a beautiful country and it's not as though the people aren't friendly and welcoming, but if you're there with the England team, you can feel you belong to the 30 most hated people in the land. It was unfortunate, too, that we were there in winter. That evening Wellington was windy as well as cold and with our friend wanting to give us 'some shit', it didn't feel like the most hospitable place in the world. Then when you wake up the next morning, there's a local newspaper outside your bedroom door and it's full of mostly negative things about the England team.

Everyone says they don't read the local newspapers, but that's bollocks. Every day, especially the day before and the day of the match, there are hours to kill and you read books, you go on the internet and you read newspapers, especially those that are lying around the hotel. We would have a bit of a chuckle because it was so partisan, but it never shocked or surprised me. If you look at England's history over hundreds of years, you can work out why some people don't like us too much. Yet nowhere else have I come across the one-eyed bias you find in the southern hemisphere. In New Zealand's case, they just didn't respect our rugby and couldn't really get their heads around the fact that we can actually play the game in the northern hemisphere. In a curious way, our 15–13 victory at the Westpac Stadium in Wellington, otherwise known as the Cake Tin, merely confirmed their impression that we couldn't play.

Conditions were terrible, and with the wind and rain, it was almost impossible for either team to play good rugby. The game is remembered for a heroic period in the match when we had two players in the sin-bin but our 13 showed a lot of character against their full 15 and actually drove them downfield in one fantastic sequence of driving forward play. People have said to me that that was a seminal moment in the evolution of the team and possibly the greatest moment from all our years together. Well, I have to disagree. I certainly can't take any credit for the courage and defiance the guys showed, because I was one of the two in the sin-bin at the time and one of the reasons why the team on the pitch had to dig deep during that part of the match. But I think people have been carried away by the fact that we won. We just did what we had to do. We were very good defensively and Jonny kicked a few terrific penalty goals to clinch our victory. No amount of bravery could hide the fact that we hadn't played any rugby. Sure, the conditions were tough but that was only a partial explanation. The truth was that, in terms of getting possession and holding on to it, we were poor. We did a few things right but generally we didn't play very well.

Not surprisingly, New Zealand's rugby cognoscenti weren't impressed and one of them famously described us as like 'white Orcs on steroids'. We had one or two forwards who weren't blessed with the best looks in the world but that was no reason to get personal. Of course, few in New Zealand could see what was obvious. We hadn't played very well but we'd beaten their team in Wellington, as we had beaten them at Twickenham seven months before when, again, we hadn't played well. Perhaps the ability to win when not playing well said something about the side?

After the game, we adjourned to the bar of Wellington's Intercontinental Hotel where it was a pleasure to meet up with Warren Gatland for a drink. Warren's a former All Black and he wanted to see his country win the World Cup, but he thought we had a big chance and it was obvious he wanted his Wasps players, Joe Worsley, Josh Lewsey and me, to do well. Clive joined us, as did a number of British rugby writers who were there to cover the tour. It seemed like a throwback to a different era, when players and journalists used to enjoy a few beers together under the Chatham House Rule. In terms of rugby, the 11 days in New

Zealand could not have gone better. We beat the All Blacks, our midweek team beat the New Zealand Maoris and there was a real sense of mission accomplished. Still, I looked forward to getting to Australia where the weather would be better and we'd no longer be the 30 most hated men in the country. Well, I was right about the weather anyway.

On arrival in Melbourne, the Australian press greeted us with a message that translated as, 'You thought the Kiwis didn't like you . . .' And off they went, telling us our nine-man rugby wouldn't work in Melbourne because their indoor stadium would keep out the weather and we would have to score tries. Then, just when we'd settled into our hotel and begun to think about the game, David Campese was resurrected, from whatever part of the world he was in at that moment, to slag off the English. I like Campese and regard him as a friend but why was he always saying the same thing? England can't run with the ball. England can't do this. England can't do that. England are crap. We'd heard it all before. Clive, of course, picked up on the reception we were getting and seemed pleased. 'Get used to it, guys. This is how it has always been in Australia and it will be even worse when we're here for the World Cup.' There wasn't much point in us saying we scored 42 points against Ireland at Landowne Road, getting three tries along the way. No point either in reminding the Aussies that we'd got a few tries when we beat them at Twickenham seven months earlier. Instead, we decided we would just go out and ram whatever pathetic little message they were trying to put across down their throats.

We played the rugby we were always capable of playing, and it was definitely one of our better performances. We set out at

100mph and ended up scoring some decent tries. For Will Greenwood's try, we created phase after phase, showed good handling skills to keep the move going at the end. We then tried a lovely little line-out move that worked nicely and resulted in Mike Tindall scoring. At that point we were in control. Australia came back at us, got a try and threatened to make a game of it but we just blew them away with an excellent try from Ben Cohen.

At different points in the matches against the All Blacks and Australians, we needed Jonny to get us points and he didn't fail. He was becoming a big factor in our team. In every game of rugby there are moments when not much is happening, just a penalty or two to each team, and Jonny had an uncanny ability to keep our side of the scoreboard ticking over.

Clive and Johnno are very different characters. After our 25–14 win in Melbourne, Martin thanked George Gregan and his Aussie team for a good game, said England was pleased to have won and looked forward to the next meeting. Clive wasn't quite so diplomatic. He reminded people England hadn't been shown much respect before the game, especially as the team had won its three previous encounters with the Wallabies and had just beaten New Zealand in Wellington. He also reminded people of the nonsense about England not being able to score tries and said the results showed that to be plain stupid. I was glad Clive gave it to them although it didn't do much for his popularity in Australia. That wasn't something he could control, anyway.

Another little motivation for us to win was Clive's decision to travel to Perth afterwards for three days of pre-World Cup reconnaissance. None of us had wanted to spend three days in Australia if we'd lost to the Wallabies. We wouldn't have been able to bear another Campese column and the endless drivel they come out with when they beat England. If they'd beaten us, they all would have come out of the woodwork. But we needn't have worried. We celebrated in Melbourne and then dragged our weary bodies and our hangovers across Australia for three days' relaxation and research. We had no match to play, no training to do, we'd beaten the All Blacks and the Wallabies at home, and, yes, we had a very good time in Perth.

A series of debriefing sessions were held between players and coaches, which were quite amusing. Basically, each player met with Clive, Andy Robinson and Phil Larder and, bizarrely, the interviews were timed for early morning. Mine was something like 8.30. We landed in Perth in the late afternoon and the meetings kicked off straightaway the next day, but that didn't stop us going out on the town on that first evening. Just outside the hotel there was an Irish pub, and after checking in, we decided to reconvene there in 20 minutes. I arrived at the rendezvous with Jason Leonard and we expected a good crowd but not everyone. There are always a few shirkers. On this occasion, though, every single player was there and we had a hell of a night. We watched England play a one-day cricket match on telly, went off for a bite to eat and then broke into different groups, some carrying on through the night. Jason's interview was very early the next morning and when he showed up, Andy Robinson remarked that he was wearing the same shirt as the previous evening. Jason agreed. It was the same shirt.

'You've only just got in?' said Robbo.

'Yeah, I have actually,' said Jason, cool as a cucumber.

Clive wouldn't have bothered what time any of us had got in

because we had done our jobs in Melbourne. I was a bit glassy-eyed from the long night and wasn't sure what to expect, but the coaches made it easy for me.

'Lawrence, you've had an excellent tour,' they said, 'really well played. We're delighted with the way you've come on.'

I thought for a second about bringing up their decision to drop me for my 50th cap but decided against it. I wasn't sober enough to have a sensible conversation and instead I thanked them and went straight off to bed. Later, I was intrigued to learn the meetings hadn't been as straightforward for other players. Joe Worsley and some of the younger players had proper meetings with the coaches, with serious analysis of their progress. Apparently, when interviewing Joe, one of the coaches made a comment to the effect that they felt they knew pretty much all there was to know about coaching.

Our coaches were very good and I had a huge amount of admiration for them. They had every right to feel satisfied with the work they were doing with the England squad. They had achieved things no previous England coaching team had managed, and they had us on course to win rugby's ultimate prize. But at times I also had a sense that maybe they were too conscious of how good a job they were doing. From his meeting with them, I think Joe got that same sense and I wondered if they weren't just a little bit too proud of their work, too sure about their ability. You can always learn new things but I have to say I didn't see any of our specialist coaches queuing up to do courses in New Zealand, or going off to some Australian club or provincial side to see what they were doing. These are people I have the utmost respect for but it was almost as if the results we were achieving had deluded them into thinking everything they were doing was brilliant. You never stop learning in this game, whether you are a player or a coach.

Clive wanted to set new standards of preparation and there is no doubt he achieved that. For a few years, the southern hemisphere countries became obsessed about what England were doing, and tried to incorporate some of our methods into their training. However, if England was to remain at the head of the pack, our coaches needed to be open to the newest techniques and set the bar even higher. I didn't feel they were always doing that. The players would sit round and talk about what our coaches did when they weren't in camp or on tour with us. You could never fault the work and commitment they put in while we were together, always there to help or do extra training with you. But we never saw them spectating or researching at our clubs and when we turned up for England duty, we would laugh about whether Phil Larder had improved his tan more than Dave Alred. I think we were all a bit jealous if I'm honest.

Yet the England environment was one we loved, totally unlike the set-up when I was first capped. Back then you couldn't wait for the week to be over so you could get back to the your club. Clive created something special and the coaches were very much part of that. As we became successful, though, some of them became contented and I'm not sure they were doing that much in the long intervals between international get-togethers. Maybe I'm judging them harshly but there were signs that made you wonder if we would be able to take things much beyond the 2003 World Cup.

16

The winning habit

t is Friday, 21 November 2003 and from where I'm sitting in the breakfast room at our team hotel, life looks pretty good. How many times in your life will you stay at a hotel that overlooks the Pacific, where young people are surfing from early morning, and know the following day you will play for your country in the World Cup final? Alice and my parents are in Australia and will be in the stadium tomorrow evening. Another reason for my cheerfulness is that I am truly looking forward to the big game. My form is good, my physical condition has never been better and when it comes to important games of rugby, I back myself. This evening at six o'clock we will have our final training session, but it will be no more than a walk-through of certain moves. Mimicking the southern hemisphere, we have taken to calling our last practice 'The Captain's Run'. It's a team run as far as I'm concerned and always will be. But that's still eight hours off and as I leave the players' breakfast area, I'm probably one of the most chilled people in the hotel.

On the way out I notice a few friends sitting down to breakfast. Steve Hayes and Terry Evans had flown in from London the previous day and, typical of Steve, he was able to get rooms in our hotel. Steve built and ran a very successful company called loans.co.uk and was chairman of the committee taking care of my benefit year; Terry is his life-long friend and they're with my then agent Ashley Woolfe. Pleased to see the lads, I join them and order another coffee. Jason Leonard is at the next table, chatting with his dad, Frank, and there's some good-humoured banter in the air. Steve and Terry are talking about the great time they'd had on their first night out in Sydney. Yarns are being spun, stories told and I see Clive walk into room, looking round as if he's not sure whom he's looking for. At this moment, Steve tells a funny story and everyone roars with laughter. Clive hears the noise, looks our way and moves on. I think no more of it. After a while, I go to my room for two match tickets I have sorted for Steve and while there, I check on a text message I'd received while chatting with the lads.

It's from Clive and I can't believe what I'm reading. 'You have the air of a man who's carrying on too many meetings outside of training. This England pack has carried you throughout this World Cup and I don't think you are ready for the game.' I can take this two ways. One, it's a clever ploy to keep me sharp; two, what the fuck is this guy on about? My reaction is the latter. I go absolutely mental, steam is coming out of my ears and I'm ready for a serious row. I try to calm myself but there's no chance of that. This is not something I'm going to let pass. I'm not putting up with this shit. Before going back down with the tickets for Steve, I text Clive: 'I completely refute and resent those comments. You have the air of a man who is stressed and paranoid. May I suggest you go for a walk on the beach? I'm perfectly ready for this game – are you?' Sending off this reply helps but I'm still furious. I think I know Clive well, so I understand he can be impulsive, but I also know he is too honest to use a text like that as some kind of motivational trick. At the time he wrote it, he believed it. What was I guilty of? Having a laugh with my mates? They are in Australia, two of them in the same hotel as the team. What am I supposed to do, ignore them? The bit that really incenses me is his line about the England pack carrying me through the whole tournament. 'You're not getting away with this,' I think.

Throughout the day, we don't see each other much but I refuse to speak with him when we do and I avoid eye contact. I want him to know how much he's pissed me off. Knowing Clive, I can see him calming down, possibly even taking that walk on the beach and realising he must have many things to sort out. The next morning, as in the day of the World Cup final, I receive another text. He apologises for what he wrote the previous day. 'Sorry for the text yesterday, I look forward to shaking your hand as you're getting off the bus this evening. Let's have a great day.' It's a ritual that as we get off the bus at the stadium, Clive shakes each player's hand or says what he feels is right at the time. By now, I've calmed down and after receiving the second text, I feel much better. I don't want to leave for the stadium still at war with Clive – we have been through too much for that. The apology is enough. Clive was just having a bit of a wobble and I suppose I was as good a target as any to let off steam at.

The thing about Clive and me is that from the moment he asked me to captain England in 1997, our relationship was never strictly professional. Alice and I have had a personal friendship with him and Jayne. When the *News of the World* was hounding me, it was Clive who opened his house to my family. He also opened up his personality and let me see the two sides to his nature – the seriously ambitious coach, but also the bloke who loves to have a good time. As human beings, we just hit it off well. He likes the finer things in life – good food, good wine, good company – and I happen to have the same tastes. Because we got on so well, I have known a side to Clive that I'm not sure any other England player saw. That didn't stop him making some tough decisions where I was concerned and there were times I felt he over-compensated when he wanted to be seen to treat me the same as everyone else.

In the early years he would phone me up and begin the conversation by saying, 'Now, don't laugh at this, just tell me what you think...' I would never laugh because I enjoy discussing his ideas, and found most of his plans interesting. Clive could start a conversation thinking one thing and end it thinking exactly the opposite. As he became more experienced, he also became more decisive about how he wanted things done and there was less need to discuss things. He didn't get on with everyone as well as we got on but that was natural. A coach generally has his sounding boards, the guys he will sell his philosophy to and rely upon to spread the message down through the ranks. I was definitely one of the believers.

Even when I was dropped for the Australia game in 2002, I didn't believe Clive's was the key voice in the decision. Sure he was convinced by the argument, otherwise he wouldn't have gone with it, but I do believe he was reluctant to take that decision. We were never just 'player and coach'. Between us, it went deeper than that. No matter how mad I was with him on the day before the World Cup final, I didn't want to get off the bus that Saturday evening without things being OK.

'Best of luck, Lol,' he said, holding out his hand. 'Enjoy the evening.'

I grasped his hand. 'Don't worry, mate, we will.'

We left London for Australia on 1 October for seven and a half weeks that would define us as rugby players. Our last day in England was spent at our training base in Pennyhill Park Hotel with our families. Alice and I had discussed bringing the kids to Australia for the later stages of the tournament if we were lucky enough to get that far. Potentially, it was a once-in-a-lifetime experience and for that reason, we wanted them there but, on the other hand, we were reluctant to take them out of school. As well as that, I find it difficult to enjoy the children when I'm preparing for big rugby matches. You want to spend time with them but you're restricted and they're too young to understand. So we decided against it and agreed that Alice would cut her trip down to 10 days so that she wouldn't be away for long. Everything was fine until our eldest, Ella, saw Neil Back's daughter on the pitch at the end of the World Cup final. Did I have a problem after that or did I what? A visit to Ella's school a week after we returned, making sure that I brought along the Webb Ellis Trophy with me, got me somewhat off the hook.

Our tournament started against Georgia in Perth, a match we were expected to win by a big score. Perth is a long way from the other major cities in Australia and as rugby union is not a huge sport there, we felt we spent the first month on the periphery of the tournament. Mentally, I had prepared myself for bedlam but it was all quite low key. Two days before the Georgia game, a few of us went out for a coffee and might have gone into Starbucks but the Georgian players beat us to it. It was that kind of city. I'd picked up a minor hamstring injury a few weeks before, missed the warm-up matches against France and Wales and was desperate to play in that first game. I got my wish and although the Georgians were big lumps that took a lot of shifting, we scored 84 points against them and achieved one of our main targets by not conceding a try. We wanted to send out a message to every team in the World Cup, telling them that the No. 1 team had arrived in Australia and was ready. Next morning dawned with a reminder of the subtleties of the Australian media as their experts dissected our 84–6 victory and found the negatives. We had a chuckle about that.

Six days later we were due back at the Subiaco Oval to play South Africa and everyone understood that our World Cup depended upon winning that match and making sure we took the right route to the final. Four years earlier we'd lost our pool match against New Zealand and given ourselves a virtually impossible task. Defeat in this match would put us on a course to meet the All Blacks in the quarter-finals and Australia in the semi-finals – not the way to go. Our preparation for the game was excellent, although I did notice Will Greenwood was not himself. For a back, Will got on surprisingly well with some of the cynical old forwards and was well liked. When he went quiet and seemed a little withdrawn the week before the South Africa game, it was clear there was some kind of problem. When a few of the lads enquired, he didn't convince anyone when he said he was fine. I spoke to Clive who told me that Will's wife Caro had gone into pre-labour and although she wasn't well, she was stable. The plan was for Will to return to England immediately after the South Africa game. I felt for the guy because he was facing probably the biggest game of his career but had something far more important on his mind. In a peculiar way, my concern for Will and Caro helped my preparation because it allowed me to see things in perspective. Yes, this was an important game but . . . I didn't know how many were aware of Will's situation but most people could see something was up. Johnno and Jason Leonard would have known about it, I'm sure. I admire Clive for the way he quite rightly always put a guy's family before his rugby and the needs of the team. Will was provisionally booked on every flight out of Perth to London in the week before the South Africa match, so that if things had taken a turn for the worse, he would be on the next flight home. The irony was that Will ended up playing a key role in the game, scoring the try that put daylight between the teams. The game was also memorable for the performance of Kyran Bracken, who was in the side because Matt Dawson wasn't fit. He played a blinder against Joost Van der Westhuizen. Joost was one of the best players in the world and a pain in the backside for the opposing No. 8. Every time we played them, he would put me under all sorts of pressure on our scrums and tended to make my life very difficult. We wanted Kyran to snap at Van der Westhuizen's heels and do unto him as he would do unto us. That's what Kyran did and he actually outplayed Joost. As well as that, Jonny kicked his goals and in games as tight as this one, that makes such a difference.

It hadn't been a brilliant performance but it was a job well done, not that the local media were going to acknowledge that. Their attitude to us was epitomised by a full-page photograph of Jonny kicking, under the headline, 'Is That All You've Got?' You just had to laugh. You wouldn't think we had beaten one of the five teams realistically capable of winning the World Cup and done so decisively, 25–6. No one in our squad was surprised or annoyed by Australian antagonism, though. We had come round to the view that if they were trying so hard to undermine us, they must fear us. We knew how hard the South Africans had played and we knew that overcoming them would only improve us. In any tournament, it's better to have tough matches in the early stages because they sharpen you. The team that wins every one of its pool matches easily is the team that will worry when it meets its first serious rival. The Aussies hadn't even noticed Richard Hill's absence through injury. He was a huge loss. Richard set incredibly high standards for himself and consistently reached them. That's the challenge for every player, to hit that level week in, week out, year in, year out. Hilly did that, which I have to say made him different. Other players tend to be far more erratic. Great one week, not so good the next. His consistency of performance marked him out as a star.

In our debriefing session on the day after the South Africa game, Clive wanted to focus on the high number of penalties we conceded and decided the best way to do this was to show each penalty on the video and get the culprit to own up. 'So, who gave that away?' he asked. Up went Martin Johnson's hand. We moved on to number two, 'And who was at fault here?' asked Clive. Again Johnno. Four out of the first five were Johnno's, which caused a lot of sniggering among the usual suspects, and Clive, realising he wasn't doing much for his captain's self-esteem, ended our little video session. 'Anyway,' he said, 'you get my point.'

At 1.30 a.m. on Saturday night, Melbourne was very much alive. Not surprisingly, I'd ended up in the questionable company of Jason Leonard, Iain Balshaw, Mike Tindall and Matt Dawson. Earlier in the evening we had won our third consecutive game at the World Cup, beating Samoa in a tough match without ever producing our best form. Samoa played well, were 10 points up after five minutes and we were still behind with 17 minutes remaining. We came through in the end, even if it wasn't scintillating, and I never felt we were going to lose. We would be criticised in the following day's newspapers and, knowing that, we were determined to make the best of our night out. We'd had a few drinks but no one was ragged and although we were talking about returning to the hotel, we decided instead to go to a nearby casino, for a laugh. A five-minute walk down by the River Yarra brought us to our den of iniquity. This is what I love about some cities, the 24-hour casino. I'm not a regular gambler but my cousin runs Napoleon's, a casino in Leicester Square, and Melbourne wasn't my first experience. We headed to the bar, which is, I suppose, an indication of our priorities. Actually, it was a bar/restaurant and we ordered food as well as drinks. While waiting for it to arrive, we agreed to empty our pockets, put all the money in the middle and gamble it.

The total came to about a thousand Australian dollars and we decided to play a game of spoof – we had to guess the total number of coins being held, in closed hands, by all the players at the table, maximum of three each. Whoever lost the first round had to go into the casino with the $1,000 and return with more. Unusually for me, I lost, so I scooped up all the dollars and headed out to the tables. This wasn't what I'd planned. I'd have preferred to stay with the guys, having a laugh, so I was determined to make it quick. I turned the $1,000 into chips, made for the roulette table and put everything on black. As the wheel was spinning, I checked to see my credit card was where it should because if black didn't come up, I'd be looking for the nearest ATM. Couldn't possibly go back with less than I came in with, no matter what. Black came up – $2,000. I hung around for a little, wanting the boys to sweat a bit, and when I returned I had a scowl on my face and tried to look like someone who'd lost everything. They looked at me, afraid to say a word, sensing the worst, and then I laughed and tossed two grand on the table. 'The standard's been set,' I said. They didn't know if they should be pleased or fearful.

Balshaw was the next man out so off he went and was gone for 45 minutes. We thought this had to be bad news but he returned with a few hundred more than he started. The procession continued until everyone had had his turn and each one came back showing a profit. Did a few of the lads lose and then head off to a cash machine? I imagine they did but we ate a lot of food, drank a lot of beer and after paying for everything, we ended up with more money than we started with. As the night wore on, the laughs grew louder and the fact that we had been pretty ordinary against the Samoans became less and less important. We were still in the World Cup, the games were tough but that is how we wanted them and we'd had a cracking night.

People might think staying out late in the middle of a tournament wasn't very professional but with evening kick-offs, we didn't get to leave the stadium until midnight. By then we'd be so revved up by the match that there was no point in trying to go to sleep. In any case, after playing Georgia, South Africa and Samoa, the pressure on us eased just a bit because our next opponent, Uruguay, was going to be the least difficult of our pool games. Clive acknowledged this by having the team stay in Surfer's Paradise for the week beforehand. Some guys had their families come to visit and the mood was definitely more relaxed.

I've always been one of those who gets better the more I play. Through the first three games I wasn't skipping through the tulips, but neither was I overly concerned. Missing the prep games had set me back but I was improving and would be fine for the knock-out stages. In any case, not many of the England players were at their best in the pool matches and I didn't feel my case was different from any number of the lads. Like most who started against South Africa, I half expected to be rested for the Uruguay game but wasn't surprised when Clive included me. He knew that I needed to play a lot to get to my best form. Since I was one of the few Test-team guys selected, I was nominated to do the press conference after the XV was announced. I went to the room and was due to speak immediately after Clive and the coaches. I passed Clive as he was leaving and sat down totally ignorant about what had just taken place.

In answer to a question about why he picked me for the Uruguay game, Clive had launched into, 'Well, I don't think Lawrence has been playing particularly well,' and proceeded to criticise my performances so far in the tournament. This wasn't something he had said to me and, suddenly, it was the story of the week and made all the more juicy because I was sitting in front of the journalists, totally unprepared for it. Clive could have pulled me to one side as he was walking out and given me a heads-up. To be honest, I would have expected him to do that, despite previous form. In such situations, I try to be positive. I told myself the reason Clive did that kind of thing was that he knew I had broad shoulders and could take the knocks. He knew, too, that I wasn't going to lose sleep over his criticism but I would be lying if I said it didn't piss me off. I knew he was never going to walk into that press conference and say, 'You know we gave away too many penalties against Samoa and Johnno was the biggest culprit,' but I don't really know why he chose to pick on me, and not for the first time. Perhaps, as I've said, it was because we actually had quite a close relationship and he felt he could do it to me and, in the long term, it wouldn't affect anything. And he was right.

My annoyance at the time was conveyed to the team's press officer, Richard Prescott. What bothered me was the way my form, which actually hadn't been bad, had been made such a public issue by Clive. Due to what he said, I was on the defensive from the moment I sat down in the press conference, and there was no need for that. Richard definitely got the message and, eventually, I'm sure Clive did. And it all worked out in the end, because Clive's decision to pick me against Uruguay and then leave me on the field for the full match meant I would be the only one to play every England game in its entirety. A fact that ultimately I was both grateful and proud of in equal measure.

When you beat a team 111–13, there isn't much you can say and, to be honest, not that much you recall. I've got one vivid memory of how well they kicked the ball. The guy who took their kick-offs just launched this torpedo that went a million miles into the air and invariably landed on me. As it came down, one of their biggest and most offensive tacklers lined me up and smashed me. It was the same guy every time and he never missed. I would run it back three or four yards and then be involved in what felt like a train crash.

By half-time we were about 50 points up and I wondered what our coaches could possibly say when the contest was already over – 'Keep it up lads, don't get complacent'? Our guys were better than that and they pointed out things we could be doing better. Andy Robinson started having a go. 'Can't we do something a bit more imaginative at the kick-offs?' Thanks, mate, it wasn't a lot of fun for me, either. Throughout the first half, I'd been listening to Iain Balshaw shouting in my ear at each of the restarts, 'Hey, Lol, give us the ball. Give it to The Gas,' meaning the quickest man on the team. With his lovely Lancastrian accent, Balsh is a genuine character, a fantastic bloke and one of my favourite team-mates.

Through that first half, I didn't think it was on and played it safe by taking it up and recycling it. Robbo's demand for something better from the kick-off got us talking. 'Right, first kick-off of the second half, I'll give to Andy [Gomarsall] or The Gas and we'll see what happens.' Again the kick was perfectly struck, miles into the air, and when it came down, they were all over us. Iain's voice was ringing louder and louder in my ear – 'Lol, Lol, give it to The Gas, give it to The Gas.' So I gave it to The Gas and The Gas got smashed by two Uruguayans, sandwiched between them and then buried. Quite badly injured, he was in no condition to continue. As he was being lifted onto a stretcher, I walked over as if to commiserate but instead whispered into his ear, 'Oye, oye, give it to The Gas,' and he just said, 'Oh fuck off, Lol.'

That might have been the end of his World Cup but, thank God, he recovered and actually came on in the final. The whole thing was hysterical and the highlight of the game for me. I love Iain to pieces, and we've been good friends for a long time. He's a real talent and one of those guys who doesn't give a shit. He brought great energy and a sense of humour to the squad and, as I can do a reasonable Lancastrian accent, I could take the piss out of him quite successfully. He was a bit of a lad, which made him a laugh to have around.

Over the years, Clive had established a very structured routine at half-time. Against Wales in the quarter-final at the Suncorp Stadium in Brisbane, we needed the interval to change things, otherwise we were going out of the World Cup. First thing was to start running for the tunnel when the whistle sounded, because we wanted to show the opposition we were still strong and well up for the battle. In the Welsh match, we were exhausted and sped off to the tunnel only because our instincts told us to. We were 10–3 down and it could have been more. Most worrying was our lack of energy in the first half, when Wales were quicker and more mentally alert than we were. A few Welsh fans were standing over the tunnel and as Will Greenwood and I went through, they started screaming abuse at us. Not to give them any satisfaction, Will and I just started laughing, as if to say, 'There's only going to be one winner today.' That was something neither of us was sure about. They focused on Will and his slight resemblance to Rodney Trotter from *Only Fools and Horses*. 'Hey Trotter, ya fackin' wanka, ya goin' fackin' lose.' It was funny but it also gave us a sense of what it would be like to lose to these guys.

As was usual at the World Cup, Clive and the coaches sat in a glass box at the back of the stand. We called it his David Blaine Box and when Clive got to the changing room at half-time he was as pale as Blaine had been after 44 days suspended over Tower Bridge. Jonny Wilkinson wasn't having a good match but then few of us were, the difference being that, in his position, Jonny could change the game, but that wasn't happening. Our line-out was good but we couldn't seem to get field position. We didn't have the dominance up front that we expected and we ended up playing too much of the first half in our own territory. The look on Clive's face was unmistakable. For the first time in the World Cup, he felt we were in a match that we could lose.

On arrival in the changing room, the next stage of our half-time routine was silence for the first two or three minutes as everyone took recovery drinks, changed shirts, organised what strapping was needed and iced their bumps or bruises. By then Clive had already spoken with Dan Luger, who had not been at his best in the first half. In a scene reminiscent of the Tony Diprose incident six years previously, Clive just said. 'Dan, you're off,' and in no time Dan had left the changing room and Clive was speaking with his replacement, Mike Catt. The final element of the half-time protocol was for Clive, and others if required, to address the group. Clive said his piece and was followed by Andy Robinson and finally Johnno, who made a powerful speech, telling us if we didn't buck up our ideas, we were on the way home. I remember thinking, 'If the worst comes to the worst, I'm not going back to England, I'm finding some other continent.'

For me, the most telling act was Clive's decision to bring on Catt. Jonny's moment would come in the semi-final against France but he was struggling against Wales and he looked like a young man under serious pressure. He had been that way from the beginning of the tournament and from where I was sitting, he didn't seem to relax much between games. It looked like he was in turmoil, apprehensive about what lay before him. I'd noticed he was finding it difficult to sign autographs for supporters and had taken to disguising himself when leaving the hotel in Brisbane, something he would also do in Sydney. Although I had no right to question how Jonny dealt with being Jonny Wilkinson – just as Jonny would never question why I felt so chilled all the time – I was worried for him. I did wonder if he made things harder for himself by being so conscious of the scrutiny and attention. I know some of that is because he worries about the effect on the rest of the lads when the spotlight is so firmly on him.

His performance against the Welsh improved once Catt came on, as they shared the burden of directing our game. A couple of raking kicks downfield by Catt did wonders for the morale of the forwards, who really wanted to play the game in their territory, and when Jason Robinson produced a moment of magic to set up

Will Greenwood for a try, the game was as good as over. It hadn't been a good performance and something wasn't right. After the game, the blood returned to Clive's face and he offered us his take on where things stood.

'Guys, I think we all appreciate how close we came to defeat this evening and how close we were to flying home tomorrow. You can enjoy tonight but tomorrow we're going to have to have a very serious conversation about where this World Cup is going and what we need to do. One thing is sure, that performance was not acceptable and it certainly won't be enough to beat France. Go away and think about it. One final thing, I've had to phone Austin Healey to get him to fly over here. We've got injury concerns, especially with Josh and Iain, so can everyone do everything possible to get themselves one hundred per cent fit and then I can send Austin straight back to London again.'

I hoped Clive was being funny about sending Austin back. If it was a joke, it was a good one and Austin would have been the first to laugh. If it was serious, it was a pretty horrible thing to say.

That night in Brisbane, a good number of us went out for something to eat. When the meal ended and the sensible guys had gone to their beds, the durable Jason Leonard, Martin 'Cozza' Corry, Paul Grayson and I decided to have just one more drink. From the restaurant, we found a pub. From the pub, we went to a nightclub and from there we ended up in some sort of pool bar. It's one of the things I like about Australia – these places where they serve food and drink through the night. We ended up getting pretty pissed and actually talking a lot of sense. We spoke about the Welsh performance and the reasons for it – our decision to train in the heat of the afternoon sun for night games was bullshit; the endless analysis didn't make you play with passion; why did we feel so bloody knackered in matches when we were meant to be so fit? As we were playing pool for drinks, we got more assertive as we went along and we were sticking the knife in here, there and everywhere. The way we saw it, the only people who hadn't made mistakes and knew how to sort things out were, quite clearly, the four men around the pool table, and we knew we had to have a strategy for the meeting the next day. There we were at 3 a.m, planning it out. 'You say this, I'll back you, then I'll say this, and you mention this,' and we all agreed, 'Yeah, yeah, fuck 'em.' Next morning we did our recovery and afterwards trooped off to the meeting. Jase, Cozza, Grays and I weren't quite as perky as we'd been the evening before and the stench of cologne was an obvious giveaway.

The meeting was serious and it was obvious from Phil Larder's analysis that he had stayed up all night and gone through the video with a fine toothcomb. He had stats on how many tackles we made, how many we missed, how many big hits, how many turnovers we'd conceded, how many charge-downs. Every aspect of our defensive performance was put under the microscope and every mistake pored over in minute detail. He named who was responsible and why. It was an impressive performance. Andy Robinson went through our attacking game and pulled it apart. Why didn't you work the blindside at that point? Why were you walking to that ruck? We lived in a team environment where no one glossed over mistakes and no one felt any need to be soft on those who weren't doing their jobs. In that room, we were all men and nothing would go beyond the four walls. If you accepted the criticism directed at you, you nodded. If you didn't, you put your hand up and explained why you thought it wasn't your fault. Mostly guys accepted responsibility because otherwise the meeting would have lasted for another two hours.

When it came to the moment for the players to respond, I blinked my eyes and tried to get rid of the haze. Jason was a little away from me and my nod to him asked if it was time for us to speak up. He mimed, 'No,' and I could tell he'd changed his mind. The coaches were pretty fired up, their tirade was justified and backed up by the stats from the game and he didn't think it was the most opportune moment to say our piece. I tried Cozza and Grays, again silently asking if we should have a go. They were with Jase – not the time, not the place. Every brain cell told me to agree with them and say nothing, but I didn't listen. I felt some kind of moral obligation to speak on behalf of the four of us and to make some of the points we had agreed the night before. So off I went. I said it didn't make sense to train in the heat of the day for games being played in the cool of the evening and I felt the players should have more of a say in how much we trained and what we did in training over the final two weeks. I also went on to say I felt that in every game so far, we seemed to lack passion. Our performances were machine-like. It was only when we played with some emotion that we were at our best.

I ended up saying we all realised we could have been out of the World Cup against the Welsh and if we didn't start displaying true commitment and drive, we wouldn't get any further. As I spoke, I could feel the passion I'd been talking about building up inside me, beginning to spill over. What I said was very well received.

Others spoke about the exhaustion they felt in the Welsh match and suggested we had spent too much time on the training ground. A certain message was coming through.

There is no doubt that what was being said was taken on board by the coaches. Probably Clive's plan was always to back off in the last two weeks, but whatever the reason was, our training was moved to cooler evening time and the sessions became lighter and less intense. Mostly they started with us walking through organisational stuff and although there was a bit of running and we still did our weights and recovery sessions, it actually felt like we had completely eased off. I thought it reflected very well on the coaches that when the big moment arrived, they were able to cut the umbilical cord and allow the players to get on with it. They still took charge of what happened on Monday, Tuesday and Wednesday, Thursday was our day off and then Friday and Saturday belonged to the 22 selected players. It must have been so hard for the coaches, having given so much to our preparation, to have to step back at the eleventh hour. These guys cared so much about the team and the tournament and it was like the last thing they did for us.

The mood was so calm and chilled in the final two weeks that it was possible to enjoy the experience of playing for a place in the World Cup final. The Manly Pacific hotel in Sydney was a place we all knew well and we felt comfortable there. It wasn't incredibly luxurious but it was set in a nice suburb and our rooms overlooked the ocean. Now we were at the business end of the tournament, England fans began to arrive in their thousands and a few hundred of them spent most of the day hanging out at our hotel and massing outside the front entrance. It added to the sense of the occasion and I certainly enjoyed having them around. If we ever needed a quick getaway, there was a back exit through the car park that we all knew about.

The team room was on the first floor and the usual routine was for us to have a meeting and then go downstairs and onto the bus that took us to training. The England supporters would see us coming and move enough to form a tunnel through which we could walk to the bus. Some players weren't comfortable with the attention and would keep their heads down as they walked. Others were able to enjoy it quietly, because the fans were good-humoured and very supportive. They would say things such as, 'You're doing great,' 'Go on and win it,' 'Best of luck at the weekend.' And you can't help but be proud in that situation. It is an honour to wear the England jersey but you must never forget that you don't own it. It has been loaned to you for a short time. The fans were all wearing England shirts and the jersey is as much theirs as it is yours. It's important to remember that.

On one of those days in Sydney, we were sitting at the back of the bus, Jason Leonard and I.

'Fucking hell, Lol,' said Jason, 'have you ever noticed the way Clive is always down last and always last on the bus?'

'I hadn't,' I said, 'but now that you mention it, mate . . .'

Jase reckoned that it was carefully choreographed and Clive, as our leader, thought it right that he should be the final one to board the bus. I thought it was probably just superstition and that he had it in his head that it would be bad luck for him not to be last on.

'The more I've got to know Clive,' I said to Jason, 'the more I've realised how superstitious he is. He stays at certain hotels, he always wears a certain jumper on the eve of the game. He has lots of these Clive-isms.'

But Jase wasn't convinced and still felt Clive was milking the situation. Every day we watched to see if Clive would be last on board and, sure enough, he was.

'Right,' said Jason one day, 'I'm going to mess him this time. I've got a plan. When we come out of the meeting, we'll find some reason to talk to Clive and then I'll remember I've left my boots in the room. But you've got to keep your eyes on Clive. You got it?'

'Yeah, of course.'

So after the meeting we're walking down the stairs with Clive when Jase remembers his boots.

'Bloody hell, I've left my boots upstairs.' We all stop but Jase says, 'No, you guys keep going. I'll see you on the bus.'

He goes back up the stairs, runs around a corner and hides there for about three minutes. We're all walking towards the bus and Clive is just behind me, but then as I'm getting on the bus, I look around and Clive's not there. A few minutes later Jason comes through the tunnel of people, his phantom boots in his bag. Of course, he notices Clive's empty seat and when he gets to the back, he's full of it. Then Clive gets on.

'I fucking told you, has to be the last on, this is all set up.'

'Nah, superstition mate, superstition.'

We told a few of the other guys and laughed all the way to the training ground. The thing is, little boys on a seven-week rugby trip must amuse themselves. Strangely, we found this very funny, and if we hadn't had moments like this, it would have been so bloody boring.

*

Alice got to Sydney the Thursday before the semi-final against France. Thankfully, it was the team's day off and I was able to be at the airport to meet her. In typical Dallaglio over-the-top style, I hired a limousine and was waiting when she arrived on her 8 a.m. flight. It was funny at the airport. England fans were everywhere and doing double-takes when they saw me – 'Was that bloody Lawrence Dallaglio? What's he doing here?'

I was thrilled to see Alice because no matter how much I enjoy the company of rugby players, after six weeks I needed to spend time with her and we had a lot of catching up to do. Even though we spoke on the phone most days, it's not the same and with young kids, there was loads I wanted to know. We went to her hotel first, which was in the centre of the city, got her checked in and then went across to Manly, so she was able to see our set-up there. Alice went for a stroll on the beach while I rested and that evening we went out for something to eat. From the moment Alice arrived, I felt more relaxed than ever and couldn't wait for the French game.

A week later Alice and I went for lunch at a lovely little restaurant called Le Kiosk, situated in Shelley Beach, about half an hour's walk from the hotel. For those who haven't been to Manly, it is one of the world's more civilised places. You walked out of the hotel, along the sea front for a bit, then turned on to a lovely path that ran by the rocks and gave you a wonderful view of the Pacific. While we were walking, this guy went past us wearing a polo-neck, some kind of hat pulled down over his forehead and dark glasses so big they looked like ski-goggles.

'Shit, wasn't that Jonny?' Alice said.

'Yeah, I think it was.'

'How scary is he?'

'I hope he is,' I said. 'He's playing for us.'

Soon after we met Marc Aspland, a sports photographer with *The Times*, who was in search of Jonny.

'He went that way,' I said, 'but be careful, you mightn't recognise him.'

I was joking with Marc, making light of the situation, but in reality I felt for Jonny, and the pressure he was putting himself under. On the walk to Shelly Bay that afternoon, I wanted to run after him, put my arms around him and say, 'Jonny mate, are you all right?'

Our preparation for the semi-final against France took place mostly inside our heads. They were being billed as the form team of the tournament and had won all of their games comfortably. On the other hand, people felt we weren't playing at our best and perhaps there was a sense that we had peaked during our midsummer tour to New Zealand and Australia. As we spoke about it, the question we continually asked ourselves was whether the French team had been tested so far in the tournament, and the answer was they hadn't. Even Scotland, who might normally be expected to make life difficult for highly rated opposition, didn't put up much resistance. Against teams they were dominating, the French did look majestic, but we approached the match in a very straightforward manner:

'Are we going to test them?'

'Yes, we are.'

'Where is their strength?'

'The scrum.'

'Where are we going to come out on top?'

'The scrum.'

As the media warmed to the French style, there was particular praise for the back row. Serge Betsen, Olivier Magne and Imanol Harinordoquy are three players whom you can't help but admire and they had looked magnificent in the tournament up to the game against us. But again, had they been tested? They hadn't. It niggled Richard Hill, Neil Back and me that in all the plaudits bestowed on our French counterparts, people seemed to forget that England had a useful back row. As a team, we had something to prove – not to ourselves but to the rest of the world. We were also motivated by the consequences of losing a World Cup semi-final. Lose and you had to stay at the tournament and play in the dreaded third and fourth place play-off. Johnno and Jase had experienced that in 1995.

'Lads,' said Jase, 'believe you me, it is the worst experience of your sporting life. And one of the worst experiences of your life, full stop.'

After my post Welsh-game speech about needing to show more passion, I wanted to make sure that I felt emotional for the semi-final because I knew I could help stir up the team. As it turned out, I was almost overcome with emotion when we walked through the tunnel and found a huge wall of white shirts surrounding us. In all our years of playing at Twickenham, we had never seen anything like this. That sight almost put me over the edge. Suddenly, I started thinking of how important this game was to me, and what it meant to have Alice and my mum and dad in the crowd. What it meant in terms of my relationship with my sister who hadn't been given the chance to experience an occasion like this. What I would have given for Francesca to be in the crowd.

I've always felt that the playing of the national anthem is a focal point for a team and as they played 'God Save The Queen', the tears were rolling down my face. It seemed every person in the crowd was wearing our white shirt, tens of thousands of people who had come from the other end of the world to support us. And, to be honest, at that moment the occasion got the better of me. Johnno later said to me, 'I turned to the side and looked at you, Lawrence, and you were in a bit of a state. I knew then everything would be all right.'

It rained that evening at the Telstra Stadium and afterwards people would say, 'Well, the rain suited England and worked against the French.' You know, I've been to France with Alice and the kids and it's pissed down quite a few times. If the truth is known, we hate playing in the rain, but there is no doubt the wet highlighted an important difference between the two teams. The French saw the conditions and thought, '*Merde!*' We looked at the rain and reckoned the French wouldn't like it. I've become good friends with Raphael Ibanez, who is a team-mate at Wasps, and he says that, mentally, England were stronger than France in Sydney, and I'm sure he's right. As soon as we got to the semi-final, we were able to move up two gears and that was at the end of a week in which we hadn't had one tough training session and were the most relaxed we had been through the entire tournament.

Early in the match we went behind to a Betsen try. It was a simple thing, a line-out throw that didn't hit the target and took a bad deflection. If it hadn't been Richard Hill's first game for four weeks, he might have reacted quicker and, typical Richard, he accepted responsibility as soon as we gathered behind the posts. 'Sorry lads, my fault.' That was the way the team operated, someone put his hand up and we all got on with it. In no time, two Jonny penalties put us back in the game and we started to get control. Certainly in those days, the French struggled when an opposition got in their faces and didn't let them do the creative things. They shrugged their shoulders and thought, 'We're not being allowed to play rugby, it's not right.' In the conditions our game was about short targets, not trying to do too much with the ball and waiting for Jonny to kick the penalties or drop the goals that would take us clear. We won without scoring a try, something that would normally be a disappointment, but on this occasion it was almost sublime to do so. It made it more painful for the French, like slow torture that went on for 80 minutes and became more excruciating as it progressed. Jonny's last kicks were nails in the French coffin. It wasn't a particularly pretty match but, for me, it was a beautiful contest.

The game was also the demonstration of Jonny Wilkinson's greatness. He played magnificently and did everything he didn't do in the Welsh game.

After we had showered, dressed and done our interviews, we made the long journey back to Manly in great spirits. The key was that the adventure was going to continue for one more week and we had one last game of rugby to look forward to. With wives and girlfriends on the bus, the trip back to the hotel lasted an hour but seemed to pass in a few minutes. We were drinking cans of beer and the mood couldn't have been better. On arrival we were all looking forward to having one or two more drinks when Clive decided to have a team meeting. It was one o'clock in the morning and this announcement didn't do too much for the party mood, but he got us all into the room.

'Right,' he said, 'well done on tonight. It was brilliant. Everything's gone well. Everyone deserves credit. It's been fantastic. We've got the best players, we've got the best coaches,' which was something he often said. He then changed tack. 'But listen, we've got to have a great week this week. It's got to go really well.'

It was a strange situation. Clive was both excited and apprehensive. Excited by what we had achieved so far and by the possibility of going all the way, but apprehensive that we could still blow it.

'I want you to eliminate everything else that is going on in your life at the moment. There's going to be loads of distractions this week and you've all got to stay focused. Make sure we get it right this week, prepare properly. Forget these bloody newspaper columns, forget any book you might be doing, basically you've got to get rid of all the bullshit.'

Clive was absolutely right but this was two and a half hours after we'd won a World Cup semi-final and I found myself sitting there thinking, 'Whoa, whoa, Clive, just calm down. What you're saying is correct but, mate, I'm still feeling the whack in the ribs I got earlier in the evening and I'm still on a bit of a high from the game and I hadn't intended coming down this quick.'

After the meeting, I caught up with Paul Monk, a lovely guy

who happens to be a friend of mine and of Clive's. I told him about our meeting and how Clive had just spelt out how we needed to stay focused and what needed to be done in the last week. 'Monkey' could see the mood had changed. With the final on our minds, it was going to be a quiet drink and off to bed.

'What's the matter with Clive?' he said. 'He's a bit stressed, isn't he? Look, let me know where he is and I'll have a word with him.' As Monkey was already after having a few drinks, this wasn't the best proposal of the night.

'Monkey,' I said, 'that wouldn't be a good idea. Actually, it would be best if you stayed out of it.'

Clive was 100 per cent right. We did have to stay focused, no distractions. We were in the World Cup final. We were playing Australia. There was nothing for finishing second.

The World Cup final didn't begin until nine o'clock at night and that made for an extremely long Saturday. You do things that kill time – extend breakfast, take a walk around the hotel, have a chat with different people, take care to get the right food and fluids and, for me, there was a decision to make about my afternoon nap. Sleep for too long and there's the danger of lethargy, so I settled for a two-hour snooze. Then there is that wonderful thing called packing. In normal times, it's a chore I dislike. On World Cup final day, it was a Godsend and I stretched it out for an hour or more. With so much time, you could actually make it a bit of a celebration. I laid all of my kit out on the bed, folded each item individually and tried to pack my two bags perfectly. No matter what happened in the final, we weren't due to leave Australia until two days later but this was still my last chance to pack. If we won the final, I wasn't going to see my bedroom for two days. Had we lost, I would have been suicidal and wouldn't have seen any point in packing.

After the big bags were done, I packed my game-day bag. Boots, gum shield, shoulder pads, wash bag, and then shoes, socks, belt, pants because we'd be changing into our team suits after the game. With so much time, you get ridiculous and I must have opened and checked that bag three times. Going through this drawn-out process, I remembered my most glorious hour as a packer. It came at the end of the 1997 Lions tour to South Africa. I was rooming with Jerry Guscott for the third Test, and after the game we had our last night out. Slightly unusually, I got back to our room before Jerry. His stuff was all over the floor and as he had broken his arm in the game, I decided to pack for him and make sure he was ready for the airport the next morning. He must have staggered in at some ungodly hour and crashed out immediately because when he awoke he was astonished to find all of his stuff packed. 'Bloody hell, Lawrence, fair play to you mate. You've packed all my things. Fantastic. What a legend you are!'

Then the ungrateful git basically spent the next five minutes unpacking everything and throwing most of the stuff over by the bin.

'What are you doing?' I said.

'Jesus, Lol, I'm not taking all this shitty kit home with me. I'll leave it for the chambermaids.'

'You know I spent hours packing that for you last night, you ungrateful sod.'

'Look, I appreciate it mate, but I'm not taking all that rubbish home with me.'

Most people would have been sentimental about Lions kit, especially after we had just won the Test series, but not Jerry 'I'll keep a bit but why would I want all this junk?' Guscott. He had a point. How much training gear do you need, how many sub-standard shirts do you want? In no time, there was a mountain of gear alongside the bin and then a black chambermaid came to do our room.

'Would you like this stuff?' Jerry asked her. She was ecstatic and started to hug and kiss him. I found the scene wonderful. Here was this black guy, who'd scored the drop-goal to win the series for the Lions in a country that had been so racist, giving all of his Lions gear to a black lady he had just met. At one point, Jerry looked at me as if to say, 'Aren't you leaving anything?' but my gear was all packed up neatly and I didn't want to mess it up.

We didn't spend that much time considering how Australia would play in the final because there wasn't any point. We were two teams that were very familiar with each other's style, although it was a little bit disconcerting that they scored an early try from what was clearly a pre-planned tactic. Stephen Larkham's floated punt was perfectly weighted and Lote Tuqiri used his height advantage over Jason Robinson to do the rest. People were surprised the Wallabies didn't try this move again but there was a reason for that. One of our aims going into the game was to put Larkham under pressure and make it difficult for him to play his normal game. He's one of the most skilful fly-halves I've played against, but he has that tall and upright posture that makes him susceptible to a bang or two. We identified him as a key player for them and one who had to be sorted out in a legal and fair way. Any time there was a chance of putting a big hit on him, it had to be taken. And if you go back to the tape of the World Cup final, you'll find that Larkham was on and off the pitch at least twice, getting knocks treated, and the interruptions would have disrupted his rhythm. There were no more clever kicks for Tuqiri.

In most of our World Cup matches, we went behind early and when Tuqiri scored, it was a case of, 'Well, here we go again.' Certainly, there was no panic. If we put pressure on the other team, Jonny is going to kick a penalty or drop a goal and that certainly simplifies things for us. As anticipated, a couple of penalties from Jonny did get us right back on track and it pleased me to have a small part in the try we scored just before half-time. Coming round the corner of a ruck, I took a pass from Matt Dawson going left, just outside of Stirling Mortlock. I was aware of Jonny coming from my left and running inside of me, ending up off my right shoulder and screaming for the pass. I threw the pass inside to him and he threw an outside pass to Jason Robinson who had stolen a yard on Wendell Sailor. That was enough for Jason. When I was younger, the former Wasps and England back-row forward Roger Uttley was always saying the thing that kills a defence is an inside-outside pass, as it turns them one way and then the other and by the time they get back, it's too late. Roger was right.

I was on the floor when Jason scored and when I later saw a recording of the try, I was struck by his emotion. Jason seldom wears his heart on his sleeve and has been scoring tries for all of his sporting life. OK, it was a World Cup final but I was still surprised by the passion when he rose, punched the ball in the air and screamed the eternal rugby cry of 'Come On.' I felt it was destiny that Jason should score in the final because of the player and person he is. For me, he was the perfect guy to finish it off. We were the stronger team in the first half but our 14–5 lead didn't really reflect superiority and Australia wouldn't have been too despondent. They were the better team in the second half. It's funny the way memories blur because a few months after the final, I couldn't recall if we actually scored in the second half (we didn't!). I do, however, have a vivid recollection of the penalty that sent the game into extra time. The touch-judge Paul Hoeness saw something wrong with Trevor Woodman's binding at a scrum and called it. How often does a touch-judge make the call on such a technical infringement, something that it is generally just a matter of opinion? My opinion is that it was an unfair call against the team with the stronger scrum. It still left Elton Flatley with a high-pressure kick to level the match. He nailed it and that sent the game into extra time.

Early in that first period, Will Greenwood famously spoke to Flatley. 'Fair fucking play, mate. You've got balls as big as a house. Great kick.' Later, Will would say he wanted England to win the World Cup, rather than Australia lose it because of a missed kick. That was very noble of him, but me, I'd have preferred it if Flatley had missed it and we'd won the game there and then. But I do understand Will's sentiments. Very sporting indeed.

What can coaches do when the World Cup final goes to extra time? Clive quickly realised 'very little'. There was the famous moment in the 13 players' victory against New Zealand in

Wellington when fitness coach Dave Reddin came on with a key message from the coaches – 'Lads, lads, tackle, tackle.' No shit, Sherlock! In our huddle before the start of extra time, Johnno spoke, Neil Back spoke, I spoke and what struck me was how calm everyone was. Clive understood how in control we felt and realised he could return to the stand. Our biggest aim when the game restarted was to get back in front and we did that through a Jonny penalty. It was an unbelievable kick, struck from a long way and it absolutely bisected the posts. That was important because it ensured Australia were still chasing the game, as they had been for the previous hour. Two minutes from the end of the match, there was a ruck, the ball was there and I felt entitled to compete for it. As I did, the whistle went. Penalty to Australia and as Will Greenwood later said, I put on my 'De Niro' face. What I felt at that moment was utter determination. 'Look mate, you can throw whatever you like at us and it doesn't matter. We're just going to accept it and still win this game.' In other games I would have remonstrated with the ref but for some reason I didn't this time.

There was an expression Clive used to love banging on about, 'Thinking Clearly Under Pressure' or T-Cup. I don't know where he got that but it sounded good and had the added advantage of being spot on. And we'd obviously paid attention because in the last minute of extra time in the World Cup final, we *were* still thinking clearly under pressure. As we stood behind the posts waiting for Flatley to tie the scores again, Johnno said we should kick the ball long because the Aussies wouldn't run it back at us and we knew that Lewis Moody was still fresh and would put pressure on their kicker. At the resultant line-out, we decided to throw it long because that was the high-risk option the Australians wouldn't expect us to take.

You think about all the jargon concerning teamwork. What is teamwork? It's knowing what the team needs from you in any situation and you being able and willing to deliver it. Steve Thompson had to make that throw, Neil Back and I had to lift Lewis Moody, Mike Catt had to punch the first hole, Matt Dawson had to make that crucial break, Johnno had to take it on one last bit and then Matt had to make a good pass at precisely the right moment. Under enormous pressure, everyone did his job pretty efficiently. That's teamwork. Jonny hadn't enjoyed a good day with his drop-goal attempts, he was actually nought from three, but what is greatness? Greatness is doing it when you absolutely need to do it. Sinking the putt on the 18th to win The Open Championship when you haven't putted that well earlier in the round. Nailing that drop-goal when you've missed with three attempts earlier in the match.

One spectacular catch from Trevor Woodman from Australia's kick-off and that was it – the World Cup was ours.

The feeling afterwards was relief, but also happiness. We stayed on the field for a bit and had a rushed medal ceremony because the extra time played havoc with television schedules. What the hell, we had the right colour medals. It's amazing, you can't pick out one person in the crowd when the game's happening and as soon as it ends, you can identify every family member and every mate from 100 yards away. For me, it was hugely important that I got to see Alice and my parents before we all trooped off the pitch.

To his credit, the Australian Prime Minister John Howard came to our changing room and apologised for the medal ceremony being hurried. It wasn't his fault and it was decent of him to come and explain what had happened. For a team that had been on the road for such a long time, it was a very special feeling to come back to the changing room with the World Cup, close the door and know that we had done it. There was some mixture of emotions in there. I remember how Josh Lewsey cried – floods of tears. Other guys were too shattered to feel anything and too drained to speak. Some spoke endlessly to friends on their mobiles. Among the coaches and players, there were just never-ending hugs and photos. Everyone was going to want reminders of this moment. For me, there can be no greater feeling. To reach the pinnacle in your sport is one thing, to reach it with so many of your mates is quite another.

The American football coach Vince Lombardi once said, 'Winning is a habit.' Even though we had won the World Cup, the feeling of satisfaction and joy was one we had grown used to. It was our fifth consecutive victory over Australia and if you discounted the prep match against France in Marseille when our predominantly second XV lost by a point to a full-strength French side, we had won every match we had played for a year and a half. We didn't always win impressively, at times it was purely a question of getting the right result, but occasionally we were good. The two best performances were the Grand Slam victory in Dublin and the victory over Australia in Melbourne. This World Cup final performance was less impressive but, invariably, that's what you get at the end of a six-week tournament. But, as a team, we had developed the winning habit.

Predictably, the celebration lasted two days. And I remember more of it than you might imagine. It started in a bar/restaurant near Circular Quay in downtown Sydney that someone very clever had pre-booked for a civilised start to the evening. When I say 'evening' I mean the early hours of the morning because with the 9 p.m. start to the game, the media interviews afterwards, the return journey to the hotel, it was around 1.30 a.m. when we got to Circular Quay. Our families were there and as entry was controlled, we were able to have relaxed conversations with the people who had done most to support us during the months and years of preparation. Afterwards, we went on to a place called the Cargo Bar in Darling Harbour and left there about 9 a.m. for another bar in the notorious but interesting King's Cross district. Alice baled out around 10 a.m. and I took her back to her hotel. 'You're still wide awake, you go back to the lads,' she said. By the time I got back to the bar, I imagined they would all have gone home but I shouldn't have worried.

In the end, Jason Leonard, Martin Corry, Paul Grayson, Mark Regan, Mike Tindall and I stayed the course. To be fair, a few wives and girlfriends were still standing and in no time it was mid-afternoon on Sunday and we were in danger of missing the bus from our hotel to the official post-World Cup banquet. Our difficulty was the enthusiasm of England's fans. They were all over us and we were thoroughly enjoying it but the hours passed and we needed to get back to Manly to change for the banquet. A police van pulled up and two female officers got out. 'Are you having a bit of trouble, lads?' they asked. We tried to say we were OK but when they offered us a lift, we jumped into their van. It wasn't the first time I had been in a police van but this was a more welcoming situation than previous experiences. They took us round by the station, got us to sign some things for their colleagues and then drove us out to Manly. Martin Corry, looking for a bit of noise, switched on the sirens and it was a bit of a laugh for the six of us to be dropped off by the police. There were 2,000 English fans at the entrance to the Manly Pacific as the police van pulled up. It wasn't what you would call a low-profile return to the team hotel.

For the time being at least, low profile wasn't possible. Some among us were slow to catch on to the fact that our lives had changed. After getting back to England, we all went to Pennyhill Park Hotel and met up with our wives, partners and children before returning to our homes. Alice and I lived relatively close by in Richmond, so we were in no rush and eventually just Clive and Jayne, Alice and I and Jonny were left.

'How are you getting back to Newcastle?' Clive asked Jonny. Very coolly, Jonny replied he would get a taxi to Heathrow and get the next flight up. 'I don't think you'll be going back to the airport and flying up to Newcastle,' said Clive. 'I suggest you order yourself a car and drive up there.' Jonny didn't have a clue what Clive was on about. 'Look mate,' Clive explained, 'your life has changed in the last three days. You can't just walk out on the street any more and you can't just turn up at an airport and expect everything to be normal. That day is gone.'

All our lives had changed, Jonny's probably more than everyone else's.

17

Pig-headed

For all of my adult life, I have been a man on a mission. My goal was to show I could play rugby at the highest level and be one of the world's best players in my position. Most of all I wanted to win because, in sport, success is often measured in titles and trophies. Professional sport, though, is like a treadmill and the relentlessness is the toughest part. It doesn't matter what you achieved yesterday, today's game is the one that counts. There is no let-up and if you want to be at the top, you daren't even stop to think about it. And that was me. I never stopped and never thought beyond what we needed to do to win the next match.

I returned home from the World Cup in Australia on Tuesday morning and was rested by Wasps for the following Saturday's game up in Newcastle. Did that mean a weekend at home with my family? No chance. I travelled to Newcastle with the team and, with Jonny Wilkinson, I was proud to parade the Webb Ellis Trophy around Kingston Park. For the difficult assignment in the north-east, I wanted my team-mates to know they had my support and the best way to show that was to make the journey. Wasps were going for their second consecutive Premiership title and we believed we had a strong enough squad to challenge also for the European Cup. Even though I'd been back in England for just a few days, I couldn't wait to get back into the swing at Wasps.

What I hadn't done was consider my family's point of view. In terms of my time and energy, they were coming off last and my relationship with Alice was suffering. After we beat Toulouse to win the European Cup final in 2004, Alice and I went for a meal in Richmond before going to meet the Wasps guys at a pub later on. Alice wanted to talk about 'us' and why she felt we had 'some serious problems'. I'm there but I'm not really listening. We'd just won the European Cup, and this was only six months after winning the World Cup with England. I could see Alice was upset but I didn't know what to say and didn't want my evening of celebration spoiled. As well as that, we had the Premiership play-off final against Bath six days later and immediately after that, I was leaving with England for another tour to the southern hemisphere. I found myself saying, 'Could we have this discussion at another time?' I know I shouldn't have been thinking like that because nothing is more important than your family. Had I been thinking straight and really listening, I would have said, 'Right, I won't go on this tour with England next week.' But I didn't see it like that.

We beat Bath to win our second consecutive Premiership, the

following evening I reported for duty with England and we departed for New Zealand on Monday. Martin Johnson had retired and Jonny Wilkinson was injured. England needed people to stand up, and big Lawrence was the man for the job, always ready for the battle. There was a genuine problem in my relationship with Alice and I was blissfully oblivious to it. That's how it can be with the man who's on a mission – single-minded but also pig-headed.

Professional rugby is a brutal environment. You learn to deal with disappointment, you cope with the constant assessments of your work, you learn to manage your injuries, and you learn to perform on the field. What I didn't figure out was how to look after me. I needed my family but didn't realise I was losing them. I became desensitised to the needs of people outside of rugby, and anything that was a distraction was ignored. Alice brought up a question I didn't want to consider and therefore the problem didn't exist. It's bizarre really because on the pitch, you confront everything, you take the opposition's challenge and you deal with it. Yet when I needed to sit down with Alice and address the concerns she had about us, I couldn't do it. She wanted a platform to express her feelings and to make me understand what it was like to be in her shoes. But no, there was another final I had to play and then charge off to Australia and New Zealand on another England tour. The man on the mission couldn't stop.

In the rugby sense, everything was going tremendously well. When Martin Johnson retired from international rugby, Clive asked me to become captain. Johnno was a huge loss and it was always going to be very difficult for England to stay at the level we had achieved in the seasons leading up to the World Cup. On a personal level, being reappointed as captain brought closure to the *News of the World* episode and the unsatisfactory way in which I had been forced out in 1999. It took five years but Clive's decision was official confirmation that I was a fit person to captain my country. I sensed Clive really wanted this to happen because he had been troubled by the circumstances in which I had been forced to give it up. I recall one conversation when he reassured me that I would, one day, captain England again. It wasn't something that concerned me too much and I certainly didn't lie in bed wondering whether I would get another opportunity. It was far more important for me to be part of a winning England team and, in any case, I had never needed to be captain in order to let people know what I thought.

Post-World Cup, we were there to be shot at and the effort of winning that tournament had taken its toll on the players. The first defeat came against Ireland in the Six Nations at Twickenham, where we had not lost for four and a half years and where we had won 22 matches. Of course, Johnno's retirement hurt the team, as did Jonny's absence through injury, but we had 11 of the side that started the World Cup final and a 12th, Neil Back, was on the bench. Confirmation that we had allowed things to slip came at the Stade de France where we suffered defeat against France in our final game. It was Clive's seventh championship and the first campaign in which the team had lost more than one game. With the benefit of hindsight, the 2004 summer tour to New Zealand and Australia was a seriously bad idea. That summer we all needed a rest, players and coaches. After winning the World Cup, the team should have celebrated its status as champions by producing a string of top-class performances. Mentally and physically, we didn't have it. Trevor Woodman, Phil Vickery, Steve Thompson and Richard Hill all picked up injuries, Neil Back retired and the pack that won the World Cup was no more.

I wanted to show I hadn't lost any hunger and luckily Wasps were doing well. By winning both the Premiership and the European Cup at the end of our World Cup season, the England players at the club made a statement. Eight of us were picked for the summer tour to the southern hemisphere, and since I've always been good at compartmentalising my rugby, I talked myself into believing it would be a good tour. 'It's only three Tests,' I thought, 'just four weeks away from home, and we've got an opportunity to take these guys on and show them why we're champions.' Having new faces in the England squad meant we would have to work harder to achieve the same togetherness but that was just part of the challenge. In the event, the entire tour proved to be too much, far too much. While the Wasps players had been involved in two major finals over the eight days before departure, many others hadn't had a match for six weeks and were very rusty. And I felt I wasn't on the same wavelength as the management team.

For the first time since I'd known him, I questioned Clive's motivation and that of some of the coaches. They were still very committed, they were still doing a professional job, but no longer with the same conviction. I couldn't mention it to them because they would not have seen it and would not have appreciated hearing that from me. Over coffee, Clive and I discussed selection for the first Test, but a rugby captain is not like a cricket captain, in that he doesn't have a role in selection. Clive would ask what I thought, I would give my opinion and that would be it. But, as captain, you want to go on the pitch with a team you're happy with, which I wasn't for that first Test. Clive chose Mike Tindall and Mike Catt in the centre, even though both had missed a lot of rugby through injury. The decision that really baffled me, though, was Chris Jones's selection over Joe Worsley in the back row.

Joe was sensational for us in the European Cup victory over Toulouse when he nullified the threat of Isitolo Maka and deservedly received the man-of-the-match award. Against the All Blacks, we would have to do a lot of tackling and in my view we had to have Joe in the side. Chris Jones is a very talented player, a guy with a lot of pace and skill, but physically at that time, he and Joe are very different animals and against the All Blacks the animal we needed was Joe. I sensed that Andy Robinson was stressing about the line-out, believing that with Joe and me in the back row, we would struggle to win our own ball. That fear tipped the balance in Chris's favour and, of course, we hardly won a line-out ball anyway. I felt sorry for Chris, who was substituted at half-time.

We lost the first Test 36–3, the second 36–12 a week later and got smashed 51–15 by Australia. The tour disillusioned me and probably many others. Playing for England is not about getting beaten by 36 points.

During the tour, there was one incident that shouldn't have happened and for which I was partially responsible. Our club coach, Warren Gatland, was back in New Zealand on holiday and he invited the Wasps crew round to a barbecue in Waikato. His wife, his parents and lots of his extended family were there and they cooked up a fantastic feast for us, something they didn't have to do. Over the food and a few beers, we were having a moan about the length of the England training sessions (deemed too long) and the number of team meetings (far too many) and, of course, Warren had a grin on his face because the complaints about the England set-up were an indirect compliment to how things were done at Wasps. It wasn't that England's preparation was wrong and Wasps' right but the winning of two major trophies in the previous three weeks justified everything we were doing at the club. England had lost two of its last three games in the Six Nations and we felt entitled to a bit of a whinge.

That kind of private conversation happens all the time and yet I should have nipped it in the bud. Even when said in private, such discussions don't help anyone and don't improve team morale. And, of course, it didn't remain private. Warren gave an interview to a journalist on the local Waikato newspaper and probably believed some of what he said was off the record. However it happened, it was embarrassing for us to see our complaints about training and team meetings appearing in the article. Clive didn't like it and I totally understood why. We had been out of order – not good from my point of view and another bad moment on a difficult trip.

I apologised to Clive, who would have been entitled to blow his top but didn't. Warren, too, was a bit embarrassed about the whole thing because he's a decent bloke and he knew, as a former international coach, that the last thing you need is some other coach undermining you. Clive addressed the issue at our next team meeting, saying he wasn't happy about what had appeared but he wanted to forget it and move on. There were many times when Clive handled things maturely and well, and this was another example.

*

During the tour I had a fair bit of time to think and it began to dawn on me there was a price to be paid for neglecting my family. I called home but conversations with Alice weren't much good for either of us. She was understandably tired of always being left behind to take care of the children by a man who regarded his rugby as the most important thing in the world. Having tried to alert me to the problem without much success, she was determined to take control. I quickly began to realise that my relationship with Alice had actually broken down. It was also clear it wasn't going to be put back together easily, but I was absolutely determined to do whatever was necessary. Back in England, I came to the conclusion that resigning the England captaincy and retiring from international rugby would be for the best. I mulled it over during the summer holidays to make sure I was doing the right thing. Then, in late August, I met with Clive in the bar at Pennyhill Park Hotel one Friday evening.

'I've got something to tell you,' I said.

'Well,' he replied, 'I've got something to tell you.'

'OK,' I said, 'you go first.'

'I'm going to resign as England head coach.'

'I'm going to resign as England captain and from international rugby.'

I don't know if he had an inkling of what I was going to say, but I did have a sense of what he was going to tell me. When trying to arrange our meeting, there was something in his voice that wasn't the usual Clive. He seemed distracted. Still, I did think, 'Typical Clive, he's beaten me to the draw again.' We talked about how things were between Alice and me and the toll it was taking. The tour hadn't been enjoyable and it was time for me to attend to more important business. He admitted he had struggled for motivation in New Zealand and Australia and we both agreed it would have been impossible for him to continue in the England job and also coach the 2005 Lions to New Zealand, which he had agreed to do. You could argue that as soon as he agreed to take the Lions job, he should have resigned as England coach, but who was going to suggest that? Clive loved doing the England job because when things were going well, it was the best job in the world. We talked about our respective situations and he told me in confidence that he was considering a possible move into football, which didn't surprise me because he had often talked about that. He asked me about the 2005 Lions to New Zealand and whether I was still interested.

'Well, you tell me,' I said. 'I'd love to go but a lot will depend on my situation with Alice.'

'From my point of view,' he said, 'the fact that you're not playing international rugby is not a concern. Provided you're playing well for Wasps, it's not going to be a problem for me.'

At the press conference, I explained my retirement from international rugby in terms of wanting to spend more time with my family. That was putting it mildly, but between Alice and me, there was no easy fix. At first I thought that by giving up England and being more attentive to Alice's needs I could turn things round, but that hope didn't last long. Things had gone too far and, in a sense, I was trying to close the stable door after the horse had bolted. When I announced my retirement, I told Alice it wasn't something I would ever hold against her and that all I wanted was to make things work between us. Retiring from international rugby wasn't going to solve the problem, I realised, but it gave me some time to work on it.

I wasn't sure where it had gone wrong. My feeling was that the woman I loved was standing up for herself. She was tired of the role she'd ended up with in our relationship. She had devoted herself to our children for eight years while I had single-mindedly tried to fulfil all of my rugby dreams. With so much on her plate and so little involvement from me, she had lost her independence, her identity, and had sacrificed her dreams. We had met, fallen in love, had three kids in no time and hadn't had the kind of courtship most couples enjoy. Alice was the mother of our three children, had been my partner for nine years, and yet there were some things about her I didn't even know. Only through the tough times did I come to realise that and to appreciate she had her own road to follow.

Her mum, Lydia Corbett, was Sylvette David, muse to Pablo Picasso. Back in the early 50s, Alice's mum lived in Vallauris in the south of France and Picasso happened to live nearby. Sylvette was 19 at the time, an extremely attractive young woman who wore her hair in a high ponytail. He was in his early 70s and after seeing her, he wanted to paint her. Although beautiful, Sylvette was shy and would only agree to pose for Picasso if her boyfriend Toby could accompany her. Picasso produced around 40 portraits and some sculptures of Sylvette and she became known as 'The Girl With The Ponytail'.

Picasso treated Sylvette with great respect and gentleness. What he gave her most of all was a love of art and the confidence to express her creative talent in paintings, sculptures and ceramics. Sylvette married an Englishman, changed her first name to Lydia so that she could not be accused of trading on her friendship with Picasso, settled in Devon and became a very successful artist in her own right. That's where Alice grew up and from her mum she inherited a love of art and a very creative talent. Alice is now a successful ceramist.

A few years ago Alice went to New York with her friend Tracy. Alice knew that a permanent sculpture of her mother by Picasso was to be found somewhere in the city and eventually she discovered it in Greenwich Village, standing 36 feet in the air. Alice was blown away by the discovery. She rang in floods of tears. 'I can't believe it! I've found Mum,' she cried. Then, a few months ago, Alice was in London's West End with her friend Aideen, walking down Cork Street, which is just off Regent Street and full of art galleries. A painting of her mum, an original Picasso, was displayed in the front window of one shop and Aideen took a photograph of Alice standing outside the window, virtually alongside a portrait of her mother. She sent the photo to my phone. 'What do you think of these two birds?' said the text message. I thought it would be lovely to get Alice and Lydia that portrait, so I called the gallery and asked if the Picasso was for sale. It actually belonged to the owner himself and he was prepared to sell it to me for £1.2 million. I suggested to Alice that she ought to have married a footballer.

Picasso gave Lydia one portrait but sadly it was sold when her first husband Toby got tuberculosis and times were tough. What Lydia treasures are the memories of the time she spent with Picasso and the inspiration she drew from him to pursue her own career. Without Picasso's influence, she's not sure she would have had the confidence to do it. Lydia now divides her time between Devon and the south of France and we visit her whenever we can.

This was Alice's background and when she graduated from art school, she had the dreams you have when you leave college. Then

Ella arrived, followed a couple of years later by Josie and, soon after, by Enzo. Alice threw herself into motherhood. It devoured her time and I never thought of what she sacrificed. I had my career, which was incredibly demanding but, at the same time, incredibly exciting. In every aspect of my life except the changing room, I was an emotional retard. While I was pursuing my rugby dream, Alice and I grew apart. There were so many tours, so many training camps, so many away games, so many times when I wasn't around. Then I'd get home for four days and, because I was a man still on a mission, I couldn't relax.

In January 2005, Alice and I went to Mauritius, just the two of us. I thought it would be a chance to work things out but we didn't do that. I wasn't able to and I sensed she wasn't ready to or didn't want to. Since the arrival of the kids, we had never been away on our own until then, and only when we were together did I realise just how much damage had been done. It wasn't a disastrous trip because we were mature about it. We were stuck there together. Both of us needed a break and if we were nice to each other, we could both have a pleasant time. But there was zero intimacy and in terms of bringing us closer together, it didn't work. We talked about spending some time apart, although that was Alice's idea, not mine. From the start I was against separation, temporary or otherwise. It didn't make sense, my rugby career was drawing towards an end and we were getting to the point in our relationship where we would have the opportunity to enjoy ourselves. Why would we give all that up? We had survived the tough years, why would we throw it all away now? It made me angry to think about it but the more I fought to keep things together, the worse things got.

Typically, I saw our relationship problems as one more hurdle to be cleared. I had never been defeated by a challenge and I wasn't going to lose this one. Alice saw the way my competitive spirit worked and she didn't want a reconciliation that would be just another battle that I had won. For her, it had to be more genuine than that. Soon after we got back from Mauritius, Alice asked me to move out, saying it would be better if we didn't live together. When you've got three children, it's not easy to separate. If you don't know how long the separation is going to be, what do you tell the kids? It was a very, very difficult time for all five of us. Of course, I resisted and I felt a fair bit of resentment. Why should I move out of my own home? Why should I live elsewhere when it was my job that got us our lovely home and enabled us to live comfortably? The more I fought, the more Alice dug in her heels.

I was getting a lot of support from friends, mine and hers, and from both our families. Everyone wanted us to stay together. Maybe there were one or two who thought we would be better apart but the vast majority wanted us to be reconciled. As happens when a couple is fighting, it can get fractious and unpleasant, and although we always tried to shield the children from our disputes, it was hard. Plenty of friends told me that in trying so hard to keep Alice, I was only driving her away and my best chance was to let her go and hope that in time, we would come back to each other. That's easy to say but I found it extremely hard to do. In the end, there was no choice because things weren't improving. Luckily, I'd bought a small house in Kingston a few years earlier. It wasn't very far away, so I moved in there. The house was a complete mess. I hadn't got round to doing it up. Plaster was falling from the walls, the ceilings needed redoing, all the rooms had to be rewired and the kitchen had to be replaced. There was a bed, a coffee table, a small television and a feeling of returning to student life. That wasn't a problem. What killed me during those early months in Kingston was waking up in a house that didn't have my kids in it. It made me feel for any man or woman who is separated from their children.

Living in Kingston was a strange existence because it was a very unhappy time in my life, but a lot of good came out of it. I was going to training at Wasps with pain etched on my face and most of the guys could see it. Their sensitivity and their efforts to make me smile showed they knew exactly what was going on but they didn't say a word and neither did I. We were rugby players, big boys, and we had to be professional about our jobs. But I was struggling. From February to the end of the season, I wasn't sleeping properly. I went to the doctor at Wasps. 'You're going to have to give me some tablets because I'm not able to sleep any more,' I told him. I'd been plunged into a state of shock and that was one of my body's responses. It wasn't as though I wanted to stay awake but I couldn't rid myself of the restlessness, or stop the endless tossing and turning. I would get up the next morning and go training, and somehow my body, put into this almost meltdown state, found extra energy levels to keep me going. At the end of a four-night cycle of lousy sleep, though, I would be so damned tired my body would just cave in.

I started seeing a counsellor in Ladbroke Grove and we had some very honest sessions. It was an opportunity for me to vent the anger I felt and to retrace some old ground to see if we could find the source of things. Men can be cold and unemotional. A lot of that is the person you are, but a lot of it is shaped by things that happen in your life. When my sister died, I didn't want to confront that internally and I kind of shut down. That made me colder and utterly incapable of facing my emotional problems. I talked to the counsellor about never having visited my sister's grave and what that meant. Plenty of things in my life had to be addressed and I'm not suggesting I have dealt with them – I don't think I'm even halfway there yet. It was good for me to talk about them because it helped me to realise that there are solutions to the complex questions that have floated around inside my head for such a long time. People look for answers when there's a crisis and once that passes, the questions get buried again. I suppose that's human nature.

I continued to speak to both our families and some close friends, as did Alice, and because I was the one desperate for us to get back together, a lot of people took my side. That didn't help at all and made Alice more determined not to be forced into anything against her wishes. Her attitude was, 'You can all get lost. I don't care anymore about what anyone else thinks,' and eventually, I began to realise that all my efforts were a waste of time. Worse than that, they were driving Alice crazy. Making an effort helped me because I needed to talk about it but it didn't help our situation. So as the months passed and February became March, and March went into April, I stopped complaining to our families and friends and started to accept the fact that things weren't going to improve dramatically. I also accepted that living apart could be for ever. I didn't stop loving Alice or longing for us to be together but I did back off a little. I thought, 'OK, you want some space. Take it. See if it's what you really want.' Once I accepted that we might never get back together, things didn't seem so bad. Was the battle about control? I don't know. But once I stopped wanting to control the situation, things felt better.

Without wanting to sound like some kind of guru, I reckon you have a three-lane highway in your life. Outside lane is your career, middle lane is family and friends, inside lane is you. I spent most of my life in the outside lane, spent a little time in the middle lane and rarely ventured into the inside lane. What became clear was that I needed to spend time in the inside lane, looking at me and thinking how I could be more aware of myself and others. As soon as I focused on that, it was obvious my life wasn't as hopeless as I made it out to be. It wasn't as though I had a woman who was trying to deny me access to the children. It wasn't as though Alice was being a complete arse. Once I stopped fighting for her to come back, the anger disappeared, the arguments ceased and we went back to being rational and civil with each other. And then a strange thing happened – I started to feel comfortable about being on my own.

All my life I had never done 'me' and in my little house in Kingston, I didn't have a choice. For starters, I made the house more comfortable. I went out and chose a new kitchen and got someone to install it. It looked fine and I felt good about that. I had the house plastered and added little bits and pieces that made a difference. It was modest but it became comfortable and the kids loved coming round to 'Dad's little house'. The kids were an inspiration. Although they were young, they were aware of what was going on and they wrote some amazing cards: 'Dad, I can't understand why you can't be at home. We really miss you.' They would make me cry and cheer me up at the same time. I went out and bought some new clothes and started looking after myself. As the months passed, I went through a period of thinking reconciliation was not going to happen and, although it pained me, I would tell myself that being on my own, when I had three lovely kids, wasn't the worst thing in the world.

During my rediscovery of the single life, Wasps ended up playing an even bigger role. People at the club sense when things are not right in your personal life and they rally round. They imagined I didn't want to talk about it and so nothing was ever said, but everything was understood. As much as a rugby club can, Wasps became my family and, in that pig-headed way of mine, I looked to rugby as a way of salvaging something from the wreckage. Walking on to the pitch I would tell myself to enjoy it, because there wasn't much else in my life that I was enjoying. But try as much as I did on the pitch, I still couldn't forget the predicament I was in. I would be walking back after we'd scored a try and a voice inside in my head would say, 'I can't believe you've got yourself in this situation.' Then another voice would say, 'Look, mate, this kick-off is coming at you, and you'd better be ready.'

In a general sense, I felt mentally fragile. As well as the situation with Alice and living in Kingston, my status in rugby changed the moment I resigned the England captaincy and retired from international rugby. I didn't become any less of a player but the perception was that I had. When people start referring to you as 'the former England captain' and 'the former international Lawrence Dallaglio', they create the perception of decline. The aura that you think you had disappears and every opposing back-row forward thinks he can have a piece of you. You're the guy on the way down. The situation wasn't helped when we lost home and away to Leicester in the European Cup. Both matches were fiercely contested and we were unlucky at home. Martin Johnson knocked the ball out of Matt Dawson's hands in front of their posts but the referee missed it and they went down to the other end and got a penalty that won them the game. I'm not complaining – we would have been delighted to get away with the same thing. At Welford Road a week later we had a chance to put things right but couldn't do it. Two losses in the European Cup and you're struggling to qualify for the knock-out stages. Losing our final game down in Biarritz made it a certainty.

The thing was, we had a decent team, more or less the same bunch of players who had won the European Cup and Premiership the season before. So we concentrated on going for a third Premiership title and, unsurprisingly, Leicester were in the way again. There had been a number of big matches between us over the previous two or three seasons and they won every one of them. The two losses in the European Cup were devastating because we had believed we were every bit as good as they were. In our final league match of the 2004–05 season, we played them at Welford Road, knowing that both teams had already qualified for the Premiership play-offs. It was a special occasion for Leicester – the final home game for both Martin Johnson and Neil Back, and also John Wells's last home game as a coach at the club. With a possible final between the two clubs just two weeks away, neither of us wanted a bad result, but that's what we got. They walloped us 45–10, our lone try coming right at the end of the match. Anyone looking at the result would presume Leicester smashed us but the game wasn't like that. We missed six tackles and they scored off every one of them. We felt the mistakes we'd made could be corrected and the weaknesses that had been exposed could be eliminated.

During the reception given by the Welford Road crowd to Johnno, Neil and John Wells, we wanted to be respectful. They played 'Simply the Best' over the public address system and we applauded. Since we had been beaten by so many points, that felt humiliating. Nothing against Johnno and Neil, who had been fantastic players for Leicester, but we would have preferred to applaud them having won the match. After doing the right thing, I gathered our players into a huddle on the pitch.

'Look,' I said, 'soak all of this up, every last drop of it, and make sure you bottle it because there's a good chance we'll meet these guys again two weeks from now. What we've experienced today is humiliation on a grand scale. And no one should forget this.'

No one who was at Welford Road that afternoon and no one who watched on television or read the reports thought we could beat Leicester. In fact, the only people who believed Wasps could turn it round were our players and coaches.

The following week we played Sale in a semi-final that decided who got to meet Leicester in the final. We won decisively and it was clear that there wasn't much wrong with our form. The build-up to the final couldn't have worked out better. Most of the rugby writers felt safe in anticipating a glorious finale to Martin Johnson's playing career. The storyline defined the occasion and gave the match added significance. Johnno would have been cringing at the way the game was being presented and very conscious that it played into our hands. It was as if Wasps, the champions who were seeking a third consecutive title, didn't exist and if they did, they didn't matter. Who cared that Warren Gatland, the most successful coach in Wasps' history, would be taking charge of the team for the last time? He was just a Kiwi that the media didn't care about. As Jim Telfer told the 1997 Lions in South Africa, 'We're just here to make up the fucking numbers.' Our motivation increased as we got closer to the final.

As a team, Wasps have always been at their best when emotionally charged. There are technical reasons for this – most obviously, our aggressive blitz defence depends upon every member of the team being alert and highly motivated. It's not something you can always be for every game but on big matches, it works brilliantly. This would be one of those games. The match held a special significance for me. Since January and the move to Kingston, there had been a lot of bad times and even though things had improved, they were far from perfect. I'd learned to live on my own but I didn't want to be on my own. Rugby was the part of my life that was visible to Alice and the kids. Ella and Josie would come with me to the final, and I hoped they would see me in a more positive light. I wanted Alice and Enzo at home to be proud of the way I played. At the time it felt like the only way I could express myself was on the rugby pitch.

There was also the debt I owed my team-mates. Every day at training, every match we played, they were there for me – many afraid to say anything but making it perfectly obvious they cared for me. We were accustomed to being in big finals at Twickenham but knew it would take something special to beat Leicester. Before we went out on the pitch, we had a talk in the changing room because there were things I needed to say to them, and vice versa.

'Clearly,' I told them, 'you know that I have had a very difficult season. You guys have seen that and your support through the bad days has helped me to keep going. But that's how it is in this club, it's what we have. We watch out for each other, we look after each other and we make sure we're there for each other. It'll be me one season, somebody else next season, but that support is always there. What I'm talking about isn't just rugby. It's something greater than that. It's something we have at this club and I can tell you, if you're ever going to have problems, this is a good place to be. I'm also telling you that this afternoon, I'm going to repay some debts because I owe you guys.'

As I finished, the emotion was obvious in my eyes. I looked at the other guys, the tears were everywhere and it was an incredibly powerful feeling. Walking out through the tunnel at Twickenham, Martin Johnson was just across from me, the Premiership trophy on a table in front of us. I could sense the cameras on him and for a moment, I thought about what a fantastic player and leader he had been for Leicester and England. He was an England team-mate I had grown to like and part of me wanted to join all those applauding him. 'OK,' I thought, just as we were about to walk out on to the pitch, 'this is Johnno's last game, show respect and allow the great man to lead the way.' I stopped for half a second and don't even know if he noticed, but he was first on to the pitch that day and he deserved to be. As soon as I did that, sentiment disappeared and a very different thought struck. 'OK, mate,' I said to myself, 'you've done that. Now let that be the last fucking backward step you take this afternoon.'

Wasps played one of their best games in that final, smashing Leicester 39–14 and on this occasion the score did reflect the match. They never got into it and we had heroes all over the pitch.

Phil Greening played brilliantly. Joe Worsley, Simon Shaw and Alex King were outstanding and Warren Gatland got the send-off his three-and-a-half year stint at the club deserved. After the game, I got Ella and Josie out on the pitch and they joined in the lifting of the trophy and the spraying of champagne. They had great fun and I enjoyed having them there. I was fortunate to be named man-of-the-match and that was lucky because I was able to give Ella the winner's medal and Josie the man-of-the-match award. Thinking of Alice watching it at home, I hoped she thought I had played well.

In the months before the 2005 Lions tour to New Zealand, I wasn't sure if I wanted to go. I thought it was more important to stay around and try to be reconciled to Alice. But as it got closer and friends convinced me to step back and give Alice space, my view about the Lions changed. Being down in the southern hemisphere would have its advantages. It would be a welcome distraction and it would allow me to get through the next two months. I worried how I would survive over the summer without rugby, which had been a refuge through the months in Kingston.

From a rugby standpoint, I was in great nick and wanted to play in the series against the All Blacks. We went for a week's intensive training in Wales and stayed at the splendid Vale of Glamorgan Hotel. At the end of that week, there was a barbecue to which the wives and partners were invited to say their goodbyes. For the first time in a long time on one of these occasions, I was on my own and I felt it.

18

Putting myself
back together

I t is the pain I remember. Mind-blowing you could call it.
Twenty minutes had passed in the opening game of the 2005
Lions Tour to New Zealand. We'd made an excellent start
against Bay of Plenty in Rotorua, I think we were 17–0 up and I
felt as fit and as sharp as at any time in my career. I hadn't played
international rugby for almost a year and I had missed it. And if
you couldn't be up for a Lions Test series against the All Blacks,
you had a pretty serious problem. We were defending when I went
to help Brian O'Driscoll who was tackling one of their centres. At
the worst moment, with my right leg caught in the ground and
facing the wrong way, I slipped. All my weight went in one
direction and basically I wrenched my right ankle virtually out of

its socket. Painful, extremely painful in fact, and the second it happened, I knew my tour was over. I also knew the damage was serious. My right ankle was broken and the dislocation had messed up my ligaments. The pain was searing, worse than anything I had ever experienced.

While I was being treated, I realised they were going to put me on a stretcher and then take me off the pitch on a golf cart. Even though my situation was grim, the thought of being carried off the field bothered me. I had played the game for 20 years and never once had I not walked from the pitch. Four years previously, just before the 2001 Lions tour to Australia, my cruciate ligament was damaged so badly it needed reconstruction, but I'd played on in that game. This was different. There was no option this time. The pain wasn't letting up and after the head Lions doctor, James Robson, manipulated the ankle back into its right place, I wasn't exactly demanding to be allowed to walk off the pitch. So the stretcher was lifted onto the golf cart and I was driven away. We waited by the tunnel leading from the pitch for what seemed like an eternity. Maybe the ambulance wasn't ready but my memory is of lying there in excruciating pain and seeing the head of the paramedic, who was supposed to be looking after me, bob this way and that as he followed the action on the pitch. I wanted to say, 'Look mate, I'm in absolute agony here,' but this was New Zealand and Bay of Plenty were attacking. The noise of the crowd and the angle of my minder's head as he followed the play told me they were close to our line.

Eventually, I was delivered to Rotorua General Hospital and was again reminded that I was in New Zealand.

'Ah, Lawrence Dallaglio,' said the doctor in charge. 'I was

watching the game on television. Expected you here a bit sooner.' Then, as he began to examine my ankle, he said, 'Any chance that I could have your Lions kit, mate?' Given that the pain was still brutal, I wasn't going to argue.

'Look, let's make a deal,' I said. 'You give me some morphine and I'll give you some of my kit that I still have.'

I had actually given my jersey to the Bay of Plenty No. 8, or at least I had asked for it to be left for him before I was carted out of the stadium. Eventually, the morphine was injected and the pain receded.

Gary O'Driscoll, the Lions doctor looking after me, wanted to ring my 'next of kin' in England to let them know I was doing OK. Of course, he knew nothing about my personal circumstances and for a second I wondered who he should call. Not having lived with Alice for six months, was she still my next of kin? I gave him her number.

'Is everything all right?' I asked, after he had made the call.

'Yeah, mate, fine. She's all right. Sounded pretty upset, though. She was asking how you were.' Apparently, Alice had been in tears in front of the television as I was being carted off.

Gary told me this not thinking it had any particular relevance. I hadn't expected Alice to be upset and it surprised me. Cheered me up, I suppose. In a very personal way, it was a seminal moment in my life. And because of this, fracturing my ankle in New Zealand took on a completely different significance for me from the one it had for everyone else. They were thinking it was a complete disaster that affected the team's chances of winning the Test series. Of course, I was disappointed from a rugby point of view but there was something more important going on in my life and I found myself thinking, 'You know, this is not the worst thing that could have happened to me.' I actually felt that the broken ankle had happened for this reason.

Having spent Saturday night in Rotorua General Hospital, I was taken by car to Auckland the following day and underwent an operation to put my ankle back together. They had to realign the joint and insert a plate, which was held in place by five screws. The operation went well but, because of the surgery, I was not allowed to fly home immediately and spent 10 days on my own in the Hilton Hotel, where the team had stayed on arrival in New Zealand. For one night Scotland's Simon Taylor was there, too, forced out of the tour because of a hamstring injury. Simon has been very unlucky with injuries and it was a huge disappointment for him. We were stranded on our own in Auckland so, even though we didn't know each other well, I called his room, suggesting we go out for a meal together. He agreed and I got on to the concierge, found the best Italian restaurant, booked it and ordered a taxi to pick us up. When I called Simon to let him know the details, he'd changed his mind and no longer felt like going out. 'Oh,' I joked, 'we'll just have to go back to being English and Scottish players who hate each other then.' Still, the restaurant was booked and I hobbled out of the hotel and into the taxi, deciding I had better get used to my own company.

During those 10 days in Auckland's Hilton I hardly saw another soul, apart from the wonderful Kiwi surgeon, Bruce Twaddle, who operated on me and came regularly to see how I was doing. He even invited me round to his house and couldn't have been kinder. Being so much on my own, though, gave me plenty of time to reflect on where things stood in my life and on what was important. I was very philosophical about the injury because, in my heart of hearts, I'd had doubts about making the tour in the first place. The injury told me to slow down and concentrate on what really mattered. My phone calls to Alice were different from what they had been. Previously when I called, we talked about the kids and how they were doing. After the injury and Gary O'Driscoll mentioning how upset she had sounded, Alice and I started to speak about us. There was a lot more warmth than there had been – I don't know what changed in her mind but I didn't really care. I was just glad that there was a spark, something that gave me hope for our future. When something bad happens, you want to be around the people you love and I could tell that my injury had an effect on Alice. Even though I was alone and pretty much an invalid in Auckland, it was a good time in my life. During the phone calls, we both realised there had been enough arguing and more than enough conflict. We both wanted to move on from that.

When I left England, I was a man living on his own, separated from his partner and three children. Given the nature of my injury, I was going to need to be taken care of when I got back. My mum, I knew, would come to my rescue. There were friends who would volunteer but I wanted to go home to Alice and the kids. At some point, we talked about what would happen and Alice just said, 'Come and see me.' We didn't talk about my moving back, or pledge this or promise that, or talk about us getting back together. It just happened. I went home and Alice looked after me. I don't know whether spiritual is the right word for this but I felt there was a meaning to everything that happened. I had just broken my ankle on a Lions tour and I was back in my own house, re-united with Alice and the kids. The injury had given me the opportunity to rebuild my life.

For the coming together to work, there had to be a lot of forgiving on both sides and we both admitted the mistakes we had made. A lot of people in our situation mess things up because they are not prepared to forget. They say they have put things in the past but when there's a disagreement, they can't help bringing up old grievances. We agreed we would not do that. We drew a line under what had happened and moved on. Both of us appreciated that we were blessed with three fantastic children, and understood that we both wanted to work things out between us. The last two years have been very good for us and we can now look back on the bad times and know that some good came out of them. We were forced to address certain aspects of our lives and deal with them. We went through painful times but they made us better. What doesn't kill you makes you stronger and all that. By starting a family so early in our relationship, Alice and I missed out on the things that couples do when they first meet, where they talk endlessly about all sorts of things. We'd never had that time and, in the end, it caught up with us. Something drastic had to happen to get things right.

While I was fulfilling my rugby dreams, Alice was looking after the kids. There is no doubt she was doing the harder job and I don't think it is any help that the person she was sharing her life with was revered by so many outside our home. Eventually, Alice started to feel that her life had been taken away. After we re-united, she was able to make time for her work and that has helped to restore her confidence. She has had successful exhibitions of her ceramics and sculptures, and has a sense of having her identity back.

*

I've had great times and disappointing moments with the Lions. The '97 tour to South Africa was one of the best experiences of my rugby life but injury prematurely ended my involvement in the 2001 tour to Australia and then the 2005 trip to New Zealand. With the benefit of hindsight, I probably should have accepted that my damaged knee wouldn't hold up for the duration of the 2001 tour but the medical people gave me hope and when you want to be part of something as badly as I wanted to be part of that tour, you seize the opportunity. The injury happened when I played for Wasps against Bath at Loftus Road in a Premiership semi-final play-off at the end of the season. It was a Sunday game and my memories are pretty vivid, mostly because of what happened afterwards.

Attempting to tackle Mike Catt, I was wrong-footed and stuck out my left leg to try to slow him down. It was a stupid thing to do. He carried on through me, turning my leg around and shifting my body weight with it. Unfortunately my right leg was planted in the ground and the anterior cruciate ligament in that knee more or less snapped. I say 'more or less' because it didn't completely rupture but was very severely torn. The pain was pretty bad but what bothered me was that the game continued while I was being treated on the pitch and Bath scored following a Wasps scrum. At the time, that pissed me off far more than the injury. After being treated, I played on for about 15 minutes but had the sensation of my knee wobbling all over the place. Turning or changing direction was impossible but I stupidly felt if I got to half-time and then iced it, I'd be able to carry on. I did survive to the interval but the ice had no impact and I had no chance of continuing. From there, things got worse. Outside the ground, on the other side of the road, a number of Queens Park Rangers fans had gathered to protest about Chris Wright's involvement in QPR. Chris had stepped down as QPR chairman a few months earlier but was still a major shareholder. Leaving the ground, I had Ella on one arm, Josie on the other, and as soon as I appeared, the abuse started. 'Ah, fucking hell Dallaglio, why don't we just fucking sell you and get rid of Wasps.' It upset me that they were swearing in front of my children and I would have loved to put the kids down and take them all on. But I bit my lip and stayed calm.

Next morning I couldn't walk and my knee was twice its normal size – not the perfect way to begin the May bank holiday. Having somehow got up the stairs on Sunday night, I really struggled to make the return journey the next morning. Alice drove me to Kingston Hospital, because I desperately needed crutches, and at the hospital, a bad story became a comedy sketch. Alice pulled up outside A&E but wasn't allowed to park there and I could hardly get out of the car. Eventually, I made it to the lady at reception.

'I'm sorry,' I said, 'but I just need a pair of crutches. I can't walk and I need help.'

'Have you been here before, love?'

'No, I haven't actually.'

'Well, you'll have to fill in these forms then.'

'Look, I don't want to cause any hassle. All I need is crutches. I don't need an x-ray or any treatment or anyone to see me. Just crutches. I'm perfectly happy to pay for them.'

'Oh, we couldn't possibly do that.'

'So, how long is the wait?'

'Three hours at the moment.'

'Please, please, is there any chance of just getting the crutches.

I know exactly what's wrong with me. I'll be getting it seen to tomorrow. I just need crutches for now.'

'No, sorry. No chance.'

'This is ridiculous. Why can't you just help by getting some crutches? I'll give you my address, I'll drop them back tomorrow. If not crutches, could I borrow a wheelchair, anything that will allow me to get around?'

'I'm sorry, sir.'

I bet John Terry and Rio Ferdinand don't spend bank holiday Mondays badgering bureaucrats for crutches and being refused. Later that day, Wasps arranged for me to have a scan at the Princess Margaret Hospital in Windsor. That was another experience. The surgeon came out of the operating theatre in his overalls, specks of blood on his white boots, took one look at the scan and said, 'You've torn your ACL (anterior cruciate ligament), ruptured it I'd say, I can get you in tomorrow.' He was doing his job in a very clinical way while I was seeing it through the eyes of a rugby player. A badly torn or ruptured ACL, followed by surgery, then six months of rehabilitation, amounted to a career-threatening situation for a 28-year-old. The prospect of going under the knife at that point scared the life out of me – for God's sake, the Lions tour was three weeks away and I was desperate.

'I'll think it over,' I said as calmly as I could, but I really just wanted to get out of there.

That night I phoned my physio, Kevin Lidlow, because I was still in agony and couldn't walk. 'Come and see me,' he said. Kevin lives in Essex and it was ten o'clock. I got a friend of mine to drive me all the way there. Thanks mate. At around 1 a.m., Kevin examined my grotesquely swollen knee.

'First thing I'm going to do,' he said, 'is put a needle in there and drain it.' He took God knows how much fluid out. It was like watching the air disappear from a tyre. Suddenly the pain disappeared and I could walk again. Kevin examined my knee and thought there was a chance we could get away without surgery. 'If it's ruptured, then you have to have an operation, but there are various degrees of rupture and some don't merit one.' That gave me a bit of hope.

Further examination showed the ligament was badly torn but not completely ruptured and between Kevin, Wasps and myself, we decided to try six weeks of intensive rehab to get my knee back in shape. The Lions coach, Graham Henry, was very supportive and his message to me was clear. 'Look, mate,' he said, 'as far as I'm concerned, you don't have to play a game until the first Test.' Clearly I was going to have to play before then but he wanted me on the tour and didn't mind if it took me until the first Test to find my best form. So I went to Australia, carrying my injury, hoping that all the rehab work I had done with Kevin would keep it together. In hindsight, it was probably the wrong decision but it was a Lions tour and I just couldn't let go.

I worked as hard as I've ever worked in my life. The Lions management brought in an independent team of medical guys to test the fitness of 18 players who were carrying injuries of one kind or another. After two days of testing, I was given the green light. In fact, of the guys with similar problems, I was the one with the strongest knees. The important point about the fitness tests was that they did not involve physical contact and, in the back of my mind, I knew the real test would come in impact situations. But I was grateful for the support shown by Graham Henry and the Lions manager Donal Lenihan, who gave me every chance to prove my fitness. Andy Robinson, forwards coach on the tour, was sceptical. It was typical Andy to scowl at injured players but his little comments upset me. 'Don't let him get you down,' Jason Leonard said to me. 'I remember Robbo reporting fit for a Lions tour but actually being injured a lot of the time and only playing about one game.'

As it turned out, the tour was a disaster for me. I played against Australia A at Gosforth and we got beaten by a side we should have smashed out of sight. Not good. I got sin-binned but of far more concern, my knee didn't allow me to do the things I needed to do. There was no one to blame except myself. Since I hadn't performed, I had to prove my fitness in another game pretty soon after that and four days later, I played against New South Wales. It was a lively encounter – the game in which Duncan McRae punched Ronan O'Gara in the head – and there were lots of little niggles off the ball, but the Lions won. In the second half, I got tackled side on and that was it. After the match and for the following few days, my knee was again up like a balloon and there was no choice but to admit defeat. I watched the first Test and then flew home. After aggravating the injury, the treatment that I had from the Lions management was top class and they were very sympathetic. Not every injured player was treated so well.

Phil Greening got injured and was told he was going to have to leave the tour, but if he wanted to stay in Australia and recover in three or four weeks, he could rejoin the squad. However, ridiculously, the Lions would not provide accommodation for him during those weeks of recovery. Phil hired a camper van and travelled round Australia at his own expense. Dan Luger fractured his cheekbone in a training ground collision with Neil Back, and was advised not to fly for a week. Again, the Lions didn't provide accommodation and Dan joined Phil in the camper van. Mike Catt was also injured and he, too, ended up in the camper van. But I don't want to talk down the Lions experience because I regard it so highly. The fact that I was injured on two Lions tours doesn't change my view in any way. Playing for the Lions is one of the game's ultimate experiences and when the 2009 Lions get on the plane for South Africa, I will be envious.

After breaking my ankle during the 2005 Lions tour, Clive Woodward asked me to present the jerseys to the players before the game against the Maoris. It was the first time a current player had presented the jerseys and I felt honoured. Before giving out the jerseys, I spoke to the players about the Lions.

'If we're really lucky, we get to put on our national jersey, which all of us have done. If we're truly special, we get to be in this room. When I got my letter a couple of months ago, it came with a questionnaire and one of the questions was, "What does it mean to you to be picked for the British and Irish Lions?" I put down, "It's the greatest honour I could ever receive as a rugby player. It's the pinnacle of my career." If I went round this room and asked the same question, I know what the answers would be. They may not be the same words but they would be pretty damn similar. This game of rugby, it's more than a game. It's your life. You make huge sacrifices to be in this room, your family make huge sacrifices, your parents, your girlfriends, your wives, your coaches, they all have made sacrifices. That's what goes into that shirt. There's people watching all around the world and they are the people who have put you into this room. Whether they're alive or whether they're dead, they're watching and you've got to make it happen. For me, this tour is now about moving up to the next level. We've had two games, we know what they're about. It's now time to turn up the fucking heat. In order to do that we're going to have to take ourselves out of the comfort zone and put ourselves in a totally new environment. It's a place you've all been before in international rugby, it's out of the comfort zone and it's going to fucking hurt. You've got to be prepared to suffer. I was in a hotel room similar to this in Australia four years ago and Graham Henry got up and what he said will live with me for the rest of my life. "In this part of the world, they don't respect you. They don't think you're good enough. They don't think you're fit enough, they don't think you're skilful enough and they don't think you're strong enough. And I should know because I'm one of them." Not my words, his words. And you know what, he's fucking right. They don't respect us, and when you come off that pitch tonight, they're going to know how good we are, they're going to know how strong we are and they *are* going to respect us. And when they wake up tomorrow morning and they're eating their breakfast, they're going to know we're here to win a Test series. When you take your shirt tonight, I want you to look at the number on the back and I want you to think about the great players who have worn that shirt, because a lot of great players have worn that shirt. You come off tonight and if you have given everything, you can add your name to that list of great players.'

I would love to be able to write that the Lions went out that evening and smashed the Maoris, but it didn't happen. They lost and that was the start of the bad times for the 2005 Lions. Captain Brian O'Driscoll was taken out in the first Test and the bit that bothered me about it was the fact that the man who did it, Tana Umaga, went on to produce a man-of-the-match performance. That was something the Lions players just should not have allowed to happen.

When Warren Gatland decided to move with his family back to Waikato in the summer of 2005, Wasps lost a man who had been central to the most successful period in the club's history. Three back-to-back Premiership titles, a Heineken European Cup and a European Challenge Cup added up to five major trophies in three seasons and it put our club right up there with Leicester as the two dominant clubs in the professional era. That success was going to make it difficult for whoever replaced Warren and you could imagine a lot of good people wondering if it was the right time to join Wasps. Warren, remember, said the deciding factor for him in accepting our offer was the fact that we had a lot of good players but were close to the bottom of the Premiership league table. He thought the only way was up for us and that kind of hard-nosed Kiwi mentality became part and parcel of Wasps under Warren.

The choice fell on Ian McGeechan as his replacement. Some questioned whether he was the right man for the club because he had been at Northampton, had also coached Scotland and the Lions and he had known bad days as well as good ones. I couldn't see the logic in that. I had worked with Ian on the 1997 Lions tour in South Africa and knew how good he was. He also had an excellent playing CV. He'd been there, done that, as both player and coach, and his experience gave him a fantastic overview. The Wasps team would soon change with a younger generation of players coming through, and Ian's wisdom in overseeing that transition was going to be of enormous benefit. Shaun Edwards was still at the club and Shaun is, to all intents and purposes, Wasps coach. He's the heartbeat of the side, the engine that drives things on the training ground. When he's referred to as the defensive coach, that's an insult. He's defence, attack, tactics, strategy, psychology, lots of things. Of course, Ian would do his share of the coaching but he was also appointed to be a leader and figurehead during a period of great change.

After being offered the job, Ian rang me and we spoke very openly about the pluses and minuses of him joining Wasps. Foremost among the minuses was the fact that we were a very successful club and that was expected to continue. If it changed, there would be pressure. But the flip side of the coin was that we still had pretty much the same squad and the players were hungry for more. I appreciated the call because it was an acknowledge-ment from Ian of the bond forged between us in 1997 and I felt he was somebody to whom I could speak honestly. I looked forward to working with him. It wasn't going to be easy as my broken ankle would keep me on the sidelines for the first two months of the season and you could count another two months before I was back playing my best rugby.

More worrying for the club was the loss of fitness trainer Craig White, who decided to stick with Warren and work with Waikato in New Zealand. When his dad passed away not long afterwards, however, he decided against going to Waikato. Once he got his head above water and realised he needed to earn a living, Craig joined Leicester. He deserved the job because he's one of the best in the business, but at the time I felt we were wrong to allow him to go to our principal rivals. As it turned out, Craig's right-hand man Paul Stridgeon took over as our fitness coach and did an excellent job.

When Warren joined, he was allowed to spend time observing how things were done at the club before actually taking control, and there's no doubt he benefited from that. The same thing happened with Ian. He joined the club before the end of the 2004–05 season and just watched as Warren and Shaun prepared us for the play-off matches in the Premiership. At the same time, the club brought in the Kiwi Leon Holden, who had been recommended by Warren and specialised in coaching set-pieces – scrums, line-outs and re-starts. Wasps draws from people a commitment you don't see at other clubs, witness Nigel Melville's recruiting of Warren Gatland before he left and then in Warren getting Leon for us. Leon had worked in New Zealand and Japan and was a very useful acquisition. He, too, stayed in the background for a few weeks before formally getting involved in our training and match preparation.

Ian McGeechan paid his predecessor a compliment by not

changing anything during his early months at the club. That showed his confidence – he didn't feel the need to prove he was the new boss. In the first season with Ian on board we targeted the PowerGen Cup, having ended up in a four-team group with London Irish, Cardiff and Saracens. In this competition, each club plays the others just once, and as we were home to Cardiff, our three games were in London. Semi-finals were held at the Millennium Stadium with the final at Twickenham. We recognised that being required to play five games, only one of which was outside London, was as straightforward a route to a trophy as you could get. After qualifying for the semi-final, we played Leicester at the Millennium Stadium. It was a fantastic match, brutal but with plenty of good rugby, and we managed to win. We then beat Llanelli in the final and three-quarters of the way through the season we had one trophy in our possession.

The players had decided to go for the PowerGen Cup and I imagine Ian was relieved the team had won something in his first season. It did lessen the pressure but perhaps that was one of the reasons we didn't win our fourth consecutive Premiership title. We got to the play-offs but didn't finish high enough to get a home draw in the semi-final and we were narrowly beaten by Sale at their ground. They needed a bit of magic from Jason Robinson to win that game but with Jason in the opposing team, you can't complain about the magic because it is more or less guaranteed from him. We were a shade unlucky in that a few minutes before Jason's intervention, Tom Voyce was going through for a Wasps try when he tore his hamstring and that cost us dearly. To their credit, Sale did a thoroughly Wasps-like job on Leicester in the final. Their top players Jason Robinson, Charlie Hodgson and Jason White were magnificent but it wasn't much consolation to us to think we'd been beaten by the eventual winners.

That season, 2005–06, I returned to international rugby. It wasn't a hard decision because the reason I had retired no longer existed. My relationship with Alice was back on an even keel and she felt I should make myself available again, if that was what I wanted. It was what I wanted. In my eyes you don't exist to play just for your club, and I didn't like being referred to as 'Lawrence Dallaglio, the ex-England captain'.

By now, Andy Robinson had taken over from Clive Woodward and he was keen for me to return. My last game for England had been on the 2004 summer tour to the southern hemisphere and 20 months later I returned with a cameo appearance from the bench against Wales at Twickenham. Brief but worthwhile might be the right description – I came on when we had an attacking scrum, and when you've got Julian White propping at tight-head, there was only going to be one plan. We drove the scrum and all I had to do was pick it up and take the try. Although it was satisfying to score, the overall situation was far from perfect.

I was back in an England set-up that was now being captained by Martin Corry, the man occupying my position, or at least that is the way you tend to see it when you are fighting for your place. When I came on at Twickenham, the crowd were very humbling, giving me a big ovation and that wasn't an easy situation for Martin, although I didn't see it like that at the time. There was even some press speculation that by bringing me on Andy was somehow damaging Martin's captaincy. Martin had played well against the Welsh but the try helped my cause. In the very next game, against the Scots, I was again on the bench and I realised that the circumstances were making it impossible for me to be my natural self. The last thing I wanted was to weaken Martin's position in any way, but in making sure I didn't do that, I found myself retreating into my shell. I didn't speak up in team meetings as I would have done in previous years. That was particularly true before the Scotland game, and it was a mistake. Ten years previously I had sat in the same Balmoral Hotel in Edinburgh, a 24-year-old playing his first Five Nations Championship, and the head coach, Jack Rowell, had turned to me and said, 'Right, Lawrence, I want you to tell us how Scotland are going to play tomorrow.' There had been no warning but Jack wouldn't have asked if he hadn't felt I could do it, and if I'd stumbled or not come up with a good assessment of what the Scots were likely to do, Jack would have shut me up pretty quick.

I had also been in the team in 2000 when we felt we were going to win the Grand Slam but didn't. Six years on, I sensed the same vague sense of complacency – we felt we were the better side and because of that, things would be all right. Sometimes you have to believe you are going to be ambushed to stop the ambush happening and I wanted to say, 'Look, guys, do you realise what we're walking into here?' But I didn't. I felt on the periphery of the team and didn't want to push myself into the centre. Not undermining Martin was in the forefront of my mind, but I was wrong. Martin is a bigger man than that and he's always been a great team player. I was disappointed with myself. Perhaps it would not have changed the result but you never know. We lost that game in Scotland partly because we weren't properly prepared for how tough the Scots would make it.

Late in the match, I went on in Martin's place but by then the Scots were leading and defending very well. They deserved their victory. After the game, the Leicester coach, Pat Howard, said that if Martin Corry had stayed on the field, England would have won. Please, do me a favour. But it's one of the things I admire about Leicester – the way they support their own guys. Howard, of course, was being clever. He knew he needed Martin Corry firing on all cylinders when he returned to Leicester and was doing what he could to ensure that happened. It was the same kind of thing when there was lots of speculation in the newspapers about me returning to the England squad and Graham Rowntree gave an interview complaining about me trying to talk my way back into the England set-up. The guys at Wasps asked what he was on about and I said, 'It's just Leicester, they back their own.'

As long as Martin was captain, he would have my total support. He's a player for whom I have a huge amount of admiration. Martin never leaves anything in the changing room – everything goes into his performance. What you love about him is that regardless of whether things are going well or badly, you get what you get with him. He's Leicester, I'm Wasps and we're both passionate about our clubs, but it doesn't go over the edge between us. Part of the reason is that he's a tremendously affable bloke and I like him a lot. I appreciate that not everyone is going to like me. There's a feeling that I can be a little flashy, a bit ostentatious at times, but that's just the way I am. I do believe I'm sensitive to other people's needs and sympathetic to their feelings but sport is still a ruthless business and anyone who is any good wants to be in the starting XV.

It wasn't a good time for England and neither was it much fun for Martin or me. In that 2006 Six Nations campaign, I spent far more time warming up on the stationary bikes that England's replacements use than actually performing on the pitch. It led to some funny texts. 'Don't think you'll be winning the Grand Slam this year but I'd back you to win the Tour de France,' wrote one so-called friend. For the match against France in Paris, I realised just before the start that I needed the toilet and dashed from the bench back inside for a minute. By the time I returned to the pitch, about two minutes had elapsed and England were 7–0 down. So I got back on my bike and things got worse on the pitch. You always want to play for your country but when you're 20 or 25 points down in Paris and you're running on with 20 minutes to go, it's not ideal. I felt for Martin because I had captained England on days when we were stuffed and it's no fun. Like me, he would never question why he's there but the thing about international rugby is that it's the most amazing place in the world when you're winning and it's horrible when you're losing. The next day you feel you can't walk down to the local shop and buy a pint of milk without that sense of shame being written across your face.

The truth was that the England set-up I returned to was very different from the one I'd left. We were struggling with injuries, a lot of players had retired and results were bad. I had a long conversation with Andy Robinson, who was a coach I admired. We had a very honest talk during which he asked what I thought he could do to improve as a coach.

'Perhaps if you were to pick up the phone and talk to players on a more regular basis it might help,' I said. 'Tell guys how good they are and generally treat them like human beings, and you'll get a phenomenal response.'

I think he took that on board and he told me what he wanted from me. In one sense, I felt like an outsider returning to the squad, and that I had to justify my presence. Andy and I should probably have been a lot more ruthless in our assessments. It would have been better if he had just said, 'Look, mate, you're thirty-three years of age, you're not going to be happy sitting on the bench, are you? You're a guy who has to be at the centre of the team or nowhere but, at the moment, I can't justify putting you in that position and I'm going to pick you only if I believe you should be in the team.'

Andy said he could envisage Martin Corry being in the second row by the time the World Cup came round but, sadly for him, he was replaced as head coach in the autumn of 2006. I felt for him because he took over England at a difficult time. Maybe he wouldn't have succeeded on his own anyway, because being England head coach involves far more than coaching and I felt Andy needed help in many of the other areas. I don't think he was comfortable in his management of the players, nor with being the key voice in selection, he didn't handle the media side brilliantly and he wasn't made for the political battles with the RFU. It may be he required a team manager who would look after a lot of these things and, if so, the RFU must accept responsibility for not providing him with adequate back-up. Andy always seemed to be doing three or four jobs at the same time and, in the end, you can't do any of them to your satisfaction. Bad results lead to criticism, and with that comes pressure and the need to win the next game. Under Clive Woodward, we had a vision of where we wanted to go. With Andy, the focus was on the next game.

Clive created an environment for England players that involved the best standards of preparation, superior to anything we experienced at our clubs. It was one way of saying that playing for your country is the ultimate achievement. A former student at the college, Andy decided to take the squad to Loughborough for a training camp. I'm sorry, but my idea of being selected for England is not sleeping in a bed where my ankles are hanging out at the end. People may consider that a glib comment but I'm from the Roy Keane school of proper training facilities. You give élite athletes élite facilities. What's that phrase Keane uses all the time? 'Fail to prepare. Prepare to fail.' Under Clive, the England set-up provided the best and expected the best in return, and that was reflected in everything we did. That didn't seem to be the case any more. On and off the field, we were letting standards fall but, of course, the two are inextricably linked. After the away victory against Italy in the 2006 Six Nations, it was decided that because Matt Dawson and I had come on so late in the game, we could return to London that night and play for Wasps the next day. That was fine but we needed to get from the ground to the airport and, standing outside the Stadio Flaminio, we realised no one had pre-booked a taxi. We waited for ages, eventually got a cab, ran like lunatics through the airport to check-in, arrived sweating like mad and missed the flight. Fucking useless!

After losing to Scotland and France, we needed to beat Ireland at Twickenham to finish the season on some kind of positive note. We were leading as the game went into the last 10 minutes and I expected to be brought on to help close things down, but it didn't happen and Ireland turned it round. Brian O'Driscoll made a fine break from well inside his own half and Shane Horgan finished in the corner. You've got to give Ireland credit for coming back but England should never have lost that game. Afterwards, I went into the toilet area alongside our changing room and spoke with Andy.

'I'm sorry you didn't get on,' he said.

'Just explain one thing here,' I responded, 'because there's something I don't understand. Of the forty-four players involved in today's match, twenty-two for Ireland, twenty-two for England, I was the only one who didn't enter the field of play. And of the forty-four players involved, I'm the most experienced, the guy with the seventy-six caps who doesn't get on the field. Surely you realised when we went in front with Steve Borthwick's try that was the time to get me on. If we'd lost then, you could have blamed me.' I didn't want to have a go at Andy because it wasn't the time to do that, and he is so passionate about England, but I was frustrated. I left Twickenham a very disillusioned man that evening. I just thought, 'Lawrence, you're fooling yourself here. This is not what international rugby is about. You haven't come back for this. This is bullshit.'

When I thought about it, I did realise my problem wasn't Andy, or at least it wasn't entirely his fault. He brought me back into the squad because of what I'd done in the past, as opposed to selecting me because I was playing out of my skin. With the benefit of hindsight, I should not have made myself available until I was good enough to make the starting fifteen. I was impatient to get back and Andy wanted me but, in the end, I don't think we did each other any favours.

*

What I've loved about Wasps from the moment I first set foot in the club is the feeling that we should always be competing for major trophies. You can't win everything but there's nothing to stop you aspiring to win every competition.

My return to international rugby in the 2006 Six Nations Championship hadn't gone well and niggling injuries at the beginning of the 2006–07 season meant I wasn't involved in the 2006 autumn Tests. They turned out to be Andy Robinson's last stand and Brian Ashton was appointed in his place. At the time of the 2007 Six Nations, I wasn't playing particularly well and couldn't really complain about not being in the England squad.

It was a tough time at Wasps, too, because with so many internationals in our squad, especially England players, we struggled when we had to play without them. To make matters worse, we seemed to have tough away fixtures every international weekend. But there is such a winning mentality at the club that we find ways of pulling things out of the fire. Too many losses on the road destroyed our chances in the Guinness Premiership and we were left with just the Heineken Cup to play for. Even there, we had lost away to Perpignan and had been written off in the tournament. To have any chance of qualifying for the quarter-finals we had to win at home against Perpignan and then beat Castres away.

Home by then for Wasps was Adams Park in High Wycombe, where we'd moved in 2002 after vacating Loftus Road to allow Fulham FC to share with Queens Park Rangers while their ground, Craven Cottage, was being redeveloped. The Perpignan game at

Adams Park was a match I felt we would win because we had been woeful at their place and every one of us walked off the pitch thinking we would love to have them on a day when the real Wasps showed up. We did beat them well on our home ground and then had the far more difficult job of winning away in Castres. It was tough but after taking a 12–3 lead early in the match, we battened down the hatches and defended well to get a vital win.

Other results went our way and from struggling to make the quarter-finals, we earned a home game against Leinster. There was a temptation to move the game to Twickenham where Leinster's fans and the Irish population in London would have combined with our support to produce a massive gate. But it would have been the wrong move and we kept the game at Adams Park, where we had been beaten just once all season. Leinster were without the mercurial talents of Brian O'Driscoll, as he was injured. Brian is very much the team's leader and talisman, but I honestly don't believe his presence would have changed the result. We were stronger than they were and we won well. It was nice that our Irish scrum-half Eoin Reddan scored two tries. He was being ignored by the Irish management team and their coach, Eddie O'Sullivan, was at the game. I couldn't resist the opportunity to praise Eoin when we briefly met afterwards. 'Not a bad little scrum-half is he?' I said. It made me smile that Eoin was one of the players Eddie turned to when Ireland found themselves in trouble at the 2007 World Cup.

Northampton produced the performance of the quarter-finals, winning in Biarritz. The first I knew was a text from my mum that said, 'You're going to Coventry.' I thought, 'What's she on about?' Heineken Cup semi-final, Coventry? Can't be. Then it made sense

– Northampton had won and with the choice of a neutral home venue, they had chosen Coventry's new football stadium. The Heineken Cup campaign had started with Ronan O'Gara making some interesting points about the Guinness Premiership and how he didn't believe the standard was as high as some people thought. His view seemed to be vindicated by the following weekend's Heineken Cup results when his team Munster beat Leicester at Welford Road and we lost down in Perpignan. I have always believed the Premiership is a pretty competitive league and although that initial series of Heineken Cup results might have made some question my belief, when we got to the business end of the tournament, three of the four semi-finalists were English and one of them, Northampton, was bottom of the Premiership. Can't be too much wrong with that league. The ground at Coventry wasn't full, the occasion wasn't what a Heineken semi-final should be, but we got through and that was the important bit.

If playing in our second Heineken Cup final wasn't enough to motivate us, there was the fact that Leicester were our opponents. They were in fine form, having already won the PowerGen Cup, and they were in the Premiership play-off final against Gloucester. People were talking about them winning the treble and when they smashed Gloucester, that talk just doubled. Suddenly they were being spoken about as 'the best ever Leicester side'. Their coach, Pat Howard, was returning to Australia at the end of the season, and it was mentioned many times how appropriate it would be for him to leave after the team had made a clean sweep of the three major trophies in English club rugby. Like two years earlier when Martin Johnson and Neil Back were playing their last game in the Premiership final, we were seen as worthy fall guys for Leicester's great occasion. It always amazes me that people don't look a little closer into these things. We had developed a knack for winning major finals at Twickenham and there was one guarantee about the Heineken Cup final – Leicester would not walk through Wasps as they had Gloucester the previous week.

One difficulty for us was that we had three weeks without a game before the big showdown while Leicester were preparing for and playing in the Premiership final. We tried to organise a practice game against Bath, who still had to play the European Challenge Cup final, but they weren't keen, preferring to play Newbury instead. We also tried to set up a game against Scotland but that wasn't possible. Making the best of a difficult situation, we arranged to play our own second team, who had just beaten Leicester in the two-leg final of the seconds' league. We played behind closed doors at Henley and it was a very useful exercise. The club asked well-respected referee Tony Spreadbury to officiate and our coaches instructed him to allow the second team to get away with all sorts of pandemonium at the breakdown, let them lie over the ball and penalise us when we didn't do anything wrong. To make sure we were up against it the whole time, having to battle constantly, as we expected to be in the final itself. It made for a very interesting game. We also practised precisely how we would play against Leicester. On line-outs where we reckoned Leicester would drive forward, we didn't compete for the ball and just worked on a blitz line-out defence, making sure they weren't able to drive forward.

In the game against the second team, we went in front in the last minute with a penalty but then didn't secure the kick-off and they ended up scoring a try in the corner. We thought the try shouldn't have been given but, sticking to our instructions that he should favour our opponents, Tony Spreadbury awarded it and the seconds beat us. It had been a very decent match and we all went to the pub in Henley afterwards and enjoyed a pint and a bite to eat.

That was the Friday and we were given Saturday and Sunday off. In our various homes, we watched Leicester brutally dismantle Gloucester in the Premiership grand final. Gloucester lost Marco Bortolami, who pulled up injured in the warm-up, and as he was the cornerstone of their team, his loss was huge. Early in the game they lost another influential player, Pete Buxton, and subsequently the team just wasn't able to cope. Even allowing for the bad luck, Gloucester produced a desperately disappointing performance. Defensively, they didn't turn up and I hovered between scowling at the television and wanting to turn the thing off. I did actually turn if off at half-time.

Despite the obvious hype about Leicester, we were very positive about our chances and determined that in the media build-up we weren't going to be bullied by talk of their prowess. Yes, they were good but they were not 'the best ever Leicester side'. In my opinion, the best Leicester side was the one that beat Stade Français in the final of the 2001 Heineken Cup in Paris. I had played against all the Leicester lads – and with a lot of them – and some are truly fantastic, but for the 2007 team to be called the 'best ever' was just wrong. And, of course, we were going to use every little bit of praise for 'great Leicester' as motivation. Add to that the anger we felt about the tameness of Gloucester's defence and it was certain Leicester were going to know they were in a match.

Selection-wise we had one decision to make and that was at prop, where Tim Payne's absence through injury left us undecided about how to replace him. A lot of people thought we should move Phil Vickery to Tim's place at loose-head prop so that Phil could take on Leicester's Julian White, who is a very powerful scrummager. I didn't have a view about who should play loose-head but felt it might be wrong to switch Phil. The former All Black great, Craig Dowd, is our scrummaging coach and I spoke with him about it.

'Why would we move one of the best tight-head props to loose-head to try to counter their strong guy?' I said. 'Let's forget about Julian White, he is what he is – an amazing player at the scrum. If we leave Phil Vickery in his best position, tight-head, we only have one problem to deal with.' With Phil in his preferred position, we gave ourselves a chance of gaining an advantage on that side of the scrum and forcing the referee to watch both sides.

Wasps have always been a player-driven club where the coaches consult a lot with the team. Craig Dowd had his own views but sensibly spoke to both Phil and Raphael Ibanez, captain of England and France respectively, and they said how impressed they were by the performance of Tom French, the relatively unknown loose-head in our second fifteen. We had a live scrummaging session that week in which all the permutations were tried. Afterwards Craig put his neck on the line and recommended to Ian and Shaun that we go with Tom and he was selected for the Heineken Cup final. It was an incredible achievement for him to get from where he had been, out on loan to

Henley for much of the season, to playing in the biggest club game in the history of rugby union. There was method in the apparent madness of pitching Tom in against Julian White. Tom is relatively small and Craig Dowd had noticed that Julian didn't always seem that comfortable against smaller guys. We wanted to pack down at a level where the only way for the scrum to go was down, because it's then a tough call for the referee. Leicester like to force the opposition upwards and they get a lot of penalties based on the perception of their superior scrum. What is really impressive about Tom French is his temperament. All through the build-up, he was totally calm and seemed utterly unfazed by the task facing him. If he was feeling nervous, he concealed that from us.

Having three weeks to prepare without distraction allowed us to think long and hard about our tactics and what would work best against Leicester. Leon Holden looked closely at their line-out and thought they over-competed in all areas, especially the front, and weren't alive to the possibility of being attacked in that area. The other coaches agreed and it seemed worth a go at least once. It certainly was, more than once. We got our two tries using that ploy and they were key to the result of the match. The other thing we worked out was that in all Wasps-Leicester games, the team that leads at half-time invariably wins the match. You had to get on top of Leicester from the first whistle, get points on the board and don't let up. Sounds basic but the key for them is getting in front, forcing the opposition to chase the game and then picking them off. No matter what, we couldn't afford to start slowly.

In the build-up to the game, much was made of the task facing

Tom against Julian White. The person who seemed least bothered by it was Tom himself. His coolness astonished us and, of course, in everyone's assessment of what might happen, no one imagined we would be quite a long way into the first half before the first scrum was awarded. By that time, we were 3–0 up, but it was still an important moment. Tom got under Julian and prevented him doing any damage to our scrum. It was the same for the first three scrums and that gave us such a psychological lift. We led 13–9 at half-time and increased that to a pretty emphatic 25–9 before the end of the game. Confronted by our aggressive tackling and our organisation, they found it hard to readjust following the Gloucester game, and we were in control for most of the match.

It had been an extraordinary occasion – 81,000 people crammed into Twickenham, making it a world-record crowd for a club match – and Wasps had once again delivered a really solid performance to outplay Leicester as well as the scoreline suggested. The club had asked us to let them know the names of family members and friends for whom we wanted to buy tickets. My list ran close to 75 names and I was reminded, like every rugby player before me, that you only realise how many friends you've got in the week before a big match.

It was our second Heineken Cup victory and I was pleased for all of the guys, particularly the older warriors Phil Vickery, Raphael Ibanez, Simon Shaw, Joe Worsley, Alex King, Fraser Waters and Josh Lewsey. I was especially delighted for Alex, who was unlucky to play rugby at the same time as Jonny Wilkinson. Otherwise, he would have been England's playmaker for many years. The thing about Alex is that in terms of getting his back line moving and enabling those outside of him to play, there is no better fly-half.

The percentages in international rugby are tighter, though, and Jonny's place-kicking and defence mean that he simply has to be England's first choice. But what a servant Alex has been for Wasps. When Rob Andrew left the club in the mid-nineties, I told Alex that the club needed a fly-half and he stepped up to the plate unbelievably well. To all the talented young players at the club, he is a perfect role model. He works incredibly hard and over the years has become physically tougher, more tactically aware. As well as being a very pleasant person, he is a fiercely determined individual. As a team-mate, you admire the fact that on the big day, he invariably delivers. You can't ask for any more and, as I keep reminding him, he is the most decorated fly-half in the country – 10 trophies for Wasps and he was present for every one of them. To think we used to say he was too nice for the cut-throat business of top-flight rugby.

So many contributed to the success. Shaun Edwards again proved how he can prepare teams to win and Ian McGeechan fully vindicated Wasps' faith in him. The evolution that the club wanted Ian to manage is taking place and young guns, such as Tom Rees, James Haskell, Danny Cipriani and Dominic Waldouck, are being brought up in the proper Wasps way. They have the potential to be the stalwarts of tomorrow. I look at them and think back to my early years at the club, waiting for my first-team debut. It came when I was 23. Today's young players at Wasps are disappointed if they haven't got a Heineken Cup winners' medal at that age. They've earned the right to be there but what I want them to realise is that they can drive the club forward as opposed to simply being part of the club's first XV. The best people to move a club on are the players because they are the ones – guys such as Rees, Haskell, Cipriani and Waldouck – who will inspire future generations.

In the lead-up to the Leicester game I had moments of genuine self-doubt. Was I still up to it? Would I be able to win my individual battle? The demons don't go away with age and what matters is how you handle them. It was my responsibility to ensure that when the young guys looked towards me, they saw someone who was totally convinced that Wasps could and would win. If there was any sign of doubt, the young guys would have picked it up in no time. My lasting memory of the after-match scene is the look of quiet satisfaction on Tom French's face. It was an outstanding performance for him to come into the team and play as well as he did, and at the end, he was still fantastically calm. His expression just said, 'I enjoyed that.' And I thought, 'I bet you fucking did.'

On 29 July 2006, Alice and I eventually got married. I say 'eventually' because it was something we should have done long before but, with rugby, there never seemed to be the right moment. It was worth waiting for. We talked about having the ceremony in Devon, near where Alice's mum lives, but ended up choosing a fantastic location on Lake Como in Italy. Our friend Andrea Riva, who has a great Italian restaurant in Barnes, was the one who told us to consider Lake Como and three months before the wedding, Alice, Andrea and I went over to see if we could find a suitable church and a venue for the reception.

Andrea had told us how beautiful Lake Como was and had shown us some magnificent photos, but we arrived in thick fog, it was pouring with rain and unless someone told you there was a lake out there, you wouldn't have known. It was OK, though. We stayed at Andrea's family home, his brother Vincenzo cooked the most amazing meal for us, we had great wine and the weather outside soon became pretty irrelevant.

The next morning dawned with bright sunshine and clear, blue skies. When we opened the curtains, the lake was right there, vast and beautiful, the mountains were in the background and you could see snow on the Alpine peaks. It was a stunning part of the world and both Alice and I fell for the place there and then. Christina Chen, who was helping us with the logistics of the wedding, suggested we had a look at Villa Balbianello, which she thought would be an amazing venue for the wedding reception. Christina was right. Once Alice and I walked in, we both said, 'Yes, this is it.' It's an extraordinary villa, set in a fantastic location – if you've seen the film *Casino Royale*, it's where James Bond convalesces after he's taken a bad beating. We chose a church that was about five minutes down the lake and that meant after the ceremony, everyone would take a boat ride on Lake Como to the reception. Of course, it all took a bit of organising and Christina was a star. I helped as much as I could but my two major contributions were signing the cheque and slipping a few hundred euro to the guy at Villa Balbianello so that the bar wouldn't close on the night of the reception. Well, it did actually close at four in the morning, by which time only the rugby players were still standing.

About 120 people came for the weekend. A lot of them had been around during the traumatic times Alice and I had endured, and it was great that they were there for what was an extraordinary moment in our lives. Because Alice and I had done so much and been through so much before we actually got round to getting married, we had a genuine relationship with every single guest at our wedding. That couldn't have happened if we had got married soon after we met. It was also a very special occasion for my mum. At first, she wasn't going to come because we weren't getting married in a Catholic church. Mum has a typical East End mentality in that if she's not happy about something, she lets you know. And her Irish Catholic roots, which have given her such strength down through the years, meant she was very unhappy about it not being a Catholic ceremony – she didn't know the bureaucratic hoops you have to go through to have a Catholic wedding in Italy. The tantrum lasted a week but I spoke with Dad and between us, we got her to relent.

I don't know how Mum sees it but I believe that since Alice and I got married, she has been a changed woman. Our wedding has helped her in a way that I'm not sure I can describe, except that I have always understood her deep sorrow at not being able to see her daughter married. Since Francesca died, weddings were always a very uncomfortable experience for her because they inspired too many emotions and too many regrets. In this respect, our wedding has helped her enormously.

It was a fantastic weekend that began on the Friday with golf for the men and an afternoon at the spa for the ladies and ended with Sunday lunch on the lake. Chris Wright – not the owner of Wasps but the former scrum-half who was my first friend at the club – was my best man. When the then England coach Dick Best came to take a Wasps training session in 1992, he asked me in front of everyone who my friends were. 'Chris Wright, sir,' I said.

And Dick famously replied, 'Wright? Lose Wright.' Fourteen years on, I still hadn't lost him. Chris delivered a wonderful best man's speech and at one point explained that everything I had achieved on the rugby field would not have been possible without the support and inspiration provided by one very special person. As he said this, he turned towards Clive Woodward and everyone then turned towards Clive. 'Of course,' said Chris, 'I am talking about Mrs Dallaglio.' Clive took it extremely well. Mum just loved it.

The very best thing about our wedding day was that our three children could be there. Not only that but they played such a beautiful part in the ceremony. Ella sang solo, she and Josie sang a duet and Enzo carried the rings and performed brilliantly in his page-boy role. When Ella and Josie sang 'Whole New World', a song from the musical *Aladdin*, the effect on all of us was quite amazing. It was a wedding ceremony and there wasn't a dry eye in the church – exactly as I would have wanted it.

19

Back from the abyss

I want to tell the story of the 2007 World Cup as I saw it. There was so much going on during the weeks of preparation and then before and after that catastrophic first loss to South Africa that every player and coach will have their view on how things were. Probably the only thing everyone will agree on is that it was a pretty amazing achievement to reach the final. I don't want to be seen as the guy lifting the lid on the inside story because that suggests I have some kind of agenda, which I don't. It pains me to say this but, given our preparation, getting to the final was a victory in itself and one that reflected great credit on some truly great players. The pain lies in the fact that second place should never be acceptable to an England player.

We go to every tournament to win and if we don't do that, we fail.

Having played in our first match against USA, I was dropped and left out of the 22 for the games against South Africa and Samoa, and then made appearances off the bench in the remaining four games. It wasn't the way I had wanted to experience the World Cup and some will say it was a tournament too far for me. That is not my perspective at all. The allure of playing for England has always been too great for me to worry about the consequences. The glass for me has always been half full – I went to the World Cup believing, like 29 other players, that I would start all of England's big games.

Given my opportunity in the USA game, I didn't do what was required and I can't point the finger at anyone else for that. You can't blame other people for your performance and no matter what your thoughts about the coaches or the preparation or the tactics, you're accountable for what you do when you've got that shirt on your back. Since my first cap 12 years before, I had been dropped once by England. That was the autumn of 2002. It hurt then and it hurt again when it happened in France. But unlike 2002, I could sort of understand why Brian Ashton left me out of the team for the South Africa game, although the way we played it could have been any one of the XV that was dropped. Had I been sitting on the bench for the USA match and seen the No. 8 on the field perform like I had, I would have expected to be in for the next game. But even though you accept the logic, it is still hard to take and I hold my hands up now and admit that I didn't react in the right way for the first two or three days. You have to put the team first but initially I was angry and hurt and I didn't try to hide it. Nor can I have any complaints about Nick Easter taking and holding on to the No. 8 jersey. He played well. Nick is an affable bloke, a rugby player in the Dean Richards mould – hard, tough and a good player. I was delighted for him as he experienced the thrill of playing for England on the biggest stage. He played his part in the victories over Australia and France.

So I don't want anyone to believe I came away from the World Cup embittered by what may well have been my last experience of international rugby. That is not the case. England got to the World Cup final and I played the last 15 minutes of the match. If it was my last performance in the international theatre, it is not exactly leaving by the side door, is it? Though we had our good days and our not-so-good days at the tournament, there were plenty of laughs. I mean, some of the England guys are sharp. George Chuter, for instance, completely cracked me up on a couple of occasions. When things aren't going as well as everyone hopes, it often produces a kind of black humour amongst people. Rugby players are no different. In the early days of our preparation, there was a sign on the changing room wall at Twickenham that just said 'STW'. For the life of me, I couldn't work it out and neither could anyone else. Our head coach, Brian Ashton, had put it up and he wasn't telling us. We lost two out of our three prep matches, and started the tournament with an average performance followed by a nightmare performance. Somewhere along the way, the Da Vinci code was cracked and 'STW' was revealed as 'Shock The World'. Everyone thought it was a pretty clever message.

Then Andy Farrell tapped me on the shoulder one evening and said, 'Know what it should say?'

'What?'

'SOS,' he said.

'SOS?'

'Yeah, Shock Our Selves.'

TO CALL OR NOT TO CALL

The relationship between a player and his coach is critical. The coach is naturally going to get on better with some players than others, especially players he may have worked with in the past, but he's got to try and build a relationship with every player in his squad. I knew Brian Ashton from the time he worked with England under Clive Woodward and thought he was a good coach. He was always considered a players' coach, someone prepared to allow players to think for themselves. When he was appointed head coach after the departure of Andy Robinson in the autumn of 2006, I had just returned from injury and was still getting back to top form. It wasn't a surprise that I didn't get into England's squad for the 2007 Six Nations Championship squad and the only contact I had with Brian's coaching team was when the forwards coach John Wells came to Wasps to do a one-on-one review with James Haskell of a game James had just played. This was Six Nations time and John sat down with me and told me where I stood. 'Look, you weren't playing well at the beginning of the season but there's nothing to say we won't pick you later on, if things pick up.' That was encouraging, or about as encouraging as it's ever going to get from John Wells. He was saying, the door wasn't closed if I got my act together.

My form did improve as the season progressed, especially after Wasps got the Heineken Cup in their sights. We had good wins at home to Perpignan, away to Castres, home to Leinster and, after beating Northampton in the semi-final, we saw off Leicester in the final. Though I was playing with a knee injury, my all-round game was solid and I was hoping I might hear from Brian Ashton after the European Cup win. It was known he was going to announce a big preliminary squad and I thought I had to be in his thinking. Was he curious about whether I wanted to go to the World Cup or not, or how I was physically? Wasps replaced me after 50 minutes of the Heineken Cup final because my knee had been giving me grief and it wasn't a secret that I had a problem. I assumed that if Brian wanted me in his squad, he must be interested in the seriousness of my injury.

There were some practical considerations for me. As I hadn't been in the England squad for 14 months, there was no basis for believing I would be in the World Cup squad. Consequently, Alice and I arranged a week away with the kids on Lake Como in Italy for soon after the Heineken Cup. When you've got kids at school, such holidays must be planned and taken during a half-term break. It left me in a slight dilemma. If I'd realistically thought there was a chance of being in the England squad, I would have had the relatively minor surgery on my knee immediately after our European triumph. But there was no contact and no hint that I was in with a shout. So I decided to forget about it, enjoy my week away with family and get the knee seen to on my return. We went to Lake Como because we had good memories of our wedding there a year before. It had reminded me of how much fun I'd had on my childhood holidays in Italy and how much I loved the country. We thoroughly enjoyed our return visit even if one long walk up a mountain, with Enzo on my shoulders, almost killed my knee. As it ached, I thought that if anyone was thinking of putting me in a World Cup squad, I was in the wrong place, doing the wrong thing.

That evening, I got a phone call from different friends who wanted to know if I'd seen the *Sunday Times*. In Stuart Barnes' column he had apparently said I should be picked for the World Cup squad and maybe even as captain, la de da de da. Whether you agree or not with everything Stuart writes, his views on the game are well respected. He is a good friend of mine but he is someone who would never be afraid to write something that might offend me. He calls it as he sees it and does that with intelligence and a sharp rugby brain. 'Barnesy,' I said to my mates, 'may be a good journalist, but he doesn't pick the England squad.' Of course I know how these things sometimes work. Stuart has a good relationship with Brian Ashton and for his column Stuart wouldn't want to be too wide of the mark. So I'm thinking, 'Barnesy may have spoken to Brian, he may have known something before he wrote that column.' Part of me wanted to pick up the phone to Brian and clear things up, one way or another. But I thought 'No', fearing that I wasn't in Brian's thinking and wincing at the thought of him trying to be diplomatic as he told me I wasn't going to make it. I convinced myself that if he was considering me, there would have been a phone call. Perhaps I'd spent too long playing under Clive Woodward who was never slow to pick up the phone.

After we got back and a few more days passed, there was still this nagging worry that maybe they were going to pick me and I still needed to get my knee done. To try to get a bit of advance information, I rang Vivienne Brown, the England team manager, who I had known from the previous regime. 'Look Viv,' I said, 'I don't want to make any presumptions here but when is the squad going to be announced because I need to know whether I'm in it or not?' 'Well, it's a bit top secret,' she said. I couldn't tell her the real reason for wanting to know. 'It's just that I've got some holidays booked and I need a bit of a heads-up here.' I was putting Viv in a terrible position. 'Well, I can't really help you on this,' but I was so desperate I wouldn't let go. 'Okay, just tell me this, am I wasting my time talking to you?' And she went, 'Well, no, but I can't say anymore.' But it was enough. I knew there was a fair chance I would be in the squad and it just baffled me why there was this great need for secrecy. I then made another call, to set up a time for my cartilage operation. I went into the hospital in the morning and walked, well limped, out in the afternoon. The England squad was due to meet up in two weeks and this was an operation I could have had four weeks before. A few days later, a letter came in the post informing me I had been selected in England's preliminary 46-man squad for the World Cup.

On the day the squad met up, Brian did come and speak with me. 'Great to have you in the squad,' he said. It was the first time we had spoken since he'd become head coach seven months previously. I wanted to say to him, 'Look, you could have given me a call.' In our chat he may have mentioned something about wanting to keep the announcement of the squad secret, but anyway I didn't push it. You sense when you speak with Brian he doesn't enjoy any kind of confrontation. And with a knee that still needed a lot of rehab, I had plenty on my plate.

WELCOME TO THE STEINER SCHOOL

Walking into the England camp under Brian Ashton, my first impression was of a man determined not to follow the Clive Woodward blueprint. Clive was successful doing it one way and I admired Brian's willingness to do it another. Of course, we still had to see how his way worked but it was very different. In one of his many meetings with the players, Clive got us to commit to certain standards of behaviour that we all agreed were appropriate for players on England duty. Time-keeping was sacrosanct but there were countless other considerations. We agreed no player would use his mobile phone around the team hotel, no player was allowed to walk through the hotel in bare feet, you adhered to the dress code and lots of things like that. It may have been strict, but at least everyone knew where they stood. Clive, we would gripe, used to have meetings about having meetings, but then you always knew what the plan was, on and off the field. For those of us who had come from this environment, Brian's England was the Steiner School of Rugby – free will and free love for all. Everything was cool and you never had to worry about missing the next meeting because there was no scheduled next meeting. It was like, 'You guys do what you want.' The empowering of players can be a very strong management tool and Brian believes in handing over the decision-making to those who will have to make the calls on the pitch.

But the time to our World Cup prep matches was short and I felt we needed more direction than we were getting. Rugby players need to have some structure, both in terms of their rugby environment and what they actually do on the training ground. And as you looked closer at our Steiner School, it was obvious all wasn't well. Our three principal coaches were Brian, John Wells and Mike Ford. Brian was head coach, John worked with the forwards and Mike was our defence coach. You expected them to be singing from the same hymn sheet and supporting each other in everything they said to the players. But I don't think that was how it was. Not from where I was sitting. Right from the start, it seemed they had different ideas about what the team should be doing. Brian wanted England playing with width and imagination, reacting to what the opposing team was doing, while John Wells had a very different view. He is the epitome of Leicester; great set pieces, a bit of dog and a lot of efficiency. If John was a football coach, you'd put him in charge of Germany and be confident he would deliver results. It could have been a marriage made in heaven, John's pragmatism allied to Brian's vision and wisdom.

But they didn't appear to gel, something that players will pick up on in a millisecond. It seemed to me that the difficulty lay in Brian's personality and issue of whether he is particularly comfortable in the role of overall boss. He knows in his own mind he is the head coach and in his particular way, he tries to tell people, but the message is too low-key for players who are used to working with strong, sometimes dictatorial coaches. On the other hand, John is a strong character and was well respected by the forwards. But for a guy who was very confrontational as a player, and is very confrontational in the way he coaches, John was surprisingly non-confrontational in terms of dealing with Brian. If he had reservations, he didn't seem able to express them to Brian. Maybe if you're not the head coach, it is hard to confront the head coach but when it's adversely affecting the team, shouldn't you try? Most of the players, especially the senior ones, picked up on the confusion caused by the lack of direction. Had a stranger walked in on any training session before the World Cup, he wouldn't have had a clue as to who was in charge. There wasn't one person who took control, who said, 'Right, this is what we're doing. This is how things are going to be from here on in. This is how we're going to play. This is our vision. This is the way I see it.' That voice wasn't heard. Without it, there was a vacuum.

Before long, it was clear that pupils at the Steiner School were far from happy.

NOT WHAT THE DOC ORDERED

About the best news I heard before linking up with the England squad was that Jason Robinson had a minor knee operation, not dissimilar to mine, a week *after* me. I thought that if he could recover in time, then so could I. That put me a week ahead of him and as we were going to Portugal for a training camp, the sunshine and intensive rehab work with the physios would quickly get me back to full fitness. Details of the trip came in a note from Viv Brown and all it said was to meet at Bournemouth Airport at such and such a time. No flight times were listed, no mention of our destination and I called Viv to get some of the details. She said I had all the details the players were getting. 'Oh,' I said, finding out absolutely nothing. Still, we showed up at Bournemouth Airport in the expectation that we were on our way to the Algarve. There was a sense of excitement: the first get-together for the World Cup squad, most likely in a nice hotel/training complex close to the sea. It bothered me a little that the other players didn't know I was recovering from my minor knee operation and it struck me that I probably should have made this public, so that they were forewarned. Instead, they were expecting me to come bouncing into the squad which I definitely didn't do.

Viv got us all together at the airport and said the flight had been cancelled. 'Bad weather, we're all going to get on a bus and stay at a hotel up the road.' It was clear something was up and I had a grudging respect for Brian's cleverness. 'Never be sure things are going to happen as you expect,' was the message and 25 minutes later our bus pulled in at a Royal Marine base. Portugal would have to wait. Inside this hangar, we were introduced to guys who would be our coaches for the next few days, and we're not talking rugby coaches. 'You'll be spending some time with these guys,' said Brian, pointing to the marines present. We were told by one of the marines that we would be doing some training manoeuvres, some exercises and there was no indication as to how much time we would spend at the camp. 'From your kit, take all your valuables, plus your mobile phones and put them in these bags. They'll be locked away and returned to you when you're departing.' Again, there was no mention of when we would leave. Everyone was panicking, 'Can I make one last call? My wife's pregnant, she's expecting me to call this evening.' We were allowed to phone quickly and then we all moved off into the unknown. There were different dormitories, some housed 12, one housed 20 of us. There were no luxuries, the bunk beds were a bit small for the taller guys, the clothes were compulsory and we had to report to the training yard at some ungodly hour the next morning, 5.30 a.m. I think. A few of us had done this with Clive in 1999 and the marines know what they're doing when it comes to getting a team to come together.

We were put into various groups and it was all well thought

out. Normally, I thrive in that kind of environment and enjoy the competition but I was in the middle of my rehab and the marine training was actually the last thing I needed. I was told to only do what my knee would allow me to do but, of course, it doesn't work like that. You're in a team, you want to contribute as much as you can and you do more than you should. And the rehab went on hold. The four days we spent in Bournemouth set me back two weeks in my rehab. That I shouldn't have been there was obvious from something I discovered on day one. We should have been a group of 46 because that was the size of Brian's first World Cup squad. But there were only 45 of us working with the marines. Jason Robinson had gone on to Portugal ahead of the squad to concentrate on his rehab.

'WHAT'S GOING ON?'

Brian Ashton, John Wells and Mike Ford are all good coaches, each with his own area of specialisation. When we began training in Portugal, each worked on a different aspect of the game but their efforts didn't seem to be co-ordinated and where Brian was concerned, players struggled to relate his training to what they would have to do in a match. Another complicating factor was the size of the squad. In my mind 46 players was 10 or 12 too many. Guys want to train with those who are likely to end up alongside them when the World Cup begins. Partnerships need to be formed, patterns of play developed and practised, and the coaches needed to start telling us how they saw us playing. What normally happens is that the head coach takes a core group of players, explains to them his vision and uses those players to disseminate his plan amongst their team-mates. This didn't happen and as we drew closer to our prep matches, anxiety levels among the players increased. Not just the players but also the other coaches. They were tacitly encouraging us to do something with suggestions that we 'needed to take control'.

We decided we had to agree on what we wanted to say to Brian and that we should get the other coaches involved as well. I suggested we head off to dinner and formulate our thoughts on where we were as a group. The lads didn't think we needed to go out and we agreed to meet in the bar of the Villamoura complex at which we were staying. We met around eight o'clock in the evening. It did feel a bit cloak-and-dagger-ish as we were keeping our voices down so that no one else in the bar could tune into what we were talking about. We were there about ten minutes when Brian Ashton walked in. It is perfectly obvious we're in a meeting that has not been authorised and his body language conveyed just how uneasy he was with what he saw. It was pretty awkward for us, too. Brian must have been thinking there's a conspiracy happening here, and you couldn't blame him. Any coach would have thought the same and it doesn't take much for unease to turn to paranoia. So I got up, I mean someone had to do something. 'Look, Brian, it's not what you think. Don't worry. All that's going on is that a group of us are talking about a few issues, stuff that we want to talk about with you and the other coaches.'

'Shall I sit down and join you?' Brian asked.

'No, no,' I replied. 'Just give us a bit of time and we'll come and sit down with you.'

It was difficult because we almost had to tell Brian to leave the bar. Amongst the players in our group there was a lot of frustration.

Jason Robinson said he needed to know who he would be playing alongside in the team, especially the guys he would be linking with, the wings and centres, and that he wanted to start building relationships with them now. But we were light years away from knowing what the starting XV might be. Normally Jason is anything but outspoken so this wasn't normal but he just felt the squad was far too big. 'I could name you twelve guys now who will not be around when the squad is reduced, so what are we doing with such a big squad?' The general view of the players was that you need to have a structured approach for the first few phases of possession and after that, the possibilities open up. Brian isn't big on structured rugby and in trying to have this dialogue with the head coach, we felt we were doing what the other coaches might have done. I was uncomfortable about my own involvement as I still wasn't 100 per cent fit and had been on the outside for over a year. Andy Farrell was probably feeling the same but the easy thing would have been to sit back and do nothing.

It seemed clear to us the other coaches weren't happy and that they quite naturally reverted to concentrating on doing their own jobs well. As I've said, the players respected John Wells and there was no doubt that Mike Ford worked hard and knew how to help a team defend better – he was going to make sure that England's defence was excellent. Perhaps the biggest plus of all was the work that Graham Rowntree did with the scrum. Graham had one of the hardest acts to follow because the previous scrum coach, Phil Keith-Roach, was loved by the players and was world class at what he did. But Graham came in and didn't try to be anybody other than the Graham we had played with in the England team a few years before. What he had was a passion for the scrum and was clearly able to turn that into an effective way of working because our scrum got stronger as the tournament progressed and was an area of the game where we did well.

I hope I'm not going to lose a friendship over what I say about Brian, who was a good coach who I believe was in the wrong role. Head coach of the England team demands management skills that, in my honest appraisal, Brian doesn't have. He could have brought someone in to make sure it got done or he could have taken it on himself. He did neither and the whole squad found itself in a kind of limbo. We did meet with Brian and the coaches but I felt we never really moved things on. Some of the suggestions were implemented, bits and pieces of others were taken on board, but we weren't as rigorous in following things up as we should have been. But when you're not sure you're going to be in the first XV, it's difficult to take a central role, and not that many guys were sure of their starting place.

Most of the teams and environments that I've known involve constant analysis and an ongoing dialogue between the coaching team and senior players. Typically, coaches want to know if they're getting their message through to the players and they need to know if players have issues. We didn't have any of that interaction and as a result, players start talking amongst themselves or going off and speaking privately with one particular coach. You start to hear the same question over and over, 'What the fuck is happening?' I've seen other coaches in the situation where players are asking that question – Clive Woodward on the 2005 Lions is a good example.

Generally speaking, when that question is asked no one knows the answer.

TRIALS AND TRIBULATIONS

Six were shed from the initial squad in the first cull. Brian opted to stick with 40 for the two prep matches against France and Wales and, probably without intending to, he turned those matches into World Cup trials for a number of the lads in the squad. That was unsatisfactory because with so many players, not everyone got a full match and some had much less opportunity than others. If you only played half a match and then didn't get selected, chances are the coaches' minds were made up before you got on. That begged the question as to why the squad wasn't further reduced much earlier. Selection would be a constant area of debate amongst the players as the tournament progressed and a lot of the time we couldn't make sense of it. I felt Joe Worsley had to be picked for the South Africa game because he is the best tackler in the Premiership and one of the most destructive tacklers in world rugby; the one certainty against South Africa was that we would be doing a lot of tackling. Shaun Perry was close to man-of-the-match in our three warm-up games, had a bad match against South Africa and was then discarded. I didn't see how he could go from being No. 1 to No. 3 after one disappointing performance.

The team captain Phil Vickery got suspended for two weeks after the USA game and was made to feel like a leper. Then he's brought back for the Tonga game but only on the bench. If you're good enough to be captain of England two weeks before, what's changed? If I had been Phil, I would have been incensed. You needed to take just one look at the two tight-heads in the squad; Phil is the starter, Matt Stevens is the better impact player. For that Tonga game, I think Martin Corry was almost embarrassed by being named captain.

As I've said earlier, I accept the reasons for bringing Nick Easter into the team after the USA game. I hadn't delivered but what pissed me off was the way Brian handled it. On the morning the team was announced for the South African pool game, I got a text from Brian. Something like, 'Can you meet me downstairs? I'd like to have a word.' My first thought was that this wasn't promising. I met Brian and he told me I wasn't in the team or replacements. A player needs a little time to adjust to news like that, especially someone like me who had played so many times and was going to be deeply disappointed. But the team meeting was due to start 45 seconds after Brian spoke to me. I was furious. I didn't want the other players to see my disappointment but with so much anger, I couldn't disguise it. I didn't appreciate the lack of consideration and I say this honestly, knowing that many other players experienced the same, if not worse. How the hell can you be cool and supportive of your team-mates less than a minute after you've had news like that? It was a disappointment too that John Wells didn't feel he needed to say anything to me. Maybe that's his style, I don't know, but as a coach, I don't think you can operate like that. Surely you need to talk to the players directly under your charge. It wouldn't have taken Einstein to work it out. 'This guy has eighty caps, he's hardly ever been dropped, he's going to be naturally disappointed, I need to go and have a word with him.'

BACK FROM THE ABYSS

Watching England get beaten 36–0 by South Africa in the World Cup hurt me more than anything I've seen on a rugby field. I wasn't playing and it still felt like a knife through the heart watching team-mates who had no idea what they were supposed to be doing. After such a heavy defeat, I thought there would have to be a lot of changes and felt I had a chance of getting back into the team. But Brian told me he thought Nick was one of England's better players against the South Africans and he wanted to stick with him. That was fair enough, a coach has the right to make that call and as the tournament went on, Nick didn't let anyone down. But part of me was beginning to wonder what I was doing at the World Cup. Why was I picked in the first place? Wouldn't it have been better to select my young Wasps team-mate James Haskell who has great potential and would have benefited from the experience of being at the World Cup?

The 36–0 loss brought the team to crisis point. There has been a lot of talk about the meeting we had the next day and it was a brutal, no-holds-barred, what-the-fuck-is-happening meeting. I felt this was almost the showdown the other coaches had been wanting three or four weeks before but it hadn't happened then. It started calmly enough with a matter-of-fact assessment of where we stood in the tournament. Then people started getting up and offering their opinions on why things had turned out as they had. One guy offered his take, then another guy his and as the meeting moved on, more and more guys started to say what they really felt. A lot of valid points were made and at some stage, everyone put up his hand and said what he was thinking. In that respect, it was a worthwhile meeting. The players didn't know what was being asked of them, but at last the confusion was out in the open.

Mike Catt, I remember, said the team wasn't playing the way Brian had always preached the game should be played. Catty felt if we were going to go out of the World Cup, we should at least go out trying to play some decent rugby. It was a tough meeting for Brian, something you realised when you heard Ollie Barkley, who had worked with Brian at Bath, say, 'Look Brian, no one's got a fucking clue how we're supposed to be playing here. If you ask the fifteen guys who played against South Africa to write down the game plan, you'd get fifteen different answers.' It was harsh, but it was true.

What was generally agreed was that we needed some structure to the way we played. At times we needed to pass the ball more, other times we needed to kick it more. We also needed to know what we were doing off first-, second- and third-phase possession. After that, we could be more spontaneous. It made me think of the time we had spent in Portugal, practising stuff that had no relevance to a match situation with players who were not going to be in the squad. It was decided that the decision-makers, the guys who played at 9, 10 and 12, would go away, have a talk amongst themselves, come back and tell us how they felt we should play and we would then spend the five days before the Samoa game practising what the decision-makers were preaching. Breaking up from that meeting, there was a sense of having taken the first step back from the abyss.

NO REGRETS

As we came out on the field for our pool match against Tonga, there was a banner on the far side of the ground that said, 'Goodbye England'. That captured the mood at the time. England were so bad against South Africa that people believed we would lose one of our remaining two pool games and not qualify from our group. Well, we'd beaten Samoa but the media pressure was still just as high. You could almost see the vultures circling overhead. But the games against Samoa and then Tonga were ideal for England because on both occasions we were staring down the barrel and that's what we needed. We had players in the team who responded to that kind of pressure. Eleven of the 22 involved on match day were from Wasps or Leicester and they helped to give the team the competitive hardness that saw them through against the Pacific island teams, who were better than people gave them credit for. Samoa and Tonga were also ideal opponents because they were strong, but not so strong that England couldn't beat them. There were moments in both games when we were under pressure but we came through and the experience turned us into a battle-hardened team. Plus the fact that it had been a long time since we won back-to-back tests and that helped our confidence.

A siege mentality had also developed within our squad. That was mostly a reaction to the scathing criticism from outside but it was also a response to the feeling within the group that we weren't getting a lot of direction from our coaches. I don't want to be too harsh on this point but when you're not clear about what's going on, when the messages you are receiving don't have the clarity you need, there is a natural inclination for players to pull closer together, a survival instinct that tells them that unless they do it themselves, they're going under. It was something I had seen in other teams, with other coaches. Incredible results are produced despite all the uncertainty and confusion within the squad. I also happen to believe that Australia underestimated us. They just didn't recognise that we had a core of strong characters who wouldn't lie down. Yet, I have to admit, I was surprised that we beat them. It was the victory that turned our World Cup around.

Graham Rowntree made a short but very relevant speech before the Australia game. We always had a meeting of the forwards before the final team meeting and, normally, Graham isn't a guy who says a huge amount. When he does speak, it tends to be to the point. 'Look guys,' he said, 'we have to have no regrets after we've played Australia because if we lose we'll be on our way home and there are some guys in this room who will never play for England again. Your last game for England and you don't want to regret things you didn't do. There's going to be columns written and books brought out and people won't be saying nice things about each other or about what's happened here. The only thing we can ensure is that we have no regrets about what we do in this game of rugby. We're all frustrated, we've all been annoyed with selection, but what's happened has happened and today we've got to put it all behind us and have no regrets about our performance.'

It was an emotional response to what everyone was feeling and the performance from the England forwards was magnificent. Victory changed everything. I had looked at Brian Ashton in the days after the South Africa game and seen the face of a man who seemed ready to jump off the nearest cliff. Martin Corry compared us to the Jamaican bobsleigh team from that excellent film, *Cool Runnings*, and when Mike Catt was asked how he felt about being selected for the Australia game, he said the coaches had to pick him because there was no one else left. Mike Ford, our defence coach, gave an interview in which he said we were short of world-class players and at this point in his career, Andy Farrell, didn't have the pace for union. We've heard this and thought, 'Thanks, mate.' It was unbelievable. Somehow we'd managed to turn our World Cup campaign into a Monty Python sketch – maybe called *The Life of Brian*? But then the team produced a magnificently gritty performance to beat Australia and Brian had done what so many coaches had failed to do, he'd taken his team to the semi-final of the World Cup. He'd achieved more than his Australian counterpart, John Connolly, more than Graham Henry and the All Blacks. Even Monty Python would have struggled to come up with this script.

BOOTLACES AND EXPLETIVES

Perhaps I was spoiled. For most of my rugby life, I wore a shirt that had a single-digit number: never a back and rarely a replacement. Then in my last couple of campaigns for England, I spent a lot of time on the bench. It wasn't easy because when you're a replace-ment you feel a little on the periphery. My contribution is most effective when I have been centrally involved in the build-up and been in a position to influence the psychology of the team. On the bench, that's not possible. I tried to get used to the new role. It's important, I told myself, to support the fifteen who start and to make sure you were ready when called upon with however many minutes remaining. By the time we got to the quarter-final, I had accepted the situation and although I believed I was still good enough to be in the starting fifteen, being on the bench was far better than being one of the eight not involved on match day. My heart went out to the guys who weren't in the 22. You think of Steve Borthwick who would have prepared for the last four years believing his moment would come at the 2007 World Cup. He probably felt very let down, demoralised and dejected.

We beat Australia primarily because they hadn't been tested before playing us and were vulnerable to a team that played with a lot of physicality. Our plan was to deny them possession. If you win the collisions in rugby, generally you win the game. Our scrum was much better than Australia's and we were far more aggressive than them at the breakdown. That meant their scrum-half George Gregan was getting the ball under a lot of pressure and it affected his performance. Andy Gomarsall won the scrum-half battle hands down. We also identified that they liked to throw line-out balls to their front jumper and drive forward from there. Simon Shaw didn't contest the throw, concentrating instead on stopping their drive, which he did brilliantly.

Coming off the bench in a tight match is tough. Part of you wants to show you should have been in the starting fifteen and you're generally very pumped up, but you've got to temper that because it can lead to the concession of penalties. We were leading by two points when Joe Worsley and I came on and, unfortunately, Joe over-competed and was penalised with only minutes to go. Not far from the touchline and quite a long way out, it was a big ask and Stirling Mortlock hadn't kicked that well through the match. But if he landed it, we were on our way home. At such moments, us Wasps guys in the England team stick together. I turned to Joe and called him every expletive under the sun. Which wasn't as good as Josh Lewsey telling Joe not to worry, as he would undo his bootlaces for him. Joe looked at Josh, wondering what he meant. 'So you'll have something to hang yourself with if Mortlock gets this.'

The kick missed but not by much and I thought I really wouldn't like to be a kicker. I heard Mortlock say afterwards that when he put the ball down, the wind was blowing in one direction but as he stood to address the ball, it was blowing the opposite way. He still only missed by about a foot.

DANCING INTO BATTLE

Two weeks into the tournament, Alice came to Paris and brought me a book. Written by Nick Foulkes, *Dancing Into Battle* is a social history based around the Battle of Waterloo. Like Alice and I, Nick Foulkes has discovered the delights of Andrea Riva's restaurant in Barnes and one evening Andrea introduced me to Nick. After I went away on England duty, Nick left a copy of the book for me at Andrea's. Alice did the rest. It was a book I enjoyed immensely and it was almost eerie that as I got to the climactic days leading into the Battle of Waterloo, we were only days away from playing France in the semi-final of the World Cup. I am reading about Wellington and Napoleon and can't help seeing Wellington as the England team and Napoleon epitomising the French and there were a lot of genuine parallels. For me, the most striking thing was how Wellington remained calm when there was so much panic and chaos around him. Yeah, it does sound a bit like the England rugby players. Wellington was going into a battle in which the odds were stacked against him. There was a big chance his army would be defeated but he acted as if he didn't have a worry in the world.

Nick's book had exactly the right effect on me as it reinforced my confidence about the French game. It's part of our history; Agincourt, Waterloo, Sydney, and it has been there for a long time, this feeling that as an Englishman, you are going to beat the French. I don't want this to come across as in any way anti-French because I love the country and Alice's mum is French. As well as that, the World Cup was tremendously well organised and their treatment of the players was top class. The travel was easy, the hotels were great, the security guys could not have been more helpful – they put on a fantastic tournament. But I'm reading about Wellington and the English aristocracy having their high society banquets in Brussels (that's where they hung out at the time) and the Battle of Waterloo that was just around the corner. I'm reading this, and thinking, 'Wellington's confident because he knows he can beat the French.'

I hadn't believed we would beat Australia, but the French were different. Mike Ford produced a comprehensive assessment of how the French would play against us and it proved to be spot-on. The game became one long battle for territory and the French were determined to kick the ball deep into our half. We didn't have much choice but to kick it back and try not to lose the aerial battle. In the end, it came down to mental toughness. They were leading 9–8 and were content to maintain their one-point advantage, but didn't know whether to sit or hold. If they had been thinking clearly, they would have tried to set up a position from which they could get the penalty or drop-goal that would have stretched their lead to four. Instead they forgot about position and tried for the drop-goal when it wasn't on. Then they brought on Freddie Michalak in an attempt to do I don't know what. Michalak was an ideal replacement in the quarter-final victory over the All Blacks because France needed a try as the risks he takes were justified when they were chasing the game. Against us, they just needed three points to give them a tiny bit of breathing space. What they didn't need was Michalak.

There were about 15 minutes remaining when I got on. 'Look guys, stay calm, it's nine—eight. And fifteen minutes is a hell of a long time, let's keep our heads. One moment is going to change this game.' We got into their half, Dan Hipkiss made a good little run, fed Jason Robinson, and their replacement hooker Dmitri Szarzewski was just a fraction too eager and was penalised for a high tackle on Jason. In fairness to Szarzewski, it's not difficult to put a high tackle on Jason because his head bobs around and never gets much above chest height. Szarzewski fell into the classic trap of coming on and wanting to show the world he should have been there in the first place. Jonny didn't miss with the penalty and we were in front. Paul Sackey and Toby Flood then tackled Sebastian Chabal into touch, there were a few words exchanged, Chabal reacted with his elbow – penalty, line-out, Martin Corry takes at the back, Jonny drop-goal.

Agincourt, Waterloo, Sydney and, now, Paris.

THE LOSING FEELING

In the end, I started to get used to my role on the bench. I never liked it but into the knockout stages I was getting the hang of it and there was a gradual acceptance of the situation. I felt we could only beat South Africa by playing our best game of the tournament and we also had to get the bounce of the ball, just as we did for Josh Lewsey's try against the French in the first couple of minutes of that game. In terms of skill, cohesion, and understanding of how they wanted to play, the South Africans were better than us. They had been together longer and had beaten us the last four times we met. The 36–0 defeat didn't bother me, though, because I had been involved in a Wasps team that conceded 45 points to Leicester a few weeks before we smashed them in the 2005 Premiership final play-off. South Africa had humiliated one England team, they would be meeting another England in the final. If things went our way, we would have every chance.

Most of all England had to get in front and force the Springboks to consider the possibility of losing. We never did that and it hurt us. We didn't give away that many penalties but we gave away a few needless ones that were within Percy Montgomery's range. And this time, the breaks didn't go our way, especially in relation to the controversial refusal to award a try to Mark Cueto early in the second half. For all of us on the bench, it was a definite score . . . but we were English. I'm sure the guys on the South African bench had a different view. It was one of those decisions you could argue about all day, not that that's a rugby player's style. Whatever the video referee Stuart Dickinson decided, that was it. We were 9–3 down at the time, a try would have made it 9–8 and if Jonny had landed the conversion, we would have been 10–9 in front. That would have changed the balance of the match and done a lot for us. We're weren't a side equipped to chase a game and the statistic that says we scored just one try in the knock-out stages of the World Cup is one you can't ignore.

Perhaps too many things had to go for us – we needed the video referee to award that try and we needed referee Alain Rolland to have taken a different attitude to Schalk Berger's coming in from the side and slowing down of the ball after Mathew Tait's excellent break. If Berger hadn't done that, Danie

Rossouw wouldn't have got back to make that last-ditch tackle on Mark Cueto. While I give Berger credit for cleverly taking his hand away immediately after slowing the ball down, I know as a back-row forward that I would have expected a yellow card. But Berger got away with it which seemed to be the epitome of the match as far as we were concerned – most of Alain Rolland's decisions went against us. This point shouldn't take away from South Africa's victory. They were the better team. Their scrum held up, they smashed the rucks that little bit harder than we did and their line-outs were outstanding. We didn't take one of their throws, they took nine of ours.

Maybe it was that our preparation caught up with us in the end because the courage of the team meant we had a lot of possession, especially in the second half, but we didn't have the slick teamwork that would have produced scores. We would get so far and then make a mistake. The calmness we had against Australia and France didn't desert us but we weren't as controlled against the Springboks. When the final whistle went, it was a horrible feeling and no matter how many people tell you that you've done well to get as far as we got, the pain of losing a World Cup final is one you take with you for the rest of your life.

Soon after we arrived home from Paris, there was a letter from the RFU and a comprehensive questionnaire regarding every aspect of England's organisation and performance at the World Cup. We were asked to assess the team's preparation and the contribution of our various coaches. The assessments and comments could be made anonymously. First thing I did was to write my name on the top of the form. Anonymity is not something you can afford in Test rugby.

Epilogue

When I look back on my time in rugby, there are many different feelings and probably the strongest is a sense of gratitude. I had a career that you wouldn't even dream about and for that, I feel both privileged and fortunate. As a young rugby player, you might think, 'I would love to play for England,' but you're never going to imagine yourself playing 85 times for your country. It was an honour on every single occasion and if love of your country makes you a patriot, I am happy to describe myself as patriotic.

My good luck was to come into the game at the time I did. I'm not talking just about arriving, more or less, in the same generation as Martin Johnson and Jonny Wilkinson, but in coming along when the amateur game was still alive and kicking. The Piccadilly Line at rush hour to get to training on Tuesday and Thursday evening, the currys we brought back to the Wasps clubhouse in Sudbury at 2 a.m., Dean Ryan showing a kid the ropes and the tricks you might get away with – great, great days. Then the game went professional and got all serious, Clive Woodward came along and created a new empire for England, in rugby.

Was I glad to be involved in that? Under Clive we won 14 consecutive matches, home and away, against the big teams in the southern hemisphere. Those were the days and I loved them. Sometimes in life you've just got to be in the right place at the right time. Of course there are a few regrets but they're nothing compared to the sense of satisfaction.

One part of the journey now comes towards an end, the playing part. I imagine nothing will replicate the joy and adrenalin buzz of being in the thick of a Test match or of that moment when you stand in the tunnel at Twickenham, ready to lead Wasps onto the pitch and into battle for another Premiership title. Boy, we had it good and it's easy to look back, but I'm also looking forward to the second part of the journey.

I don't know what it is going to involve except that it will be rugby because the game remains my passion. Having spent my career at Wasps, I would like to continue my post-playing career at the club. I appreciate that not all elite players make elite coaches but I have a desire to learn and the coaches who most impressed me were the ones who kept their minds open and never stopped wanting to learn. If coaching is the future, all I can say for sure is that there will be no lack of effort and no lack of passion.

Who knows for sure what the future holds? All that is certain is that rugby will be a part of mine. It's in the blood, I suppose.

Vital statistics

Name: Lawrence Bruno Nero Dallaglio
Born: 10 August 1972, Shepherd's Bush, London
Height: 6'4"
Weight: 17.5 stone/111kg
Position: No. 8

WASPS APPEARANCES

	All games			League			Cup			Europe		
SEASON	App	T	Pts	App	T	Pts	App	T	Pts	App	T	Pts
1993–94	8+2	2	10	8+2	2	10						
Middlesex Sevens winners												
1994–95	21	6	30	16	5	25	5	1	5			
1995–96	20	5	25	17	4	20	3	1	5			
1996–97	28	2	10	22	1	5	2	–	–	4	1	5
Courage League champions												
1997–98	28	2	10	17	1	5	4	–	–	7	1	5
1998–99	26	7	35	22	5	25	4	2	10			
Tetley's Bitter Cup winners												
1999–00	27	5	25	17	3	15	3	1	5	7	1	5
Tetley's Bitter Cup winners												
2000–01	22	5	25	16	4	20	1	–	–	3	1	5
2001–02	6+1	–	–	6+1	–	–						
2002–03	28+1	6	30	20+1	2	10	1	–	–	8	4	20
Zurich Premiership champions/Parker Pen Challenge Cup winners												

	All games			League			Cup			Europe		
SEASON	App	T	Pts	App	T	Pts	App	T	Pts	App	T	Pts
2003–04	15+1	5	25	8+1	3	15				7	2	10
European Cup winners/Zurich Premiership champions												
2004–05	28+2	2	13	22+2	1	8	1	–	–	5	1	5
Zurich Premiership champions												
2005–06	25+2	–	–	16+2	–	–	4	–	–	5	–	–
Powergen Cup winners												
2006–07	22+4	2	10	13+3	–	–	1	1	5	8+1	1	5
European Cup winners												
TOTALS	305+13	49	248	220+12	31	158	29	6	30	54+1	12	60

REPRESENTATIVE MATCHES

DATE	TEAM	OPPONENT	VENUE	TOURNY	RES	SHIRT	SCORING
22/03/1991	England Colts	Argentina Youth	The Stoop		W	8	
13/03/1991	England Colts	Italy Youth	Cambridge		L	8	Try
17/04/1991	England Colts	France Juniors	Gujan-Mestras		L	8	
27/04/1991	England Colts	Scotland Under-19	Stirling		L		
06/04/1992	England Colts	Wales Youth	Fylde		L	8	
03/05/1992	England Under-21	Netherlands	Leiden		W	8	
16/04/1993	England 7s		Murrayfield	WC7	W		
01/05/1993	England Under-21	French Military	Twickenham		W	8	
16/10/1993	London Division	Northern Division	Newcastle		W	7	
05/03/1994	England A	France A	Paris (Stade Jean Bouin)		L	Rep	
18/05/1994	England XV	Free State	Bloemfontein		L	6	
31/05/1994	England XV	South Africa A	Kimberley		L	6	
07/06/1994	England XV	Eastern Province	Port Elizabeth		W	6	
19/11/1994	London Division	South-West Division	Bristol		W	7	Try

Date	Team	Opponent	Venue		Result	Score	
26/11/1994	London Division	Northern Division	The Stoop		W	7	
20/01/1995	England A	Ireland A	Donnybrook		W	6	
03/02/1995	England A	France A	Leicester (Welford Road)		W	6	
19/02/1995	England A	Italy A	Gloucester		W	7	
18/11/1995	ENGLAND	South Africa	Twickenham		L	Rep	
29/11/1995	London Division	Samoa XV	Twickenham		L	6	Try
16/12/1995	ENGLAND	Samoa	Twickenham		W	7	Try
20/01/1996	ENGLAND	France	Parc des Princes	5NC	L	7	
03/02/1996	ENGLAND	Wales	Twickenham	5NC	W	7	
02/03/1996	ENGLAND	Scotland	Murrayfield	5NC	W	7	
06/03/1996	Barbarians	East Midlands	Northampton		L	8	
16/03/1996	ENGLAND	Ireland	Twickenham	5NC	W	7	
23/11/1996	ENGLAND	Italy	Twickenham		W	7	Try
30/11/1996	England XV	NZ Barbarians	Twickenham		L	7	
14/12/1996	ENGLAND	Argentina	Twickenham		W	7	
01/02/1997	ENGLAND	Scotland	Twickenham	5NC	W	6	
15/02/1997	ENGLAND	Ireland	Lansdowne Road	5NC	W	6	
01/03/1997	ENGLAND	France	Twickenham	5NC	L	6	Try
24/05/1997	British Isles XV	Eastern Province Invitation	Port Elizabeth		W	6	
31/05/1997	British Isles XV	Western Province	Cape Town		W	6	

Date	Team	Opponent	Venue	Comp	Result	No.	Notes
07/06/1997	British Isles XV	Blue Bulls	Pretoria		L	6	
14/06/1997	British Isles XV	Natal Sharks	Durban		W	6	Try
21/06/1997	BRITISH & IRISH LIONS	South Africa	Cape Town		W	6	
28/06/1997	BRITISH & IRISH LIONS	South Africa	Durban		W	6	
05/07/1997	BRITISH & IRISH LIONS	South Africa	Johannesburg		L	8	
12/07/1997	ENGLAND	Australia	Sydney Football Stadium		L	6	
15/11/1997	ENGLAND	Australia	Twickenham		D	6	Capt
22/11/1997	ENGLAND	New Zealand	Old Trafford		L	6	Capt
29/11/1997	ENGLAND	South Africa	Twickenham		L	6	Capt
06/02/1997	ENGLAND	New Zealand	Twickenham		D	6	Capt/Try
07/02/1998	ENGLAND	France	Stade de France	5NC	L	6	Capt
21/02/1998	ENGLAND	Wales	Twickenham	5NC	W	6	Capt/Try
22/03/1998	ENGLAND	Scotland	Murrayfield	5NC	W	6	Capt
04/04/1998	ENGLAND	Ireland	Twickenham	5NC	W	6	Capt
28/11/1998	ENGLAND	Australia	Twickenham		L	6	Capt
05/12/1998	ENGLAND	South Africa	Twickenham		W	6	Capt
20/02/1999	ENGLAND	Scotland	Twickenham	5NC	W	6	Capt
06/03/1999	ENGLAND	Ireland	Lansdowne Road	5NC	W	8	Capt
20/03/1999	ENGLAND	France	Twickenham	5NC	W	8	Capt
11/04/1999	ENGLAND	Wales	Wembley Stadium	5NC	L	8	Capt
21/08/1999	ENGLAND	United States	Twickenham		W	8	
28/08/1999	ENGLAND	Canada	Twickenham		W	8	
07/09/1999	ENGLAND XV	Premiership XV	Anfield		W	8	2 Tries
18/09/1999	ENGLAND XV	Premiership XV	Twickenham Twickenham		W	8	Try
02/10/1999	ENGLAND	Italy	Twickenham	RWC	W	8	
09/10/1999	ENGLAND	New Zealand	Twickenham	RWC	L	8	
15/10/1999	ENGLAND	Tonga	Twickenham	RWC	W	8	
20/10/1999	ENGLAND	Fiji	Twickenham	RWC (P/O)	W	8	

24/10/1999	ENGLAND	South Africa	Stade de France	RWC (QF)	L	8	
05/02/2000	ENGLAND	Ireland	Twickenham	6NC	W	8	
19/02/2000	ENGLAND	France	Stade de France	6NC	W	8	
04/03/2000	ENGLAND	Wales	Twickenham	6NC	W	8	Try
18/03/2000	ENGLAND	Italy	Rome	6NC	W	8	
02/04/2000	ENGLAND	Scotland	Murrayfield	6NC	L	8	Try
31/05/2000	Barbarians	Scotland XV	Murrayfield		W	6	
04/06/2000	Barbarians	Leicester Tigers	Twickenham		W	6	2 Tries
17/06/2000	ENGLAND	South Africa	Pretoria		L	8	
24/06/2000	ENGLAND	South Africa	Bloemfontein		W	8	
18/11/2000	ENGLAND	Australia	Twickenham		W	8	
25/11/2000	ENGLAND	Argentina	Twickenham		W	8	
02/12/2000	ENGLAND	South Africa	Twickenham		W	8	
10/12/2000	Barbarians	South Africa XV	Cardiff		L	7	
03/02/2001	ENGLAND	Wales	Cardiff	6NC	W	8	
17/02/2001	ENGLAND	Italy	Twickenham	6NC	W	8	Try
03/03/2001	ENGLAND	Scotland	Twickenham	6NC	W	8	2 Tries
07/04/2001	ENGLAND	France	Twickenham	6NC	W	8	
19/06/2001	British Isles XV	Australia A	Gosford		L	6	
23/06/2001	British Isles XV	NSW Waratahs	Sydney Football Stadium		W	6	
07/04/2002	ENGLAND	Italy	Rome	6NC	W	Rep	Try
09/11/2002	ENGLAND	New Zealand	Twickenham		W	8	
16/11/2002	ENGLAND	Australia	Twickenham		W	Rep	
23/11/2002	ENGLAND	South Africa	Twickenham		W	Rep	Try
15/02/2003	ENGLAND	France	Twickenham	6NC	W	Rep	
22/02/2003	ENGLAND	Wales	Cardiff	6NC	W	8	
09/03/2003	ENGLAND	Italy	Twickenham	6NC	W	8	
22/03/2003	ENGLAND	Scotland	Twickenham	6NC	W	8	
30/03/2003	ENGLAND	Ireland	Lansdowne Road	6NC	W	8	Try
14/06/2003	ENGLAND	New Zealand	Wellington		W	8	
21/06/2003	ENGLAND	Australia	Melbourne		W	8	
12/10/2003	ENGLAND	Georgia	Perth	RWC	W	8	Try
18/10/2003	ENGLAND	South Africa	Perth	RWC	W	8	
26/10/2003	ENGLAND	Samoa	Melbourne	RWC	W	8	
02/11/2003	ENGLAND	Uruguay	Brisbane	RWC	W	8	
09/11/2003	ENGLAND	Wales	Brisbane	RWC (QF)	W	8	

Date	Team	Opponent	Venue	Tournament	Result	Shirt	Notes
16/11/2003	ENGLAND	France	Sydney	RWC (SF)	W	8	
22/11/2003	ENGLAND	Australia	Sydney	RWC (F)	W	8	
15/02/2004	ENGLAND	Italy	Rome	6NC	W	8	Capt
21/02/2004	ENGLAND	Scotland	Murrayfield	6NC	W	8	Capt
06/03/2004	ENGLAND	Ireland	Twickenham	6NC	L	8	Capt
20/03/2004	ENGLAND	Wales	Twickenham	6NC	W	8	Capt
27/03/2004	ENGLAND	France	Stade de France	6NC	L	8	Capt
12/06/2004	ENGLAND	New Zealand	Dunedin		L	8	Capt
19/06/2004	ENGLAND	New Zealand	Auckland		L	8	Capt
26/06/2004	ENGLAND	Australia	Brisbane		L	8	Capt/Try
05/03/2005	Northern Hemisphere	Southern Hemisphere	Twickenham		L	6	Capt
23/05/2005	British Isles XV	Argentina XV	Cardiff		D	Bench	
04/06/2005	British Isles XV	Bay of Plenty	Rotorua		W	8	
04/02/2006	ENGLAND	Wales	Twickenham	6NC	W	Rep	Try
11/02/2006	ENGLAND	Italy	Rome	6NC	W	Rep	
25/02/2006	ENGLAND	Scotland	Murrayfield	6NC	L	Rep	
12/03/2006	ENGLAND	France	Stade de France	6NC	L	Rep	
18/03/2006	ENGLAND	Ireland	Twickenham	6NC	L	Bench	
03/12/2006	World XV	South Africa XV	Leicester (Walkers Stadium)		L	8	
04/08/2007	ENGLAND	Wales	Twickenham		W	19	Try
11/08/2007	ENGLAND	France	Twickenham		L	8	
18/08/2007	ENGLAND	France	Marseille		L	19	
08/09/2007	ENGLAND	United States	Lens	RWC	W	8	
28/09/2007	ENGLAND	Tonga	Parc des Princes	RWC	W	18	
06/10/2007	ENGLAND	Australia	Marseille	RWC (QF)	W	18	
13/10/2007	ENGLAND	France	Stade de France	RWC (SF)	W	18	
20/10/2007	ENGLAND	South Africa	Stade de France	RWC (F)	L	18	

Tournament Key

RWC – Rugby World Cup; WC7 – World Cup Sevens; 5NC – Five Nations Championship; 6NC – Six Nations Championship

Index

Note: 'LD' stands for Lawrence Dallaglio.

THE AUTOBIOGRAPHY

MARTIN JOHNSON

Martin Johnson had always been feared by opponents, revered by rugby fans and venerated by team-mates for his strength and desire for victory. But when he led England to World Cup triumph in November 2003, the rest of the country realised just why this was and elevated him to the status of national icon.

In this honest and typically forthright autobiography Johnson reveals what motivates him, and pulls no punches with his candid views about the state of the game.

NON-FICTION / AUTOBIOGRAPHY 978 0 7553 1187 3

MY WORLD

JONNY WILKINSON

With his outstanding performances throughout his career to date, and his dramatic last-minute drop goal to win the 2003 Rugby World Cup for England, Jonny Wilkinson guaranteed his place among the world's sporting greats and became an icon for his generation.

In *My World*, for the first time, in his own words, Jonny opens up to reveal the man behind the celebrity. He talks about his hopes and fears, his motivations and what it takes to be a true champion and offers a glimpse into the life of a rugby superstar, both on and off the pitch. In this fully updated edition, Jonny examines how his life has changed since writing the book, talking candidly about the series of career-threatening injuries that he has fought back from.

NON-FICTION / SPORT 978 0 7472 4278 9